# Win the World
# or Escape the Earth?

# Win the World or Escape the Earth?

## The End Time Controversy

Ian Rossol    Tony Wastall

River Publishing & Media Ltd
Barham Court
Teston
Maidstone
Kent
ME18 5BZ
United Kingdom

info@river-publishing.co.uk

ISBN 978-1-908393-14-2
Printed in the United Kingdom

# Dedications

### Ian's dedication

To Marj, my bride of 25 years: Your passion for us to pursue his presence together brings delight to my heart. I love you and love our pilgrimage into more of the Kingdom.

### Tony's dedication

To all the saints who are standing against the tide of end-times escapism and believing that through the church God's glory will cover the earth as the waters cover the seas; that this book might affirm and encourage them in their faith.

# Contents

# What others are saying about this book

Many dubious books have been written on the end times – books which sow confusion and anxiety in the minds and hearts of believers. *Win the World or Escape the Earth?* is a rare and welcome alternative. It addresses all the relevant biblical passages in a wise and thoughtful way. If you or someone you know has been unsettled by writers such as Tony and Ian or the preachers who espouse their views, then here is the much needed antidote. By handling these questions responsibly and with discernment, Rossol and Wastall demonstrate that a right understanding of God's plan for the end of the age does not instil fear, but rather inspires faith.

**Timothy Larsen, PhD, FRHistS**
McManis Professor of Christian Thought,
Wheaton College, Wheaton, Illinois, USA

A North American pastor recently caused a sensation by declaring that the Rapture would take place on a given date, and an extraordinary number of people believed him and were duly disillusioned when it didn't happen. Many people, especially outside America, had no idea what this 'Rapture' was supposed to be, and the media understandably treated it as a great joke. But the Dispensationalist thinking that lay behind this misguided 'prophecy' is surprisingly influential, especially in American evangelical Christianity, and has had a seriously damaging effect on attitudes towards Middle Eastern politics.

Here is a book which painstakingly explains where such thinking has come from and teases out the issues of biblical interpretation that it raises. It provides a wholesome alternative approach to understanding what the Bible teaches about the future. The authors handle the biblical text with reverence and care, leavened with a healthy dose of common sense. I hope it will be widely read, especially in those circles where Dispensationalism still reigns supreme.

**Revd. Dr. R T France**
**Former Principal of Wycliffe Hall, Oxford**

This is a masterful work and a great contribution to the Body of Christ. *Win the World or Escape the Earth* says it clearly. We have our work cut out for us, but Jesus Christ is Lord and He will expand His Kingdom until it fills the earth. Thank you Ian and Tony.

**Harold R. Eberle**
**President of Worldcast Ministries and author of *Victorious***
**Eschatology**

What we believe about the end of the world has everything to do with how we behave in our daily lives. Jesus clearly defeated Satan on Calvary's cross, yet pessimistic perspectives of the last days have resulted in a powerless Church battling a dangerous devil. Prevalent eschatological perceptions have somehow managed to commission Satan to carry out his devious plot to terrorise the planet. *Win the World or Escape the Earth?* is a clarion call to rise up, destroy the works of the devil and complete our divine mission to make disciples of all nations.

Tony and Ian's vast insights into the last days are accurate, refreshing and inspiring. They uncover theological errors that have been propagated for generations, resulting in fearful and defeated believers. This book is a must read for everyone who hungers for a fresh approach to their divine call. This book will rock you! Caution: be prepared to have your worldview seriously challenged.

**Kris Vallotton**
**Co-Founder of Bethel School of Supernatural Ministry, Senior Associate Leader of Bethel Church, Redding, California**

Tony and Ian have given us a first class introduction to Eschatology – the study of the last things. However, "Win The World or Escape The Earth?" will also help the more "in-depth inquirer" to sort out the many interpretations and end-time sound bites which fly like bees around the attractive honey pot of this truth and often do damage to those who sincerely approach the subject. And if these commendations are not sufficient, this work will, above all, enable the reader to engage in a balanced understanding of Christlike life and service. This is a "best buy" book!

**Roger Forster, founder of Ichthus Christian Fellowship.**

# Acknowledgements

Many people have helped and assisted us in bringing this book to print. We want to acknowledge some of them in particular. A big thank-you goes to Laura Barrett, Liz Carvell and Faith Rawley for their many hours work on the manuscript. Our thanks go to R T France and Tim Larsen for their valuable suggestions. We want to thank Jonathan Bugden and Tim Pettingale of River Publishing, for their partnership in this project. Finally, we want to acknowledge the role of our friend and mentor David Matthew for his invaluable contribution. Thank you David, for helping us craft our ideas, for copy editing our draft manuscript, for your work on the glossary and for encouraging us to persevere.

# Preface

The 2005 film version of H.G. Wells's novel *War of the Worlds* contains many unforgettable scenes. In one of the most graphic, dock worker Ray Ferrier (played by Tom Cruise), along with his daughter Rachel, is fleeing the terrifying alien machines that are running amok, killing and destroying everything in their path. Ray and his daughter take refuge in the basement of a house owned by a kind stranger, Harlan Ogilvy.

There are some striking parallels between the scene that unfolds and the church landscape today. Harlan Ogilvy's house even reminds one of a chapel perched on a hillside, with Harlan, 'the pastor' urging the desperate father and daughter to take shelter inside in the hope of being rescued from the destruction being wrought in the earth.

Ray's relief quickly evaporates, however, as he faces as many threats inside the house as he did outside. First, the aliens send in a probe which worms its way around and from which the inhabitants barely avoid detection. Next, four demon-like aliens enter and proceed to ransack the rooms. But worse is to come for Harlan who, already suffering from shredded nerves, suffers a complete breakdown and begins shouting and ranting. A row ensues and in desperation Ray is forced to kill Harlan in order to save Rachel and himself.

It is only when Ray is finally forced outside the house in search of Rachel and faces the enemy head on, that he finds hope and eventual triumph, despite the horrors and hardships that await him.

Many today view the church as a haven in a world under enemy control. Some of us even call our meeting rooms by the name 'sanctuary'. The irony is that when church is viewed in this way, it ceases to be a refuge and instead becomes a place of greater danger. Pastors and people alike battle against invasive enemies from beyond the church doors, and even small congregations fight among themselves for control of the little they have.

In stark contrast, others are waking up to the reality that the scene of God's activity is chiefly 'out there' in the world, where the powers

# Introduction

## Tony's story

'Tony, have you heard? Jesus is coming any time now! The rapture could be just around the corner and then comes the great tribulation'.

The year was 1971. I was a young Christian who had recently experienced an encounter with the Holy Spirit that ignited my passion for Christ and a desire to serve him. My friend was insistent: 'Have you bought the book yet? Everyone is talking about it. You'll discover exactly what is going to happen'. I flicked through the paperback that was thrust into my hand. There were references to beasts, wars and disasters, a lot about Russia, China and Israel; and plenty about the book of Revelation. It was amazing! I soon bought my own copy and devoured it eagerly.

*The Late Great Planet Earth* by American author Hal Lindsey was indeed a sensation. Its breezy, confident style not only captured the imagination of the church, it went on to become the non-fiction best seller of the 1970s, selling 9 million copies by 1978 and 28 million by 1990. It was translated into 54 other languages.

Lindsey's sequel, *Countdown to Armageddon*, was on the New York Times bestseller list for 20 weeks. For the first time ever, ordinary men and women felt that they could grasp complex Bible prophecies which had made little sense until then.

Hal Lindsey provided ready answers for the turbulent times we were living in. According to Lindsey, we were in the last of the last days. The oil crisis, the Middle East wars, conflicts between communism and the West; they were all there in the Bible prophecies, indicating that Jesus was about to wrap things up. And so, for my church youth group and friends everywhere, the message of *The Late Great Planet Earth* was believed without question, and unfolding events in the 1970s were followed carefully for signs of the antichrist appearing and armies amassing on Israel's borders.

I had come to Christ at a young age and was part of a town-wide youth network from many church backgrounds. Regardless of denomination, we were deeply influenced by the 'rapture message' of *The Late Great Planet Earth*, the 'Jesus Movement' from California and musicians like Larry Norman.

What troubled me, however, was that as the years went by, fewer and fewer of Hal Lindsey's confident predictions seemed to stack up, all the more so as world events took a different path in the 1980s. Thawing relations between the Soviet Union and the West culminated in the collapse of the Berlin Wall in 1989. Suddenly, the world looked a very different place from that described by Hal Lindsey in 1971.

My time at Bible College in the mid-eighties gave me the opportunity to study the return of Christ in much greater depth. I discovered that the message of *The Late Great Planet Earth* and its kind formed part of a system of belief known as dispensationalism. I learned how what began as a fringe movement in the 1800s came to dominate the church within a matter of a few decades, until today it is considered by many to be orthodox and mainstream.

I was also privileged to come under the teaching of men like Ern Baxter, Arthur Wallis and Bryn Jones. They boldly proclaimed a different kind of Christian hope, in which the church triumphs in the world instead of escaping it, and the nations are transformed by the gospel of God's kingdom. This only served to deepen my hunger for the truth and set me on a pilgrimage to discover what future really awaits the church of Jesus Christ.

## Ian's story

In the Pentecostal church in which I was raised, discussion of future events associated with the return of Christ frequently figured in Bible study discussions. As a young believer, I was not aware of the many theological assumptions that were commonly held amongst Pentecostals and that I had subconsciously embraced. I had inherited, from my grandfather, a first edition *Scofield Reference Bible*, which was revered among my fellow-Christians for its biblical insights. I had no idea at the time that Scofield's theological system was known as dispensationalism. Only later did I realise that through all those years my view of the Scriptures had been defined by dispensational theology, particularly when it came to understanding the return of Christ and events leading up to it.

My recollection of church life in the early 1970s was of endless discussion and speculation concerning the end times and the application of biblical prophecy to current affairs. The events of 1967 and the Six-Day War between Israel and its Arab neighbours had made the issues surrounding the state of Israel headline news in the popular press and focused people's attention on the idea that this was a sign of the coming of Christ.

Then I was introduced to Hal Lindsey's book *The Late Great Planet Earth,* with its bold assertion that current events pointed to the imminent return of Jesus. The formation of the State of Israel in 1948 was proof in his thinking that the rapture, the antichrist and the great tribulation were just a few years away.

Lindsey confidently predicted that the world was going from bad to worse, the church was losing ground to the devil and the antichrist was already alive, residing incognito somewhere in the world. In the Pentecostal churches of my locality, whole Bible studies were often devoted to debating the contents of Lindsey's book in the light of the prophetic Scriptures.

I remember long discussions on the possible identity of the antichrist. The majority of the older members of the Bible study believed that the then current U.S. Secretary of State, Henry Kissinger, was the most likely candidate. The younger members of the group like me were puzzled by this. We viewed Mr Kissinger as a skilful international diplomat and wondered what monstrous activities he might have engaged in to deserve being dubbed the antichrist!

Along with much else that was discussed at that time, the identity of the antichrist has had to be revised in the light of unfolding world events. Since then other candidates have been proposed for the job but after a season of popularity they have all fallen out of favour when predicted historical events did not unfold as anticipated.

The future was viewed by all of us with foreboding and a sense of gloom. Our sole consolation was that Christ would rescue us in the rapture, remove us from an evil world and transport us to eternal bliss in heaven. Our main assignment in the face of this bleak outlook was to be faithful to the Lord and win souls for Christ before it was too late. Our vision of the future could best be described as hopeless if it were not for our Lord's intervention.

My personal convictions regarding dispensationalism began to be undermined during my time at university. In hearing me speak about the imminent rapture, a faithful Christian friend asked me how I saw the 'until' verses in the New Testament regarding the coming of Christ. He pointed out that Acts 3:21 states that Jesus must remain in heaven *until* the time comes for God to restore everything, and 1 Corinthians 15:25 says, 'He must reign *until* he has put all his enemies under his feet'.

I had to admit that Christ's return could not be immediate if the New Testament taught that certain prophetic expectations had yet to be fulfilled. In addition, I began to appreciate that the dispensationalist view that the church would fail in its mission appeared incompatible with the sovereignty of God and the promise of Jesus that he would build his church, which could not be overcome by Hades' diabolical activities.

And so my personal journey of revelation got underway as I began to study the Scriptures with a new openness and was exposed to teaching from other church streams.

## Our journey

Both of us were deeply influenced by the rapture culture of the 1970s. But a journey of discovery meant that the persuasive message of *The Late Great Planet Earth* became less and less convincing in the light of global events in the subsequent decades. A re-reading of the book in the early 1990s – soon after the removal of the Berlin wall and the collapse of communism in Eastern Europe – highlighted the fact that many of the predictions could not possibly be fulfilled. Here is a sample:

> One of the most active areas of evangelism for the communist gospel is in Africa. As we see further developments in this area in the future we realise that it will be converted to communism. (page 68)
>
> Libya will join Russia in attacking Israel. (page 69)
>
> Germany and the Slovak countries will join hands with communist Russia. Also, Cossacks will invade Israel on horseback. (page 70)
>
> Leadership of the West will shift from the USA to Rome in its revived form. By 1980 we will have a United States of Europe. (page 96)[1]

Other people have written extensively exposing the predictions contained in *The Late Great Planet Earth*, their findings, unfortunately, being largely ignored by the Christian public. At present Hal Lindsey is still actively writing and broadcasting as an end-time prophecy expert! Lindsey is one of a long line of 'prophecy teachers' who claim to be able to provide a road map to the return of Christ. His writings made a great impact on many impressionable young people, ourselves included. We just went along with the crowd, believing that the rapture of the church was imminent and that the antichrist would soon be appearing.

*The Late Great Planet Earth* proved to be the first rumblings of a literary avalanche of books on Bible prophecy, books that became more and more extreme in their claims as the years went by. Of these, perhaps one deserves special attention: the amazing *88 Reasons Why Christ Will Return in 1988*, by Edgar C. Whisenant.

Whisenant was a former NASA engineer and a keen Bible student. His book confidently asserted that the rapture of the church would take place some time between the 11th and 13th September 1988 during the Jewish feast of Rosh-Hashanah. 300,000 copies of the book were mailed to pastors across America and it went on to sell a staggering 4.5 million copies.

Some sections of the church in the USA were galvanised by the book's claims. As the dreaded date approached, Trinity Broadcasting Network regularly screened instructions to believers on how to prepare for the rapture. When October 1988 passed with no rapture, Whisenant was unrepentant. He went on to publish a whole series of further books, all claiming to offer revised insights into the date of the rapture. *The Final Shout: Rapture Report 1989* was the first. This not surprisingly predicted the rapture in – wait for it – 1989! Next up was *23 Reasons Why a Pre-tribulation Rapture Looks Like It Will Occur on Rosh-Hashanah 1993*. Finally we had *And Now The Earth's Destruction by Fire, Nuclear Fire*, published in 1994.

The most amazing thing is not Whisenant's audacity in continuing to turn out such books, but the Christian public's gullibility, in continuing to buy them as they did.

A fundamental question began to emerge in our minds from the rubble of broken promises and unfulfilled prophecies. How could the Bible itself be the source of such confusion? This question provoked an investigation by both of us into what lay beneath the particular ideas held by these prophecy teachers. It became apparent that there were recurring absolutes held in common by them all. These could be summarised as follows:

## The rapture

All the prophecy teachers held that Jesus does not just return once at the end time, but twice! The initial visit was termed the 'rapture', a secret event in which the church would be caught up in the air to be with the Lord. Meanwhile, back on the earth, a seven-year period of tribulation would be unleashed on the remaining population. A shadowy figure known as the antichrist would rise to prominence. The Jewish nation would be converted and there would continue to be people who came to Christ; these were termed 'tribulation saints'. A great battle would ensue in the Middle East with nations besieging Jerusalem, but then Jesus would return again, this time in a blaze of glory to defeat the armies and judge his enemies.

## The millennium

The return of Jesus to the earth would be followed by a golden age of 1000 years, referred to as 'the millennium', an idea taken from Revelation chapter 20. During this time Christ would reign physically from a rebuilt temple in Jerusalem through the Jewish nation. The church would be absent, allegedly removed from the earth as the 'New Jerusalem' spoken of in Revelation 21. The millennium would end with another massive confrontation. This time, Satan himself would be released to gather rebellious people from across the earth, who would then march on Jerusalem in a massive show of force. Jesus would bring the rebellion to a swift end, with Satan being cast into the lake of fire. There would then be a resurrection from the dead of all humanity to appear before God's seat of judgment before he ushered in eternity.

## Israel

All the prophecy teachers laid great stress on the Jewish nation continuing to be God's chosen people. Yes, the church was important, but its role in the end times, they declared, would be eclipsed by the nation of Israel. Such teachers emphasised the obligation of all believers to support the cause of the present-day State of Israel because of its divine calling. Such actions would attract a special blessing from God. Additionally, some of these voices were very insistent that any other viewpoint was unbiblical and anti-Semitic, and would attract the judgment of God for not supporting his 'chosen people'.

It became clear that all of these beliefs hinged on a certain way of interpreting the Bible in general and Bible prophecy in particular.

The prophecy teachers insisted that the Bible should be interpreted *literally* except where explicitly stated otherwise. If this rule was compromised, their system simply didn't work. We noticed that each teacher had his own way of 'literally' interpreting Bible prophecy depending on current world events, but no-one seemed to question this.

Digging beneath the surface we discovered that these core beliefs formed part of a system of teaching known as *dispensationalism*. It had arisen during the 1800s and gained greater and greater popularity through the decades of the 20th century. Every time the world was threatened with war or danger, like the two World Wars, there was a heightened fascination with Bible prophecy and an eagerness to interpret events in the light of it.

'The beast' or 'antichrist' seemed to feature prominently each time and that label has been pinned on many historical figures including Hitler, Mussolini, Mao Tse-tung, Mikhail Gorbachev and Henry Kissinger. The Pope, too, has been a favourite candidate due to his religious power base in Rome and the global influence of Roman Catholicism.

We discovered that dispensationalism had its roots in the teaching of a Church of Scotland minister by the name of Edward Irving. We will look into his fascinating life in more detail in the following chapter. He came to prominence in the 1820s, and after his premature death in 1834 his followers formed a new denomination, the Catholic Apostolic Church (CAC).

In Irving's day, the study of Bible prophecy gained its impetus from the Napoleonic wars, and it was commonly felt that Napoleon himself – or, after his death, perhaps a member of his family – could be the antichrist. It all seemed to make sense at that time: the uniting of Europe under a powerful leader, the persecution of the church, and the world going from bad to worse.

The CAC built their whole structure on the expectation of the imminent return of Christ. Twelve apostles were appointed and a complex hierarchy set up to govern the Church. As they believed the time of the rapture would soon come, they saw no need to prepare for church growth or world mission. They existed as a 'faithful remnant' waiting to be 'raptured' away.

Throughout the remainder of the 19th century the CAC held tenaciously to its convictions that the rapture was looming, while at the same time slipping further into obscurity. The last 'apostle' died of darkness are being defeated through ordinary heroes like Ray Ferrier. Just like Ray in the film, many believers today are discovering that the seeds of the enemy's downfall have already been planted, waiting for us to exploit them. They are realising that far from being a remnant under siege, the church is God's unlikely army, rescuing men and women from death and claiming back the earth itself from Satan's oppression.

How did we come to such differing views of how the future will play out? Why are some believers convinced that the world is going to ruin, while others believe the Bible offers overwhelming hope for humanity? This is the subject of our book.

Every restoration in the fortunes of God's people has been preceded by the voice of the prophets calling them to repentance, faith and action. So too today, our generation owes a debt to those pioneers of a message that challenged the pessimism and escapism of their day and believed God for a recovery of the church's glory and power. Many 'John the Baptists' could be named, but in particular we want to honour Arthur Wallis, one of the fathers of the Charismatic Movement of the 1960s and 70s. His vision and voice were instrumental in the emergence of many vibrant 'new church' expressions which transformed the Christian landscape in many nations.

We honour Arthur for his willingness to respond to fresh light concerning God's purpose rather than be restricted by the prevailing mood of the day. Like Ray Ferrier in *War of the Worlds*, his courage became an inspiration for others to follow. Through his message of restoration at the popular Dales and Wales Bible Weeks, Arthur, along with Bryn Jones, Hugh Thompson, David Matthew and many others, contributed to the biblical understanding that underpins this book. The last 40 years have seen the emergence of a generation who are courageously occupying the arena that the enemy seemed to dominate and are finding, to their joy, that it is there for the taking.

in 1901 and the church fell into rapid decline. Today, nothing is left of it and Irving and his followers are regarded as a quirk of church history. Certainly dispensationalists prefer to distance themselves from him, but it was the Irvingites who undoubtedly set the scene for many others who followed.

Dispensationalism itself, however, did not die out but flourished in the hands of others to the extent that what began as a fringe movement came to dominate the church within a matter of a few decades. The 20th century saw its continued advance and establishment as part of mainstream Christianity.

More recently, the invasion of Kuwait by Iraq, the 9/11 terrorist attack and the Iraq War each fuelled a new crop of books on the end times by a more recent generation of prophecy teachers, all confident of having the keys to understanding events surrounding the return of Christ.

Finally, it is worth mentioning Tim LaHaye's *Left Behind* series of novels. They are set in the alleged seven-year period between the rapture and the return of Christ, sometime in the not-too-distant future. They are imaginative and captivating but based entirely on the dispensational view of end-time events.

The influence of these books has been incalculable. The first one appeared in 1995 and LaHaye and co-author Jerry Jenkins have gone on to write a total of twelve, plus spin-off youth books, audio books, devotionals and comics. In all, there have been sales of 65 million. Jerry Falwell is quoted as saying of the first book, 'In terms of its impact on Christianity, it's probably greater than that of any other book in modern times outside of the Bible'.[2]

Some may ask, 'Does all this really matter? Surely all prophecy, true or false, will take care of itself, and dispensationalism doesn't seem to have had a negative effect on the testimony of the church at large'. It is clear, however, that dispensationalism has indeed adversely affected large parts of the church. By supplying a grid in which end-time events fit our particular world today, some sections of the church have become more excited with preparing to leave Planet Earth than transforming it, and seem more interested in the antichrist than the Christ.

Our aim in writing this book has been to make a complex and challenging subject understandable by the church at large. Dispensationalism has already been adequately questioned by some fine theologians. The problem, however, is that the arguments over end-time teachings like the rapture or the millennium are not being fought and won at the theological level but at the popular level. People prefer a good story to sound theology!

Through Christian TV channels, books on biblical prophecy and from pulpits every Sunday, the Christian public is bombarded with dispensational teaching, to the degree that in many circles people are not even aware there is any other viewpoint!

Books like the *Left Behind* series have exerted enormous influence on a largely uninformed Christian public. The fact that they are labelled as fiction does little to prevent their readers from absorbing the underlying assumptions – which for 1800 years of church history were unheard of.

Dispensationalism is a vast subject with many interlocking themes. We will tackle them one by one, seeking to demonstrate how they work together to form a belief system that only holds up when every part is in place. At the same time, we ourselves want to avoid unwarranted dogmatism. We respect the fact that no one knows exactly how events will unfold as we approach the great day when Jesus returns. Rather than replacing one flawed system with another, we want to stir up a passionate commitment to advance the kingdom of God in the power of the Spirit and win the world to Christ.

## End notes

1. *The Late Great Planet Earth*, Zondervan, 1970
2. *Time Magazine*, 8th September 2007

Chapter 1

# The story of dispensationalism

Most of the teachings of dispensationalism were unheard of before the 1830s. As we have seen, it was largely through a Church of Scotland minister, Edward Irving (1792-1834) that they first came to prominence. Although he is little known today, Irving's influence in the first part of the 19th century was considerable and an understanding of his life is essential to our subject.

Irving trained under Dr Thomas Chalmers in Edinburgh before taking up the pastorate of the Church of Scotland congregation at Caledonian Chapel in London in 1822. He was an eloquent and commanding preacher and soon attracted such large crowds that a new church was built in Regent Square in 1827 to accommodate the growing numbers.

Irving was a colourful and highly controversial character, a charismatic pioneer advocating speaking in tongues and other spiritual gifts, decades before the Pentecostal revivals of the early 1900s. He was also a man with a quest to better understand the end times. He was gripped by the urgent tone of biblical prophecy and a belief that world events in his day were pointing to the return of Christ.

The popular view in the early 1800s was that the gospel would flourish and that a victorious church would usher in the return of Christ. This hope was spurring on the great missionary movement into every corner of the world.

Irving took a different view, however. He envisaged the world becoming darker and increasingly hostile to the church. He also held that the church itself would largely fall away, with Christ returning to rescue just a faithful remnant. It is important to understand at least some of people who shaped Irving's convictions – they were a colourful crowd!

The first of these was Samuel T Coleridge, the great English poet and philosopher. Originally a Unitarian, Coleridge had ruined his life and health with alcohol and narcotics before turning to the Anglican

Church for help. He was also taken up with transcendentalism and German philosophy. Coleridge heard of Irving's reputation in the mid 1820s and began attending his church.

A deep friendship developed between the two men, with Irving becoming entranced by the poet's philosophical ideas. Among these was the conviction, contrary to the mood of the day, that the world was heading for worse and worse conditions that would culminate in terrible suffering for mankind. Irving even went so far as to dedicate a speech at the London Missionary Society to Coleridge, acknowledging the poet's role in the formation of his ideas.

Another major influence in his life was Manuel Lacunza, a Spanish Jesuit who wrote a book under the pseudonym of Juan Josafat Ben-Ezra entitled *The Coming of the Messiah in Glory and Majesty*. Irving was introduced to his ideas in 1826 and was so impressed by Lacunza's work that he mastered Spanish in order to publish it in English. Irving added a 203-page preface in which he presented his own views on the end of the world, namely the apostasy of the Christian Church, the subsequent restoration of the Jews and the imminent return of Christ.

The third influence on Irving's mind was a self-taught student of Bible prophecy named Hatley Frere. He was from a notable family and became a close friend of Irving's from his time in London. Like Coleridge, Frere had a pessimistic view of the world. His ideas, however, were based on his own interpretation of Bible prophecy and the books of Daniel and Revelation in particular. Mrs. Oliphant, Irving's biographer, writes regarding the friendship:

> Mr. Hatley Frere, one of the most seditious of those prophetical students…has propounded a new scheme of interpretation, for which, up to this time, he has been unable to secure the ear of the religious public…. Mr Frere cherished the conviction that if he could but meet some man of candid and open mind, of popularity sufficient to gain a hearing, to whom he could privately explain and open up his system, its success was certain.
>
> When Irving, all ingenuous and ready to be taught, was suddenly brought into contact with him, the student of prophecy identified him by an instant intuition – 'Here is the man!'
>
> He disclosed to his patient hearer all those details to which the public ear declined to listen; and the result was that Mr. Frere gained a disciple and expositor; and that an influence…

24

of the most momentous importance.... took possession of Irving's thoughts.[1]

This association proved to be crucial in the way Bible prophecy was to be handled, and therefore in the development of dispensational thought itself.

Frere's conviction was that the majority of Bible prophecy was already fulfilled and that the coming of Christ could be no more than a few years away. And so Irving embarked on his obsession with end-time events. He related his indebtedness to Frere in the following terms:

> I had no rest in my spirit until I waited upon you and offered myself as your pupil, to be instructed in prophecy according to your ideas thereof.... I am not willing that anyone should account of me as if I were worthy to have had revealed to me the important truths...only the Lord accounted me worthy to receive the faith of these things which He first made known to you...
>
> And if He make me the instrument of conveying that faith to any in His church, that they may make themselves ready for His coming, or to any of the world, that they may take refuge in the ark of His salvation...to His name shall all the praise and glory be ascribed...[2]

These, then, were the chief influences upon Irving in the early 1820s: hardly what might be termed orthodox! Let us see how Irving himself contributed to the development of dispensational thought in the minds of others, an influence that spread far and wide within a very short space of time.

During his third year in London, Irving was introduced to Henry Drummond, a London banker and at one time High Sheriff of Surrey. He was also the leader of a missionary organisation known as the Continental Society.

Henry Drummond arranged for a conference to be held at his country seat, Albury Park, some 30 miles south of London, for the study of prophecy and the end times. It took place in November 1826 with around twenty men attending and lasted some six days. It proved to be pivotal in crystallising among those present the view that the end times had arrived. As they saw it, the church was heading for apostasy, the antichrist was about to be revealed, and the Lord would soon return for his beleaguered people.

It was also at this time that one of the most unusual teachings of all was introduced by Irving: the idea that Christ's return would be in two stages. The first stage, in which the church would be secretly removed from the earth, soon became known as the rapture. This was separated by a few years from the second stage, regarded as the return of Christ in glory. This notion, hitherto unheard of and outside of all orthodox doctrine, would within a few decades be embraced by large sections of the church.

It is difficult to pinpoint with accuracy the precise time and manner in which Irving conceived this rapture teaching. Dave McPherson has sought to show that the teaching originated from a prophecy brought by a 15-year-old girl named Margaret McDonald in Port Glasgow. The McDonalds belonged to a group of Irving's disciples who had been experiencing charismatic manifestations and Irving was keen to authenticate what was taking place among them[3]. In reading a transcript of the prophecy it seems that this *could* have been the source of the teaching.

What is clear is that this was the period when Irving embraced 'rapture teaching' as part and parcel of his emerging system of thought. With this vital component now in place, one can see that by around 1830, Irving's views on the end times are largely indistinguishable from those of dispensationalism as it emerged at the end of the 19th century.

Irving died at the age of just 42, in a state of considerable anguish from the loss of his baby son and the sting of criticism and rejection. He was a radical pioneer and proud mind, a deeply flawed man who nevertheless exerted considerable influence with his ideas on the return of Christ. The Church of Scotland expelled him just two years before his death and congregations loyal to his teaching formed the Catholic Apostolic Church just one year later, in 1835.

## J. N. Darby and the Brethren movement

One of those influenced by Irving was an Irish Anglican vicar, John Nelson Darby, who went on to do more than anyone else to shape and expound the premillennial teachings that Irving had begun to explore and which came to be known as dispensationalism.

Darby was born in London in 1800 into an Anglo-Irish land-owning family. He embraced Christianity as a student and was ordained into the Church of Ireland in 1825. However, he soon resigned from the denomination and began to develop his own theological ideas. Among these were the rejection of the clergy-laity divide, the unity of all believers, the imminent return of Christ for his bride, and the need for the church to prepare for this event by separating herself from a corrupt world.

Darby's views struck a chord with other young men in Dublin, who began to meet to 'break bread' in order to express their unity in Christ. They played down the official ministerial titles that many of them bore and met simply as brothers in Christ – brethren. And so by 1832 the first Brethren assembly was born.

One of those influenced by Darby was Lady Powerscourt, who was also a friend of Irving. She hosted a series of prophetic conferences at her estate, Powerscourt House in Enniskerry, County Wicklow, in which Darby was a keen participant.

As Darby emerged as a natural leader among the Brethren, his teaching on dispensationalism became widely accepted within this movement, as well as influencing Christians from other denominations. All of Irving's views on the return of Christ were present in the teachings of Darby, who went on to develop and disseminate them through his expansive writings:

- A 'secret rapture' of the church prior to the public return of Christ
- A period of tribulation followed by the return of Christ in glory
- The division of history into separate dispensations of time
- The distinct place of ethnic Israel in the plan of God
- A Jewish millennial reign of Christ on earth before the final judgment

It would be wrong to suggest that all the leaders of the Brethren movement were happy about Darby's interpretation of the Scriptures. One notable opponent was George Müller, the founder of the famous children's homes in Bristol and a man honoured widely for his vision and pioneering faith.

Of course, today's dispensationalists are eager to distance themselves from any suggestion that Darby's views were influenced by someone as unstable as Irving. John Walvoord wrote in 1976:

The often repeated charge that Darby secured his pre-tribulationism from Edward Irving has never been actually documented. One can hardly account for the wide acceptance of pre-tribulationism by Plymouth Brethren, who are devoted students of the Bible, to the offering of this view by a person who had no reputation for orthodoxy.[4]

But considering the widespread dissemination of Irving's views during the 1830s and the attendance of both Irving and Darby at the Powerscourt conference, it is highly likely that the former influenced the latter. Iain Murray writes as follows:

> This was just the period when Irving's influence through his preaching and writing, through the Albury Conferences and through 'The Morning Watch', was at its height. Amongst these Brethren, all earnestly exercised about spiritual things, Irving's warnings on the worldliness of organised religion and his reiteration of the Biblical teaching that the Bridegroom's advent is the blessed hope, received a ready hearing.[5]

Darby possessed qualities that Irving lacked and it was largely through him that dispensationalist views made rapid gains during the middle decades of the 19th century, affecting large portions of the Christian community in Britain, particularly the Church of England.[6]

## North America and C. I. Scofield

Now we must turn our attention to North America, where Darby's teachings were particularly well received. The 1870s saw the growth of the 'Bible Conference Movement' across the USA, with large numbers of believers gathering for the teaching and expounding of Scripture. The popular Niagara Bible Conference was one of the best known. These conferences, with their emphasis on literal Bible interpretation and their cross-denominational appeal, were fertile ground for the spread of dispensational views.

One of the participants in the conferences was Cyrus I. Scofield, who formed a board of Bible conference teachers that in 1909 helped to produce the famous Scofield Reference Bible. This edition was the King James Version of the Bible with explanatory notes by Scofield on the same page.

The notes presented the system of Bible interpretation that we have described above as dispensationalism. It encouraged people to understand the Scriptures from a dispensational perspective and quickly became popular across the United States, and subsequently in the United Kingdom.

Due to the Scofield Bible's success and influence, the majority of Evangelicals in the 20th century in the United States adopted a dispensational approach to the interpretation of Scripture, in particular Christians in Presbyterian, Baptist and Congregational circles. The same influence in the United Kingdom resulted in much of the Pentecostal movement embracing this system of theology, as also did many Charismatics in the latter part of the 20th century. The Scofield Bible has sold millions of copies and done more than anything else to help make dispensationalism synonymous with mainstream Christian thinking.

Several Bible institutes founded in the late 19th century also contributed to the spread of dispensational theology. The most famous of these, perhaps, was the Moody Bible Institute in Chicago. In 1924 Dallas Theological Seminary was founded specifically to advance dispensational theology in a formal academic setting. Lewis Sperry Chafer, one of the early principals of Dallas Seminary, further promoted dispensationalism through his eight-volume systematic theology.

Other Bible schools in the USA have become well known for their dispensationalist teaching, among them Grace College, Grace Theological Seminary, Northwestern College, Biola and Grand Rapids Baptist Seminary.

The rapid spread of dispensationalism has been assisted by two broader issues that have helped make it one of the most significant trends of 20th century Christianity:

### Defence of fundamentalism

The early decades of the 20th century saw the authority of Scripture come under increasing assault from liberal *'higher criticism'*, which eroded traditional beliefs like the virgin birth of Christ, the reality of miracles and the authenticity of biblical prophecy. The response to this came to be called *'fundamentalism'*, a movement dedicated to defending the authority of Scripture and the evangelical doctrines of Christianity.

Dispensationalism became an accepted part of this defence of the faith by fundamentalists. Its broad denominational base and literal interpretation of Scripture helped unite them as they withstood the modernist onslaught. In turn, dispensationalism profited from its association with the fundamentalist movement.

### Events in the Middle East

Events in the Middle East in the first half of the 20th century seemed to point to the fulfilment of biblical prophecy as understood by dispensationalists. The pressing need of a homeland for the scattered Jewish people, particularly after the Holocaust, focused attention on the Jewish cause and accelerated the process of finding one in Palestine. When this finally came about in 1948, many thought the return of Christ could be at most just a few short decades away. Successive Middle East conflicts in the 1960s and 70s seemed to confirm the view, pushing the dispensationalist publishing industry into overdrive!

The Jewish cause is without doubt still one of the core passions of dispensationalists, holding as they do that much end-time prophecy relates exclusively to the Jewish people and thus to their politics. We will examine the Israel question in depth in a later chapter.

## An outline of dispensational theology

Before we look at more recent developments it would be helpful to give an overview of classic dispensationalism as taught in the Scofield Bible.

Scofield taught that history may be divided into periods, or dispensations. He describes these dispensations as, 'the ordered ages which condition human life on the earth'.[7] Beginning with Adam and Eve in the garden, he describes a total of seven such dispensations. We list them below with the title Scofield gave each of them, the time period covered and the scripture reference indicating where he believed each one commenced:

| | | |
|---|---|---|
| 1. Innocence | Creation to Fall | Genesis 1:28 |
| 2. Conscience | Fall to Flood | Genesis 3:23 |
| 3. Human Government | Noah to Babel | Genesis 8:21 |
| 4. Promise | Abraham to Egypt | Genesis 12:1 |
| 5. Law | Moses to John the Baptist | Exodus 19:8 |
| 6. Grace | Church age | John 1:17 |
| 7. Kingdom | Millennium | Ephesians 1:10 |

According to this system, we are currently living in the sixth dispensation, the Church age, which will be followed by the last and seventh dispensation, the millennium.

A dispensation, according to Scofield, is 'a period of time during which man is tested in respect of obedience to some specific revelation of the will of God'.[8] Each one can also be identified by its own divinely-given mandate to mankind, and each one ends with man's failure to fulfil the divine calling. In the first dispensation, Adam and Eve failed in their task by eating the forbidden fruit, which resulted in the need for a second dispensation. This one, too, ended in man's failure. Thus man's failure and God's judgment, according to Scofield, run through the whole course of history – including the present church age which is destined to end in the same way.

For dispensationalists, the next great event on the prophetic calendar is the removal of the church from the earth so that God can usher in his millennial kingdom. This removal, the rapture, is the secret coming of Jesus for believers only, who will be caught up to meet him in the air, from where he will take them to heaven. The future hope for dispensational Christians therefore becomes escape from the earth so that life can be enjoyed in heavenly bliss.

Underpinning Scofield's dispensational scheme was the belief that two parallel purposes of God run throughout time and eternity. These are expressed in the formation of two peoples who will forever maintain their distinction. One purpose relates to the earth and involves an earthly people, the Jews, with earthly objectives. The other purpose relates to heaven and involves a heavenly people with heavenly objectives: the Christian Church.

The future hope of the church according to dispensationalists is therefore its removal from the earth in order to gain its heavenly inheritance with Christ forever. The Jews, by contrast, as heirs to the promises given to Abraham, will inherit the earth, ushering in a Jewish millennial kingdom. This duality of purpose is further expressed in that the church is considered to be the heavenly bride of Christ, whereas the Jews are viewed as the rightful wife of Jehovah.

Dispensationalists believe that since the Old Testament prophecies predict a future Jewish millennial kingdom, there are no outstanding promises left for the church to receive before the coming of the Lord. A secret rapture of the church from the earth, a seven-year period including the tribulation, and finally Christ's visible appearance to judge the nations and renew the earth; these combine to ensure that the destinies of the church and the Jews are kept separate.

## More recent developments

Dispensationalism has not stood still. By the latter part of the 20th century, a number of significant developments had taken place within that tradition. The resulting variations have created a virtual minefield for anyone trying to grasp what dispensationalism looks like today. For the purpose of this brief history we will limit ourselves to the most significant of these.

The classic dispensationalism of Darby, Scofield and Chafer could never have survived in its original form. It contained too many inconsistencies and contradictions for it to retain its credibility. Furthermore, its pessimistic appraisal of the church has been eroded by the Pentecostal and Charismatic revivals of the last 100 years. These have invigorated the church worldwide with confidence, faith and a passion for the gospel. The global church is rising up, not fading away!

The first major revision of dispensationalism began to appear in the 1960s with the emergence of revised dispensationalism. Its most influential proponents would include Charles Ryrie, who produced the popular Ryrie Study Bible, John Walvoord, J. Dwight Pentecost and Alva J. McClain.

Revised dispensationalists abandoned the doctrine of there being two eternally different groups of people through whom God was working, the church and the Jewish nation. They affirmed that salvation was only through Christ and that Jews had no head start simply because they were Jews.

They also began to move away from the highly privatised view of Christianity of former dispensationalists. The church, they conceded, was not a beleaguered remnant but a growing body with social responsibility towards a world that God was redeeming.

Methods of Bible interpretation changed too. Dispensationalists have always prided themselves on their 'literal' method of Bible interpretation. At the same time, the Brethren Church was renowned for its colourful Bible typology. These two methods of approaching the Bible became less and less compatible and revised dispensationalists began to drop much of the typology of their forebears in approaching the Scriptures. This process has exposed dispensationalists to greater scrutiny in the way they build their doctrinal case.

The most complex area of change concerns the kingdom of God. The Classic dispensationalism of Darby and Scofield held that there were actually two kingdoms: the *kingdom of God* was a spiritual, invisible kingdom, present now and received in the hearts of men and women when they accept Christ. The *kingdom of heaven* was very much an earthly kingdom, visible, political and still in the future. It was in fact the Jewish millennial kingdom that Jesus would rule over on his return.

Revised dispensationalists realised that this dual view of the kingdom was simply untenable. They began to drop references to a *kingdom of heaven* and *kingdom of God* and grapple with other ideas of the kingdom that could still support a dispensational framework. The result was confusing and, for many, just too complex to grasp. So at the popular level of Christian prophecy teachers, the old language has remained and much of the theological discussion left to one side.

In the 1980s and 1990s another revision began to emerge in the form of progressive dispensationalism. Influential in its ranks are Robert L. Saucy, Darrell Bock and Craig Blaising.

In progressive dispensationalism the dualism of an earthly and heavenly people has virtually vanished. The church is seen as a vital part of the one plan of redemption. Its arrival at Pentecost did not require a separate or secondary plan of redemption as the earlier dispensationalists had held. Furthermore, the church is acknowledged as the fulfilment of the New Covenant promises set out in the books of Jeremiah and Ezekiel. It is the 'one new man' that Paul speaks about in Ephesians, comprising both Jewish and Gentile believers.

Progressive dispensationalists still maintain that God has a distinct end-time purpose for the Jewish nation. They also believe that when Paul said 'all Israel will be saved' (Romans 11:26) he was referring to the whole ethnic nation of Israel.

Progressive dispensationalists understand the dispensations as successive but not separate arrangements in the plan of redemption. They foresee a Jewish millennial kingdom being inaugurated at the return of Christ but view it as an outworking of the one kingdom of God through the ages.

Clearly then, dispensationalism today is far from a unified set of ideas. While changes have taken place at the theological level, many have continued to retain the ideas of earlier forms of dispensationalism, particularly at the popular level of the pulpit, Christian TV and books on the end times. Indeed it is popular literature that has contributed most to promoting dispensationalism. Let's remind ourselves of some of the key works.

Hal Lindsey's best-selling book *The Late Great Planet Earth* applied dispensational theology to then-current world events, like the restoration of the state of Israel, the politics of the Cold War and the nuclear arms race. Lindsey, a graduate of Dallas Theological Seminary, exerted a profound influence upon Christians in the 1970s and 80s through this and his other books.

Then in the 1990s and 2000s came the best-selling *Left Behind* series written by Tim LaHaye and Jerry B. Jenkins. These novels graphically portray a dispensationally-conceived future, beginning with the rapture and continuing through the series with a description of the great tribulation and society's response to the world-dominating reign of the antichrist.

All of these developments make the task of evaluating dispensationalism today all the more challenging. So what are we left with? What are the main pillars holding up the dispensationalist house, the tenets on which all dispensationalists agree? Surprisingly, despite all the twists and turns, what remain are the same key issues that Irving and Darby taught in the mid-1800s and noted earlier in this chapter.

We will look at each of these in more depth as well as examining other major themes of dispensationalism such as the Olivet discourse and the tribulation. First of all though, we will need to look at the bible itself: how do we understand it and its teaching on the return of Christ? Our task in all of this is not to replace one dogma with another or dispensationalism with another 'ism' of our own, but to open up our subject objectively in a way that will shed light rather than generate heat.

### End notes

1. Margaret Oliphant, *The Life of Edward Irving*, 1864, pp 104, 105
2. Oliphant, op cit, p 107
3. Dave McPherson has written many books seeking to expose pre-tribulationism and secret rapture theology, including: *The Incredible Cover Up* (1975), *The Great Rapture Hoax* (1983) and *The Rapture Plot* (2000). Sadly, his decades-long conspiracy hunt of dispensationalists has undermined an otherwise helpful contribution to the debate.

4. John Walvoord, *The Blessed Hope and the Tribulation*, p 48
5. *The Puritan Hope*, p 199
6. E. B. Elliott, writing in 1851, noted with concern, 'In the year 1844, the date of the first publication of my work on the Apocalypse, so rapid has been the progress of these views in England, that instead of its appearing a thing strange and half heretical to hold them, as when Irving published his translation of Ben Ezra, the leaven had evidently now deeply penetrated the religious mind; and from the ineffectiveness of the opposition hitherto formally made to them, they seemed gradually advancing toward triumph.' *Horae Apocalypticae, A Commentary on the Apocalypse* 4th edition, 1851
7. Scofield's note on Ephesians 1:10
8. Scofield Bible, p 5

# Chapter 2

# Christ, his covenant and his kingdom

This chapter is all about the Bible and specifically how we approach it. Our basic understanding of God's Word determines what we see when we read its pages – the lens through which we view it. Are we looking at a timetable for our impending departure from Planet Earth, or following a master-plan for the redemption of the world? To set out an alternative approach to God's Word than that offered by dispensationalism, we are going to apply a wide-angle lens and take in the full sweep of the Bible.

The flip side to this approach is to get close up with a zoom lens. This is where the subject of Bible interpretation (hermeneutics) comes in. We have devoted a separate appendix to this important issue and encourage our readers to explore it.

Bible interpretation is governed by rules or guiding principles. They make surprising common sense and are in fact identical to those for interpreting any historic or legal document. Once clear on these basic rules, one can have far greater confidence in handling specific passages of Scripture. The beliefs and doctrines of dispensationalism are due largely to its particular rules of Bible interpretation. It is almost impossible to tackle dispensationalism without appreciating this fact.

So far we have pulled no punches in identifying dispensationalism as a negative influence in the Christian landscape. However, so as to avoid the snare of conducting a crusade against a section of God's church, we want to acknowledge the positive contribution it has made: a solid defence of the Christian faith, countless passionate evangelists, a love of God's Word and a call to holy living. Many holding to dispensationalist views have been at the forefront of church planting and missions. The tone of urgency at its heart has focussed numerous believers on the brevity of this life and the priority of the next.

But dispensationalism remains inherently pessimistic and speculative in its view of the world. If you believe that the next event on God's calendar is the rapture of the church, it is difficult to have faith for more than the urgent and immediate. The best hope is that Jesus will rescue us from the grim situation coming on the earth before it is too late!

The idea that the church has already done all it can do continues to rob believers of their destiny to bring transformation to a world in darkness. One of today's most popular dispensationalist prophecy teachers recently concluded that 'by evangelizing the world in preparation for the "time of the end", the church has accomplished what God called it to do'.[1]

## Christ, the centre of all things

So what is the Bible all about? In a word – Christ! Unless this is clear in our thinking we risk being 'tossed around by every wind of doctrine'. Jesus is there all the way through, from the tree of life in the garden, to the Lamb on the throne of heaven. He is in the furniture of the tabernacle, the robes of the priests, the sacrifices of Leviticus and the laws of Moses. He is in the history of Israel and the declarations of the prophets. He is as much the subject of David's psalms as of Paul's epistles.

When Jesus spoke to the two disciples on the Emmaus road, Luke records that, 'And beginning with Moses and all the Prophets, he explained to them what was said in all the Scriptures concerning *himself.*' (Luke 24:27). The person of Christ is woven into every book of the Bible. Even the book of Revelation is in fact the 'revelation of Jesus Christ' (1:1) and not, as some would have us think, the revelation of the antichrist, rapture or tribulation.

To fully grasp the significance of Christ and all he accomplished, we must begin with the expectation carried by the Old Testament prophets. By investigating what they saw, we will understand the foundations of God's plan for the present and the future. From the Old Testament prophets a burden emerges for the coming of God's servant, the Messiah. This is powerfully announced in Isaiah 9:6-7:

> *For to us a child is born, to us a son is given, and the government will be on his shoulders. And he will be called Wonderful Counsellor, Mighty God, Everlasting Father, Prince of Peace.*

> *Of the increase of his government and peace there will be no end. He will reign on David's throne and over his kingdom, establishing and upholding it with justice and righteousness from that time on and forever. The zeal of the Lord Almighty will accomplish this.*

This coming 'Son', given by God, will be no ordinary human being. Let's look more closely at two features in particular that stand out. First of all, the titles 'Mighty God' and 'Everlasting Father' indicate that the Messiah has divine attributes. He is coming as king and will completely change society, ushering in an age in which he will administer his kingdom with justice and righteousness, from that time and for evermore.

Isaiah fills out his vision of the future under the Messiah in chapter 11:1-9. In verse 1 he proclaims, 'A shoot will come up from the stump of Jesse; from his roots a Branch will bear fruit'. That shoot was of course his son, King David. The prophet likened the Messiah's reign to that of David, who established God's kingdom on the earth during his lifetime. That administration of the kingdom became the high water mark of the government of God in Israel's history.

Although the tree of David was ultimately cut down by the Babylonian captivity, Isaiah assures us there would emerge from the remaining stump a shoot that would bear fruit for God, a person whom Isaiah identifies as 'the Branch'. This was fulfilled in Jesus, born of David's line and destined to sit on David's throne. Jeremiah also signals the emergence of this 'righteous Branch':

> *The days are coming,' declares the Lord, 'when I will raise up to David a righteous Branch, a King who will reign wisely and do what is just and right in the land. In his days Judah will be saved and Israel will live in safety. This is the name by which he will be called: The Lord Our Righteousness.* (Jeremiah 23:5-6)

The prophets concur that the life of this king would be characterised by the presence of the Spirit – 'the Spirit of wisdom and of understanding, the Spirit of counsel and of power, the Spirit of knowledge and of the fear of the Lord' (Isaiah 11:2). Because of his righteous reign and the justice that he would bring, life in the future would be very different from how it was at the time the prophets were writing. With vivid prophetic imagery Isaiah declares, 'The wolf will live with the lamb, the leopard will lie down with the goat, the calf and the lion and the yearling together; and a little child will lead them'. (Isaiah 11:6).

Isaiah returns in 53:2 to the 'shoot' expression he used earlier but with a startling new revelation – the Messiah must suffer for his people. Isaiah 53 contains a graphic description of the punishment, humiliation and ultimate crucifixion of the Christ, indicating that although the coming Messiah would be a king, salvation of his people would come through his own vicarious suffering.

Secondly it is not only his kingly titles that are relevant here, for the prophets also reveal the Messiah as the mediator of a New Covenant. Isaiah says that God describes him as 'my servant, whom I uphold, my chosen one in whom I delight; I will put my Spirit on him' (Isaiah 42:1). Then he goes on to say in verse 6, 'I will keep you and will make *you* to be a covenant for the people and a light for the Gentiles' (the same phrase is reiterated in Isaiah 49:8). So, not only would there be a New Covenant, but the New Covenant would be a *person*, the Messiah! He would give his life to establish a new basis of fellowship and relationship between God and his people.

Malachi saw a similar thing when he prophesied: '"Then suddenly the Lord you are seeking will come to his temple; the *messenger of the covenant*, whom you desire, will come," says the Lord Almighty' (Malachi 3:1).

At the time of Malachi, 400 years before the birth of Christ, there had emerged among the faithful community of God's people a strong desire to see the promised Messiah revealed. Malachi affirms to this believing community that the Lord would indeed come, but he sets no timescale to the event. Malachi does, however, identify the Messiah as the 'Messenger of the Covenant'. This would be an important aspect of the Messiah's ministry.

So Christ is indeed the subject of the Bible. He is present on every page. But, as we have seen, the Old Testament prophets also link Christ to the position of King in the kingdom of God and mediator of a New Covenant. These two themes, covenant and kingdom, are of great importance because they reveal the structure and story of the Bible – what Christ is doing and how he is doing it. We can summarise as follows:

**Christ**      **the subject of the Bible**
**Covenant**    **the structure of the Bible**
**Kingdom**     **the story of the Bible**

This is what we are going to explore further in this chapter, beginning with covenant – and especially the wonderful New Covenant.

## Christ and the covenants

The word 'covenant' is little used in everyday life today, but in biblical times the concept was widely understood and applied right across civilised life. Let's begin with a definition:

*A covenant is an agreement binding two parties together, entered into under certain terms and invoking blessings (benefits) if the covenant is kept and curses (sanctions) if it is broken.*

It is through covenant alone that men and women can experience relationship with a holy God. Biblical covenants are not thrashed out by both parties equally, however. God himself stipulates the terms; they are non-negotiable by us. The Bible covenants form the very structure of God's revelation to humanity and have been central in the development of theological understanding. Indeed, so great has been the significance of covenant that the 16th century Reformation gave rise to a widely held school of thought known as *covenant theology*.[2]

Dispensationalists have always acknowledged the importance of the covenants but have placed them second to their own scheme of dispensations, an idea that has led to all manner of problems as people have tried to accommodate the two systems at the same time.

We recommend the works of O. Palmer Robertson for an excellent introduction to understanding the biblical covenants. In his book *The Christ of the Covenants*, he sets them out as follows:

| | |
|---|---|
| **Adam** | **The covenant of creation** |
| **Noah** | **The covenant of preservation** |
| **Abraham** | **The covenant of promise** |
| **Moses** | **The covenant of law** |
| **David** | **The covenant of the kingdom** |
| **Christ** | **The New Covenant** |

Unlike Scofield's dispensations, the biblical covenants build successively upon each other, each contributing to a progressive revelation of God to man. To quote Robertson:

*The covenant structure of Scripture manifests a marvellous unity. God, in binding a people to himself, never changes. For this reason the covenants of God relate organically to one another. From Adam to Christ, a unity of covenantal administration characterises the history of God's dealings with his people.*[3]

We are going to take a brief survey of these Old Testament covenants.

## Adam

Although there is no formal covenant-making event recorded between God and Adam, it is clear that a covenantal relationship existed. God commissioned Adam (Genesis 1:27), he blessed him (Genesis 1:28) and he warned him of the consequences of disobedience (Genesis 2:17). Hosea 6:7 actually refers to this covenant with Adam when it says of the people of Israel 'Like Adam, they have broken the covenant'.

## Noah

The covenant God made with Noah is found in Genesis chapter 9. It is really a commitment by God to preserve creation until his promises and purposes for the earth are fulfilled – regardless of humanity's failings. It reaffirms God's purpose for men and women to 'Be fruitful and increase in number and fill the earth.' (Genesis 9:1). It also establishes the principle of human government: 'Whoever sheds the blood of man, by man shall his blood be shed' (Genesis 9:6).

## Abraham

Next to come was the Abrahamic covenant. In Genesis 12 God revealed himself to Abram and promised to bless him and his family and make of them a great nation. Further chapters of Genesis expand on these promises to include a national inheritance, blessing for all nations through Abram and victory over his enemies.

The Abrahamic covenant was a *grant covenant*, where God's promises are unconditional. The covenant blessings were instead entered into by faith. This is significant because Abraham becomes the father of *all* who relate to God by faith. The New Testament writers constantly point us back to Abraham as the foundation of our New Covenant relationship with God.

## Moses

By contrast, the Mosaic covenant was a *bilateral covenant*, the kind by which a king would allow his subjects to enjoy life under his reign in exchange for loyal service. Its blessings were conditional on the people's obedience. When God brought Israel out of Egypt to lead them into the Promised Land, he established a new level of relationship with them through the Mosaic covenant. God's intention was that he would be their God and they would be his people, a kingdom of priests and a holy nation (Exodus 19:5-6). Moses received the detailed statutes and laws of this covenant at Mount Sinai, by keeping which the Israelites could enjoy fellowship and communion with a holy God.

### David

The final Old Testament covenant was the one God made with David. This covenant concerned itself with prophetic anticipation of the coming of the kingdom of God in the Messiah. In Psalm 89 we read how God promised David that from his line Messiah would come and reign on his throne. In the fullness of time, Christ would fulfil the prophetic scriptures concerning David and his reign.

The 'Old' covenant referred to by the New Testament writers is the Mosaic Covenant and Israel's track record in obeying it was at best chequered. Yes, there were times of revival and restoration under the judges, David and some of the other kings, but by the time the prophetic writings of the Old Testament were given, the people had departed from both the spirit and the letter of the covenant and spiritual decay had set in. God said to them through Jeremiah:

> In the time I brought your forefathers up from Egypt until today, I warned them again and again, saying, 'Obey me.' But they did not listen or pay attention; instead, they followed the stubbornness of their evil hearts. So I brought on them all the curses of the covenant I had commanded them to follow but that they did not keep. (Jeremiah 11:7-8)

The covenant given at Sinai was no longer a means by which God and his people could relate, since it was now well and truly broken through the people's disobedience (Jeremiah 31:32). God had been devoted to his people like a faithful husband, but Israel had gone after many lovers (Hosea 3:1).

Although the Israelites broke the covenant, God's redemptive plan to have a people for himself continued. To achieve this, a new covenant would have to be established on an entirely different basis. Jeremiah anticipates the inauguration of this great moment:

> *'The time is coming' declares the Lord, 'when I will make a new covenant with the house of Israel and the house of Judah. It will not be like the covenant I made with their forefathers when I took them by the hand to lead them out of Egypt, because they broke my covenant, though I was a husband to them,' declares the Lord. 'This is the covenant I will make with the house of Israel after that time,' declares the Lord. 'I will put my law in their minds and write it on their hearts. I will be their God, and they will be my people.'* (Jeremiah 31:31-33)

We instantly recognise this as the New Covenant, a fact that is confirmed by the writer to the Hebrews. The New Covenant, he declares, is the one that Christ established through the sacrifice of his life on the cross, thus making the former covenant, given at Sinai, now obsolete (Hebrews 8:13).

Isaiah and Ezekiel, like Jeremiah, see the requirement for a new covenant. Isaiah 42:6 and 49:8 describes, as we have already seen, the covenant as a person, Messiah. Ezekiel 37 speaks of an everlasting covenant which will unite and fulfil the previous covenants in itself.

So, not only would there be a New Covenant, but the New Covenant would be a *person*, the Messiah! He would give his life to establish a new basis of fellowship and relationship between God and his people.

Indeed, the New Covenant in Christ completely fulfils the old Mosaic covenant, to the degree that the Old has now become redundant as a means by which people relate to God. The only covenant in operation now is the New Covenant and with it comes a new priest, Christ, ministering from the order of the priesthood of Melchizedek. The Aaronic priesthood with all its ceremonies and institutes no longer serves any purpose at all. Those days are gone for ever!

With the New Covenant also comes a new spiritual temple, the church, the people of God, both Jew and Gentile, bought with the blood of Jesus. There is no longer any need for a physical structure in Jerusalem. And should a new one ever get built in Jerusalem, as dispensationalists expect, it will have no relevance to the purposes of God. The new covenant prevails in all things. It is therefore misleading and confusing to find some Christians advocating a return to Jewish customs and ceremonies that the Bible itself declares to be of no value!

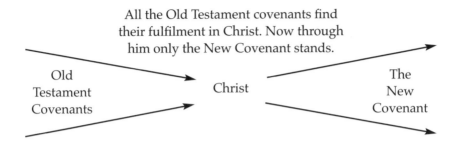

All the Old Testament covenants find
their fulfilment in Christ. Now through
him only the New Covenant stands.

Old Testament Covenants → Christ → The New Covenant

## Christ and the kingdom

The biblical covenants give us a structure by which we can understand the Bible. We have seen already that Christ is the subject of God's word, but what of the story itself – what is Christ up to in the earth? This is where we introduce the amazing activity of God's kingdom.

We saw earlier that the Old Testament prophets viewed the coming Messiah as king, and so it is obvious that he must have a kingdom over which to reign. The Messiah's kingdom, they insisted, would differ from every other in that it would never end. Isaiah declares, 'He will reign on David's throne and over his kingdom, establishing and upholding it with justice and righteousness from that time on and *forever*' (Isaiah 9:7). So when is this kingdom introduced to the world and in what shape and form? Is it here already or does it await a future millennial reign, as dispensationalists believe the Old Testament prophets announced? Perhaps the prophet who can help us the most with this kingdom drama is Daniel.

King Nebuchadnezzar of Babylon was troubled one night by a strange dream and was at a loss as to its meaning. Daniel chapter 2 describes how he summoned his wise men to provide him with the interpretation. None were able to help the king in his request except Daniel, to whom the Lord gave an understanding of the dream and the key to its interpretation.

Daniel explained that the king had seen a large statue with its head made of pure gold, its chest and arms of silver, its belly and thighs of bronze, its legs of iron and its feet partly of iron and partly of baked clay. In the dream, a rock was cut out, but not by human hands. The rock struck the statue on its feet and smashed them, resulting in the whole of the statue being broken to pieces and swept away by the wind without leaving a trace. However, the rock that struck the statue went on to grow into a huge mountain that filled the whole earth.

Daniel identified the head of gold as King Nebuchadnezzar. He explained that three kingdoms would follow his, represented by materials inferior in quality to the golden head. Then, Daniel prophesied, in the times of the kings represented by the iron mixed with clay, the God of heaven would set up a kingdom that would never be destroyed. It would crush all the other kingdoms, bringing them to an end, but the kingdom of God represented by the rock, would grow and endure forever.

The majority of Bible scholars agree about the kingdoms that followed the Babylonian head of gold. The silver represents the Medo-Persian Empire; the bronze depicts the rule of Alexander the Great and the Greeks; and the iron represents the Roman Empire. According to Daniel, it was during the time of these kings – the Roman Emperors – that God would set up a kingdom that would never be destroyed.

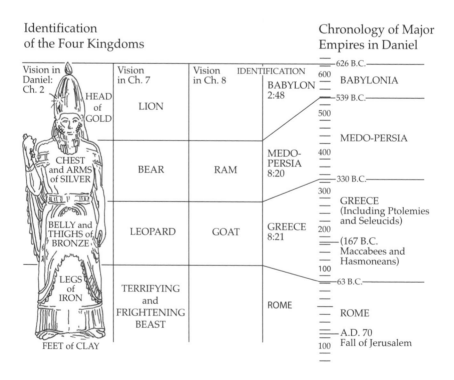

Identification of the Four Kingdoms

Chronology of Major Empires in Daniel

| Vision in Daniel: Ch. 2 | Vision in Ch. 7 | Vision in Ch. 8 | IDENTIFICATION | |
|---|---|---|---|---|
| HEAD of GOLD | LION | | BABYLON 2:48 | 626 B.C. — 600 BABYLONIA — 539 B.C. — 500 |
| CHEST and ARMS of SILVER | BEAR | RAM | MEDO-PERSIA 8:20 | MEDO-PERSIA — 400 — 330 B.C. — 300 |
| BELLY and THIGHS of BRONZE | LEOPARD | GOAT | GREECE 8:21 | GREECE (Including Ptolemies and Seleucids) — 200 (167 B.C. Maccabees and Hasmoneans) — 100 |
| LEGS of IRON / FEET of CLAY | TERRIFYING and FRIGHTENING BEAST | | ROME | 63 B.C. — ROME — A.D. 70 100 Fall of Jerusalem |

This took place in the coming of Jesus into the world. He is the stone 'cut out by no human hand', destined to judge the kingdoms of this world. The clear implication of Daniel's interpretation is that the kingdom of God has already been established in the earth through the coming of Christ as a man. But just as the stone grew to become a great mountain, the kingdom that Jesus introduced did not come at that time in its fullness but is in the process of increasing.

Daniel also indicates that this kingdom has a people. He says, 'nor will it be left to another people.' (Daniel 2:44). So Jesus will grant his followers to be heirs of his newly established kingdom, something we find agrees perfectly with the New Testament revelation of the church as his kingdom people.

Dispensationalists believe Nebuchadnezzar's dream refers to the coming of the kingdom in the future, the alleged 1000-year reign of Christ. It is common for them to read into the passage the idea that there will be a re-formed Roman Empire at some stage in the future, at which time Christ will set up his millennial kingdom on earth. We can do no better than quote Professor Jay E. Adams in addressing this point:

> The time of the establishment of this kingdom is specifically given. It is during the days of the ascendancy of the fourth kingdom: 'in the days of those kings' (Daniel 2:44). By no ingenious method of interpretation can this be made to mean some yet future date, more than 1,900 years after the fall of the fourth kingdom. To pretend that the Roman Empire continues today is sheer nonsense. There has been no fourth kingdom for centuries.
>
> The prophecy speaks of the same kingdom that John, Jesus and Paul announced. It is the kingdom the apostles preached, and the one Revelation depicts as replacing the Roman Empire. According to Mark 1:15, Jesus preached that the 'time is fulfilled, and the kingdom of God is at hand'. If he did not refer to Daniel's promises of this kingdom, to the fulfilment of what prophecy did he refer? There is but one kingdom predicted. If the kingdom of Christ in the present age is not that kingdom – what is?[4]

If our understanding of Daniel chapter 2 is correct, we should expect to find it in the New Testament. Indeed, the gospels are first to teach that Jesus brought his kingdom with him at his first coming. Christ's forerunner, John the Baptist, proclaimed, 'The kingdom of heaven is near' (Matthew 3:2). Later, when Jesus was outworking the commission the Father had sent him to complete, he said, 'If I drive out demons by the Spirit of God, then *the kingdom of God* has come upon you' (Matthew 12:28).

When asked about the timing of the kingdom of God and its appearance, Jesus responded by saying that the kingdom does not come with careful observation. Instead, he asserted, the kingdom was already among them (Luke 17:21). This should not surprise us. As Jesus is the King, wherever he is and wherever the will of God is done, there the kingdom has already come!

Furthermore, the kingdom that had arrived in Jesus' first coming to earth became a primary feature of his teaching during the three and a half years of his public ministry. Matthew 13 records seven of his parables, each of which explains the characteristics and nature of a kingdom which had already come among them.

Christ's passion for imparting an understanding of his kingdom remained undimmed following his resurrection. He was with his disciples for a period of forty days prior to his ascension. What did he talk to them about? The primary theme of his conversation was again the kingdom of God (Acts 1:3).

What we have discovered so far presents us with something of a conundrum. If the kingdom of God arrived at Christ's first coming, why did it not come *in its fullness* at that time, but awaits a greater fulfilment at his future coming? We must now turn our attention to the very important issue of explaining how these two stages work.

## The kingdom, 'already here' and 'not yet here'

Although the Old Testament prophets were accurate in their description of the coming kingdom of God, they did not necessarily understand *how* it would come. They saw the kingdom as belonging to a future golden age quite separate from their own 'present age'. That future age would herald a number of things:

The coming of the Messiah (Isaiah 11:1-9)
The establishing of the age of righteousness and peace (Isaiah 11:4-9)
Judgment and justice being enacted on the earth (Isaiah 2:4)
The resurrection of the dead (Psalm 16:9-11)
The Day of the Lord (Joel 2:11)
The Spirit being poured out on all flesh (Joel 2:28)

The coming of the kingdom as understood by the Old Testament prophets can be represented in the following way:

| Present Age | The End | Age to Come |
|---|:---:|---:|
| | **X** | |
| | | =Kingdom of God |

Characteristics of the age to come:
– Messiah coming – age of righteousness
  and peace (Isaiah 11:1-9)
– Judgment (Isaiah 2:1-4)
– Resurrection of the dead (Psalms 16:9-11)
– The day of the Lord (Joel 2:11)
– Gift of promised Holy Spirit (Joel 2:28)

How should we understand what the prophets saw? Do we relegate all these features to a future millennial age or has Christ introduced some of them already? Clearly, some are here now, at least in part, but others are not, and won't arrive till Jesus returns. There is no contradiction here. Jesus repeatedly distinguished between two ages, the present age and the age to come. More than once he contrasted life 'in this age' with that of 'life in the age to come'. For example:

> 'I tell you the truth, no one who has left home or brothers or sisters or mother or father or children or fields for me and the gospel will fail to receive a hundred times as much in this **present age** (homes, brothers, sisters, mothers, children and fields – and with them, persecutions) and in **the age to come**, eternal life.' (Mark 10:29-30)

Whereas in this age, he says, people will be persecuted for following Christ, in the age to come they will know the fullness of eternal life and all opposition will be absent. Jesus' disciples understood the distinction:

> The disciples came to him privately. 'Tell us,' they said, 'when will this happen, and what will be the sign of **your coming** and of **the end of the age?**' (Matthew 24:3)

They grasped that this age would come to an end when Christ returns at his second coming, not his first. Jesus further clarified the matter:

> 'The people of this age marry and are given in marriage. But those who are considered worthy of taking part in **that age** and in the **resurrection from the dead** will neither marry nor be given in marriage, and they can no longer die for they are like the angels.

*They are God's children, since they are children of the resurrection.'*
(Luke 20:34-36)

The coming of Christ will trigger the resurrection from the dead of all humanity to face the final judgment. In the future age people are described as 'God's children' and are known as 'children of the resurrection'.

The Old Testament writers saw the age to come separated from this age by a single arrival of the Christ, often referred to as 'the day of the Lord', when he would set up his kingdom. The New Testament writers accept the same basic model, but under the Holy Spirit's direction they introduce a significantly new dimension. The kingdom would come in two stages; invading the present age by Christ's first coming and being consummated in the age to come by his second coming.

Jesus himself taught this. Not only did he speak of the kingdom present now, but also of a future coming of the kingdom. For example, in the parable of the Minas (or talents) he spoke of a man of noble birth who went to receive a kingdom and return (Luke 19:11-27). On other occasions Jesus spoke about entering the kingdom as a future event (Matthew 7:21, 25:34).

The rest of the New Testament paints a similar picture, one of a kingdom that is here, yet not *in its entirety*. It awaits a final consummation.

It is this understanding of the kingdom, *already arrived* in the person of Christ but *yet to come* in its fullness, that could not have been fully anticipated from the Old Testament alone and which is unwrapped for us in the New Testament. This change of perspective brought through the New Testament is depicted by the diagram below.[5]

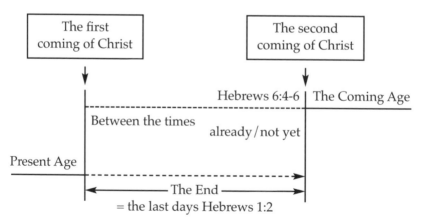

50

Instead of one 'coming of the Messiah', we now understand that there are in fact two: his physical birth as a man 2,000 years ago, and his still-future return in glory. The vertical line to the left represents the timing of his first coming, when the kingdom was inaugurated. The second vertical line indicates the future return of Christ, when the kingdom will be consummated. The horizontal lower line represents the present evil age, which continues today even though the kingdom of God has arrived in Christ. The higher horizontal line represents the presence of the kingdom of God. It came with Christ and continues after his second coming into the fullness of life in the age to come.

At this present time, therefore, we are positioned between these two appearances of Christ in the overlap of two ages! 'Already' Christ has come. 'Not yet' has he come a second time. 'Already' the kingdom has arrived in the life and ministry of Jesus. 'Not yet' has the kingdom been fully manifested as it will when he returns to judge the earth and usher in the age to come. The whole of this period we are in is actually 'the last days'.

In this overlap of two ages there are two kinds of people living on the earth. Some live outside of Christ and remain wedded to the present evil age. Others have responded to the reality of Christ's first coming and have placed their faith in him. They now belong to the kingdom of God. The writer to the Hebrews describes these people as having 'tasted the powers of the coming age' (Hebrews 6:5). They no longer live according to the flesh, the power of this age, but rather according to the Spirit, the power of the future age. This results in the manifestation of love, joy and peace that the Spirit always brings.

To summarise, the New Testament writers teach us that as believers in Jesus Christ we live:

- In the overlap of two ages
- By the Spirit and not by the flesh
- In the 'already' and 'not yet' of the kingdom

The reality of living in the 'already' but 'not yet' is best expressed by the New Testament writers when they speak about the resurrection. Believers have already been 'raised up with Christ and seated with him in the heavenly realms' (Ephesians 2:6). Resurrection to new life is something we enjoy now because of our relationship with Jesus Christ. The apostle John puts it in these simple terms: 'He who has the Son has life; he who does not have the Son of God does not have life' (1 John 5:12).

Our spiritual resurrection, the receiving of the life of Jesus and the presence of the Spirit, has therefore already taken place. The physical resurrection of the body, has, by contrast, not yet occurred and awaits the return of Jesus and the consummated kingdom. At that time, 'when he appears, we shall be like him' (1 John 3:2) – in character, yes, but also in enjoying a body like the one he himself had following his resurrection (Philippians 3:10-11).

The privilege of those living in Christ is firstly to enjoy the kingdom of God here and now. According to Paul, life in the kingdom is not about rules regarding what you can or can't eat and drink; it is about living in the righteousness, peace and joy that come from the person of the Holy Spirit, who now dwells in us (Romans 14:17).

Secondly, because we experienced an invasion of kingdom power into our lives when we received Christ, it is our privilege to demonstrate that life and power to those still shackled by sin and darkness and to offer them a better way to live – in the freedom that Christ bought through his blood. This is our mandate, to extend the kingdom here and now on the earth until Jesus returns in glory.

## Conclusion

We have shown how the twin themes of covenant and kingdom provide a means of unlocking the purpose of God in the Bible. The covenants are the structure of the Bible and indeed of history itself. They are like the chapters of an amazing book in which God is revealing his plan and purpose for the world. Just as the chapters of any book build one upon the other, so God's covenants build successively toward the great climax of the New Covenant in Christ and then his final return in glory.

If God's covenants are the structure of the book, then God's kingdom is the story. We may say that the great narrative we are part of is that of the coming of the kingdom of God into the world here and now. Jesus taught us to pray, 'your kingdom come, your will be done on earth as it is in heaven' (Mathew 6:10).

The implications of our study are far reaching but also very practical. They affect not only our understanding of events surrounding the return of Christ and what he will achieve when he appears, but also our present lifestyle and priorities. Our present priorities and behaviour will reflect our expectation of the future.

Rather than looking to be rescued from this present evil generation, we expect to win it for Christ and his kingdom.

With our understanding of God's purpose as revealed in his Word and with tools to interpret it at our disposal (see Appendix), we are now in a much better position to approach the specifics of our subject. What do the Scriptures clearly say about Christ's return, and how do we understand some of the issues surrounding it, and over which there has been such a frenzy of speculation?

## End notes

1. *Countdown to the Apocalypse*, Grant Jeffrey, p 140
2. Covenant theology has many valuable qualities but we are not fully committed to the scheme due to some of its inherent weaknesses. For an excellent overview of covenant theology, see the essay by Willem Van Gemeren, 'Systems of Continuity' in the book, *Continuity and Discontinuity*, edited by John S Feinberg. Prominent in covenant theology's weaknesses, Van Gemeren identifies:
    - Emphasising covenant as a contract rather than an expression of love
    - Dead orthodoxy
    - Extreme continuity with Old Testament law leading to errors like infant baptism as a New Covenant equivalent to circumcision
3. *The Christ of the Covenants*, p 45
4. *The Time of the End, Daniel's Prophecy Reclaimed*, p 20
5. This is based on a diagram that appears in Gordon Fee's book *Paul, the Spirit and the People of God*.

Chapter 3

# What the Bible clearly teaches about the Second Coming

The return of Christ should be the most inspiring and most eagerly anticipated event in the calendar of the church! Yet for generations believers have been divided and confused over this subject. With the advent of dispensationalism, fear and pessimism have been added to the end-time menu. Despite this, there is so much in the Bible that speaks simply and clearly on the subject of Christ's return, if we approach it with an open heart and mind. In this chapter we will seek to establish what Scripture plainly states, so that on this foundation we can tackle some of the more obscure and controversial matters.

## The world to which Jesus returns

We have observed that there is a relationship between the events of Christ's return and our understanding of the condition of the world to which he returns. If you expect evil to flourish and Satan to have the upper hand, you will more naturally believe the dispensationalist idea that Christ is coming to rescue his people from enemy threats and God's judgments. If on the other hand you expect the world to be increasingly transformed by the power of God, you can easily foresee Christ returning for a victorious church advancing a conquering kingdom. Furthermore, you will spend your life in pursuit of such a vision rather than hiding in a church building waiting for safe passage to heaven!

Who has the upper hand in the world that Christ returns to – God or Satan? Will the kingdom of God fill the earth before Jesus returns or will darkness cover the planet? Dispensationalism has, over the last 150 years, deeply eroded the expectation of many of God's people concerning the end times. Instead of faith, there is fear. Rather than abounding hope, there is apprehension and speculation.

Jesus taught us to pray, 'your kingdom come, your will be done on earth as it is in heaven' (Matthew 6:10). If the kingdom of God does not come until after Jesus returns, there is no particular reason for such an injunction. But just as he came to introduce his kingdom to the earth, he expects his people to continue where he left off, taking that kingdom to the four corners of the world in the power of the Spirit.

Firstly then, we want to discover some of the clear statements of Scripture concerning what God will achieve on the earth *before* the point at which Jesus returns, prior to looking at the actual return and beyond.

## The church comes to fullness

The New Testament paints a consistent picture of Christ returning for a glorious church. Far from being a beleaguered remnant or even simply holding its own in the world, the body of Christ is destined to emerge in fullness and glory in the earth. What does this look like?

### Unity

Jesus prayed that his people might be perfectly joined in love (John 17:20-23). He taught that the world would believe in him when his people are united in this love (John 13:34-35). We cannot imagine Jesus being denied the answer to his prayer or his reward for the suffering he endured at the cross. There is only one body, one bride, one people, one temple. The apostle Paul teaches that the church will come to 'unity in the faith ...' in this age (Ephesians 4:13).

### Maturity

Paul says Christ will present to himself a radiant church, 'a bride without stain or wrinkle' (Ephesians 5:27). She will not be blighted by the spots of adolescence or the wrinkles of old age. Instead she will 'grow to become in every respect the mature body of him who is the head, that is, Christ' (Ephesians 4:15), and God is constantly working in his people to bring them to this state of maturity (Hebrews 6:1).

### Power

The church is God's instrument and channel of power in the world.

When the Holy Spirit descended on the disciples at the day of Pentecost, he elevated them to the same mission and anointing as Christ himself. Before his ascension Jesus commanded his disciples to wait in Jerusalem until they received the Holy Spirit (Acts 1:4). It was this power that enabled them to be his witnesses 'in Jerusalem, and in all Judea, and Samaria and to the ends of the earth' (Acts 1:8). We are the extension of Christ and his ministry to the world he died to reach.

## Multitudes are won to Christ

The gospel is advancing as never before in the history of the world. With more than 2 billion believers, the world is being reaped for Christ before our very eyes. But does biblical teaching match this historical evidence? We believe it does.

There are many Old Testament scriptures that speak of the world being won to the Lord. David records God the Father promising the Son, 'Ask me, and I will make the nations your inheritance, the ends of the earth your possession' (Psalm 2:8). Isaiah, speaking of the future church, declares:

> Arise, shine, for your light has come, and the glory of the Lord rises upon you. See, darkness covers the earth and thick darkness is over the peoples, but the Lord rises upon you and his glory appears over you. Nations will come to your light, and kings to the brightness of your dawn. (Isaiah 60:1-3)

When we cross into the New Testament we find Jesus' church commissioned to take the gospel to the ends of the earth (Matthew 28:18-20). The Acts of the Apostles is the record of the early church's achievements in doing this in their day. Paul evidently believed the fruit of the gospel would continue to grow in the world (Colossians 1:6). Peter declared that the Lord is not slow in keeping his promise but 'is patient with you, not wanting anyone to perish, but everyone to come to repentance' (2 Peter 3:9). The Acts of the Apostles even records examples of whole geographical regions turning to God, for instance Samaria (Acts 8:4-8), Lydda and Sharon (Acts 9:35) and Ephesus (Acts 19:17-20).

## Justice and righteousness in the nations

The Old Testament is full of prophetic imagery of God's people taking the lead role in discipling the nations in the ways of God.

Take Micah's prophecy for example (it is worth reading the whole chapter!):

> *In the last days the mountain of the Lord's temple will be established as the highest of the mountains; it will be exalted above the hills, and peoples will stream to it. Many nations will come and say, "Come let us go up to the mountain of the Lord, to the temple of the God of Jacob. He will teach us his ways, so that we may walk in his paths." The law will go out from Zion, the word of the Lord from Jerusalem.* (Micah 4:1-2)

Dispensationalism consistently relegated scriptures like this to a role for the nation of Israel in an alleged future Millennium. But the New Testament presents the church alone as the people commissioned with such a task. Jesus himself could not have been clearer when he said:

> *All authority in heaven and on earth has been given to me. Therefore go and make disciples of all nations, baptising them in the name of the Father and of the Son and of the Holy Spirit, and teaching them to obey everything I have commanded you. And surely I am with you always, to the very end of the age.* (Matthew 28:18-20)

For God's kingdom to come on earth as it is in heaven, the very nature of that kingdom, righteousness and justice must be displayed in the nations of the earth, not just in Christian congregations.

In his book *Transformations*, Ed Silvoso presents a compelling theology of nation-discipling and provides up-to-date examples of the process in action. There is incontrovertible proof of the gospel's power to transform communities and nations, not just to convert individuals. Silvoso writes:

> Jesus did not only come to save souls (as important and precious as that is), but also to seek, find and recover everything that was lost. This introduces a key insight that is needed to capture the full scope of the atonement and that is corroborated by Colossians 1:20: "For it was the Father's good pleasure to reconcile all things to himself, whether things on earth or things in heaven". This last sentence underscores the totality of the reconciliation effected by the Lord. Heaven and earth encompass the entire universe.[1]

We do not suppose that evil will be entirely eradicated from the earth in this age. Jesus spoke in his parables of wheat and weeds growing together in the field of the world (Matthew 13: 24-30, 36-43). But at harvest time, the weeds are taken out of a world which is identified as 'his kingdom' (verse 41), not the devil's.

## What happens when Christ returns?

Having lifted our expectations for what God intends to achieve before Jesus returns, we are able to appreciate the actual events of his return to planet earth. Dispensationalism presents the return of Christ as a complex sequence of events that takes place over a very specific time period. The secret rapture of the church is followed by a seven-year period of time in which the antichrist comes to prominence and intense tribulation ensues. Finally Christ returns to rescue the Jewish nation and defeat a rampaging devil.

Once we step away from the dispensational system there is a surprising amount of agreement – even among those who hold differing views of his return. We appreciate that it is not possible to accommodate every shade of opinion in this chapter, and we want to avoid any dogma of our own. Despite this, there is plenty in the Scriptures upon which to base our hope. We will begin by examining some of the words used in the Bible.

### The words used to describe his coming

The New Testament uses three Greek words in the main to describe the coming of the Lord. Each of these words carries a distinct emphasis, so it is worth discovering what they mean to fully understand the nature of his return.

### Parousia

This is the most commonly used word in the New Testament concerning Jesus' second coming. Its basic meaning is 'arrival' or 'presence' and in secular Greek the word implies 'active continuing presence upon arrival'. This word was used when a ruler or dignitary visited a city. The city gave itself to much preparation, in anticipation of his coming, even to the extent of not only cleaning the city but erecting new buildings in honour of his visit. The Greek word *parousia*, therefore, affirms that this is not a fleeting visit but rather a coming with subsequent residence. Significantly, *parousia* is used by Peter to describe the Lord's incarnational first coming (2 Peter 1:16).

The importance of *parousia* in the New Testament to describe the coming of the Lord is demonstrated by the fact that three Apostles, in addition to Paul, use it in their writings – James (James 5:7), Peter (2 Peter 3:4) and John (1 John 2:28).

## Epiphaneia

This word literally means 'a shining forth', and like *parousia*, is used both for Jesus' first and second comings. Regarding Jesus' first coming, Paul writes:

> *This grace was given us in Christ Jesus before the beginning of time, but it has now been revealed through the appearing (epiphaneia) of our Saviour, Christ Jesus who has destroyed death and has brought life and immortality to light through the Gospel.* (2 Timothy 1:9-10)

Not only was Christ's first coming a 'shining forth', but Paul affirms that his second coming will also be the same: 'In the presence of God and of Christ Jesus, who will judge the living and the dead, and in view of his appearing (*epiphaneia*) and his kingdom...' (2 Timothy 4:1). Paul further asserts that his coming will be a wonderful joy for believers and he himself lived in anticipation of Christ's shining forth at his return:

> *I have fought the good fight, I have finished the race, I have kept the faith. Now there is in store for me the crown of righteousness, which the Lord, the righteous Judge, will award to me on that day – and not only to me, but also to all who have longed for his appearing (epiphaneia).* (2 Timothy 4:7-8)

## Apokalypsis

This word means 'unveiling' or 'uncovering'. It carries the implication that Jesus has been veiled and not yet seen for who he is, but in his coming again he will manifest the glory which has been his since the beginning of the world. Paul describes this event in 2 Thessalonians 1:6-7:

> *God is just: He will pay back trouble to those who trouble you and give relief to you who are troubled, and to us as well. This will happen when the Lord Jesus is revealed* [apokalypsis] *from heaven in blazing fire with his powerful angels.*

What has been hidden from humankind concerning the nature and glory of Jesus will be revealed to all on that day.

The Greek word *apokalypsis* has come down to us in the English language as our word 'apocalypse'. The book of Revelation is known as an apocalypse because it unveils the truth of who Jesus is and what he does, so that believers aren't blinded by current events that are taking place in the visible realm.

## The nature of his coming

The fact that Jesus is returning again to the earth was made clear by two angels immediately after his ascension to glory. The disciples were looking heavenward in amazement as Jesus became hidden from sight by a cloud. Two men dressed in white suddenly appeared beside them and asked the disciples why they were gazing into the sky. The angels stated, 'This same Jesus, who has been taken from you into heaven, will come back in the same way you have seen him go into heaven' (Acts 1:11).

If Jesus is going to return in the same way in which he was taken, as stated by the angels, we can safely draw certain conclusions about the nature of his appearance:

*First of all, it will be personal.* The angels said 'This same Jesus', indicating that he himself will return rather than appearing in a different guise. It will be the same person that came out of the tomb on Easter Sunday who will descend from heaven; the same person who is now seated at the right hand of God who will come again for his people.

*Secondly, it will be physical.* Jesus ascended from the earth in a physical body. Following his resurrection, he invited Thomas to see and to touch his hands where the nails had scarred him and invited him to place his hand into his side where the spear of the soldier had pierced him. Clearly Christ's physical body in its resurrected form is different from every other human body, since it has the capacity to enter a room when the door is locked. Nevertheless it is physical and in this form he will return to the earth.

*Finally, it will be public.* When Jesus ascended it was not a private event taking place away from the public gaze. If his ascent into heaven was not secret but public, then his return to earth will also be public.

> *For the Son of Man in his day will be like the lightning, which flashes and lights up the sky from one end to the other.* (Luke 17:24)

### The order of events

Perhaps the most explicit statement on the return of Jesus is made by Paul in 1 Thessalonians:

> *For we believe that Jesus died and rose again, and so we believe that God will bring with Jesus those who have fallen asleep in him. According to the Lord's word, we tell you that we who are still alive, who are left until the coming of the Lord, will certainly not precede those who have fallen asleep. For the Lord himself will come down from heaven, with a loud command, with the voice of the archangel and with the trumpet call of God, and the dead in Christ will rise first. After that, we who are still alive and are left will be caught up together with them in the clouds to meet the Lord in the air. And so we will be with the Lord forever.* (1 Thessalonians 4:14-17)

This passage links together, in one place, certain events in a single order:

- There is the cry of an archangel and sound of the trumpet
- Jesus descends to the earth
- The dead in Christ rise first
- We who are alive join them to meet Jesus in the clouds
- We shall be with him forever

The events are sudden and swift. When everything is in place, Jesus will come without warning for his bride. We may not know the exact day or hour of his coming (Matthew 24:36) but that does not mean we will be caught unawares. There is every reason to believe that as events move rapidly to their fulfilment on earth, we will have an increasing sense that the time is approaching for Jesus to appear from heaven.

Unfortunately, from this same wonderful scripture, dispensationalists have devised their teaching of a secret departure of the church prior to the return of Christ in glory, effectively turning this scripture into a statement about the rapture only. It is an issue that cannot be ignored, the proverbial elephant in the room!

We are going to look at the subject of the rapture in depth later. But for now, note that nothing is mentioned in this passage about a second phase to the coming of Christ, and nothing is mentioned about the church disappearing from the earth. Furthermore, the words we have examined give no evidence of a separate secret rapture, just one glorious event.

## Dispensationalist view of the last days (simplified)

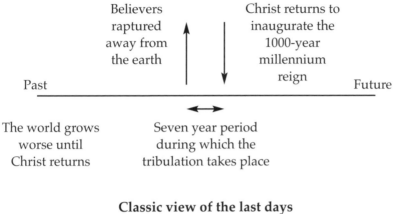

The world grows
worse until
Christ returns

Seven year period
during which the
tribulation takes place

## Classic view of the last days

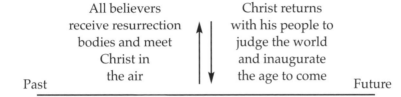

The kingdom of God increases in
the world until Christ returns

# What happens after Christ returns?

Christ returns to the earth for a clear purpose. Again there are a number of issues on which Christians do not fully agree, in particular surrounding the teaching of the Millennium. Dispensationalists believe there will be a literal 1000-year reign of Christ from Jerusalem before a final confrontation with the devil and the inauguration of the age to come. As with the subject of the rapture, we cover the Millennium in a chapter of its own. But turning away from this contentious issue for a moment, what do the Scriptures *plainly* state Jesus will accomplish after his return? They are clear about several such matters.

## *Believers receive resurrection bodies*

Paul writes about this on two occasions:

> *But our citizenship is in heaven. And we eagerly await a Saviour from there, the Lord Jesus Christ, who, by the power that enables him*

> *to bring everything under his control, will transform our lowly bodies so that they will be like his glorious body.* (Philippians 3:20-21)

> *Listen, I tell you a mystery: We will not all sleep, but we will all be changed – in a flash, in the twinkling of an eye, at the last trumpet.* (1 Corinthians 15:51)

All who belong to Jesus will have their bodies transformed to be like his resurrection body. For Paul this redemption of our bodies signifies the final act in our adoption as sons of God (Romans 8:23). This will take place at his appearing because John states that, 'when Christ appears, we shall be like him, for we shall see him as he is' (1 John 3:2). Receiving our resurrection bodies at the return of Christ means that the sons of God whom Paul talks about in Romans 8 will then be revealed. These resurrection bodies will be free from the power of sin because we ourselves will have been delivered from sin's presence. The created order will then be liberated from its bondage (Romans 8:19).

We know our future resurrected bodies will be like Jesus' glorious body because Paul says Jesus is 'the first-fruits of those who have fallen asleep (1 Corinthians 15:20). So what will those bodies be like? Two things become evident, continuity and discontinuity. First there will be continuity in that we will be able to recognise each other. When Jesus was standing at the lake shore of Galilee, cooking fish for breakfast following his resurrection, he was recognised by John who exclaimed, 'It is the Lord!' (John 21:7). The offer to Thomas to touch his hands and side indicate that there was continuity and his body had not been made in a completely different form, as compared to before his resurrection (John 20:27).

But Jesus' body also expressed discontinuity because he was able to appear and disappear in a manner that did not occur prior to his resurrection, as with the disciples in the upper room and the two travellers on the Emmaus Road.

### Rewards for the righteous

Jesus promises to reward those who have been faithful in the task he's given them to do. He explained this issue of reward for faithfulness in the parable of the talents. The talent was a considerable sum of money worth approximately fifteen years' wages. To one person he gave five talents, to another two and to another one. To the people who put the talents to work the master gave praise and the commendation: 'Well done good and faithful servant! You have been faithful with a few things; I will put you in charge of many things. Come and share your master's happiness!' (Matthew 25:21).

The master makes this same statement to the person who had five talents and to the one who had two, indicating that the issue is not how much each of us has but whether we have been faithful to handle correctly what we have been given. The crux of the issue is essentially faithfulness of service and not the amount of possessions. The person given one talent was called wicked and lazy not because he had only one talent but because he was unfaithful in its use and did not put it to work.

The reward of believers at the return of Jesus is based on personal faithfulness. God wants us to bring honour to him by using what he's given us, and thereby being able to share in his delight and happiness in enjoying his rewards.

Jesus tells a similar parable in Luke 19, but in this case instead of the master giving different gifts to different people he gives the same gift, ten minas, to ten servants, with the command to put the money to work until he returns. One servant earned ten more, another five more and yet another returned his mina because he had hidden it in a piece of cloth.

Because of his faithfulness, the servant who had earned ten minas was put in charge of ten cities. The servant who had earned five more minas was given charge of five cities. Again the reward is based on faithfulness, and in the age to come the reward for faithfulness will be increased responsibility and sphere of influence for the King. Responsibility in this age, with the gifts that God has given us, determines what we will carry as responsibility in the age to come.

## Punishment for the unrighteous

Throughout Scripture God is presented as the judge of the whole earth who will one day exercise his rightful judgment: 'he comes to judge the earth. He will judge the world in righteousness and the peoples with equity' (Psalm 98:9).

The New Testament reveals that Jesus will in fact be that judge (Acts 17:31) and Jesus himself went on to elaborate concerning that event:

> *When the Son of Man comes in his glory, and all the angels with him, he will sit on his glorious throne. All the nations will be gathered before him, and he will separate the people one from another as a shepherd separates the sheep from the goats. He will put the sheep on his right and the goats on his left. Then the king will say to those on his right, 'Come, you who are blessed by my Father; take your inheritance the kingdom prepared for you since the creation of the world'... Then he will say to those on his left, 'Depart from me, you who are cursed, into the eternal fire prepared for the devil and his angels.'* (Matthew 25:31-34, 41)

Judgment is inescapable! But thankfully it will be delivered at the hands of the one who loves us and gave his life for us. Every man and woman will stand before him to give an account of their life. They will then be separated, the righteous from the unrighteous, for eternity.

There should however, be no fear of judgment for those who have received Christ as Lord of their lives because they have already passed from death to life. They have already come out from under judgment. Jesus said:

> *Those who believe in the Son are not judged; but those who do not believe have already been judged, because they have not believed in God's only Son.* (John 3:18, GNB)

## *Destruction of the devil*

At the cross Satan was defeated by Jesus but not destroyed. We know that the devil is still at work in the world at present. But equally we believe that the power of the Holy Spirit in the church is pushing back the frontiers of darkness and overcoming Satan. We do not subscribe to a view of the end-times that empowers a defeated devil! Finally at Christ's coming he will be judged and condemned for eternity:

> *And the devil, who deceived them, was thrown into the lake of burning sulphur, where the beast and the false prophet had been thrown. They will be tormented day and night for ever and ever.* (Revelation 20:10)

Every last pocket of resistance to the reign of Christ will be wiped out. Death will be swallowed up in victory (1 Corinthians 15:54-57). Every knee will bow before him (Philippians 2:10). Injustice and unrighteousness will be a thing of the past (2 Peter 3:13).

## A renewed earth

The apostle Peter describes the Lord's coming again in 2 Peter 3:10-13:

> But the day of the Lord will come like a thief. The heavens will disappear with a roar; the elements will be destroyed by fire, and the earth and everything done in it will be laid bare. Since everything will be destroyed in this way, what kind of people ought you to be? You ought to live holy and godly lives as you look forward to the day of God and speed its coming. That day will bring about the destruction of the heavens by fire, and the elements will melt in the heat. But in keeping with his promise we are looking forward to a new heaven and a new earth, where righteousness dwells.

There is a popular idea, with no sound basis, that when Jesus returns his people will go to heaven with him and the earth will be destroyed. This is not what Peter says here. Instead we are presented with a picture of the earth being purged and renewed at Christ's coming.

Not only will this new earth be the home of righteousness but sin in every form will be absent. At his first coming, Jesus completely dealt with the *penalty* of sin on the cross. But at his second coming he will deal with the *presence* of sin by removing it forever. The new earth will completely reflect the nature and atmosphere of heaven.

God's presence pervades every aspect of life and activity in heaven. Following Christ's return to earth the nature of heaven will be re-established on the earth. Heaven and earth will know a unity of fellowship and purpose where all things are brought under the rule of King Jesus (Ephesians 1:10).

Because the earth will become a home of righteousness, not only will sin be removed, but its consequences too. All tears will be wiped away, since joy is found in the presence of God. Death will be no more, because the life-giver will be present and emotions that are associated with death and its process – mourning, crying and pain – will be banished forever from the earth (Revelation 21 and 22).

If this is to be the condition of the earth in the age to come, Peter poses the question, 'What kind of people ought you to be?' His answer is, 'You ought to live holy and godly lives' (2 Peter 3:11-12). Even though we are not yet delivered from the presence of sin, believers have already tasted the powers of the coming age. We are called to demonstrate the lifestyle of that age in this present evil age and by so doing, to attractively express the life of Jesus here and now.

In addition to Peter, Paul also sees a future time when the earth will be renewed. He states in Romans 8:19-22:

> *For the creation waits in eager expectation for the children of God to be revealed. For the creation was subjected to frustration, not by its own choice, but by the will of the one who subjected it, in hope that the creation itself will be liberated from its bondage to decay and brought into the freedom and glory of the children of God. We know that the whole creation has been groaning as in the pains of childbirth right up to the present time.*

The creation became subject to bondage because sin was introduced into the world through Adam's disobedience. Adam was made from the ground and fashioned by God from the dust of the earth. God breathed into him and he became a living being made in God's image to rule over the created earth on God's behalf.

When Adam fell, sin not only entered into his life personally but also entered the realm over which he had been given authority. The created world became corrupted and since that time has been subject to bondage and decay. Now as a direct result of Christ's victory at the cross, creation itself will be delivered from sin's consequences. The actions of the last Adam, Christ, have nullified those of the first Adam!

## Conclusion

Although there are warnings in Scripture about Satan's presence and activity in the world, the tenor of the Bible is optimistic and positive concerning the future. It presents a picture of Jesus returning for a ready church that has transformed society by the power of the gospel. The idea that the world will grow darker and darker before Jesus returns offers no hope to billions of unreached people. It makes no contribution to the transformation of our cities. It adds nothing to the discipling of the nations.

The church is the light of the world and the salt of the earth. A direct commission from Christ rests on his people to disciple the nations (Matthew 28:18-20) and nothing less than its completion before Christ returns will vindicate the work of the cross.

The return of Christ is one glorious event that will signal the resurrection of the dead, rewards for the righteous, punishment for the unrighteous, the destruction of Satan and the inauguration of the age to come. The fact that Christ is returning to the earth should be a provocation to holy living and passionate commitment to his purposes.

## End notes

1. *Transformations*, Ed Silvoso, page 56.

# Chapter 4

# The book of Daniel and the prophecy of seventy weeks

Until now we have been doing the necessary groundwork on our subject. We have introduced dispensationalism and explained how to understand the Bible in terms of the centrality of Christ, his Covenant and his Kingdom. Now it is time to tackle some of the more challenging and contentious aspects of our subject, beginning with the book of Daniel. It is here that the appendix may prove useful in understanding how to interpret the Scriptures.

Of all the Old Testament books, Daniel stands unique as a piece of apocalyptic literature. It differs from the other Old Testament prophetic books in that it speaks so specifically and graphically about the future. It really is like reading history in advance.

For this reason the book of Daniel has become a rich source for those searching for answers about the end times. One prophecy in particular has become pivotal for dispensational teachers in supporting their claims about the return of Christ: the 'seventy weeks' passage in chapter 9. It describes how Daniel was shown a future time-line of events for the nation of Israel. Dispensationalists claim that in this time-line, God literally "stopped the prophetic clock" for a period of 2,000 years, so that end of the passage describes the events surrounding the second coming of Christ, rather than his first coming. We are going to examine this very carefully as so much else hinges on it.

As a young man Daniel had been taken into exile by King Nebuchadnezzar's Babylonian army that had overthrown Jerusalem. In Babylon he was selected, along with several friends, to serve in the royal court. The providence of God saw him promoted to the highest levels there, so that he even had personal audiences with the king. Daniel received all his revelations while in exile, and lived to see the reign of Cyrus of Persia, making him about 90 years old when he died.

The book of Daniel has similarities with the New Testament book of Revelation. Indeed, it is widely accepted that, in writing Revelation, John drew heavily on Old Testament prophetic imagery to describe what he saw, including imagery from the book of Daniel. In the opening chapter of Revelation, for instance, John hears a voice speaking to him from behind. On turning to identify the speaker he describes him as someone 'like a son of man' (Revelation 1:13). This is a clear allusion to Daniel who sees one 'like a son of man' coming with the clouds of heaven and approaching the Ancient of Days (Daniel 7:13).

Similarly, the beast with ten horns that John sees coming out of the sea in Revelation 13 resembles that of Daniel chapter 7. John describes this beast as resembling a leopard, with feet like those of a bear and a mouth like that of a lion. In Daniel's vision of four great beasts coming out of the sea, the first was like a lion, the second like a bear, and the third like a leopard. Then a fourth beast emerged that had ten horns. The similarities are unmistakable.

Daniel interprets his vision of the four beasts as predicting four successive kingdoms that will rise in the earth. These share the characteristics of the four kingdoms in Daniel's interpretation of Nebuchadnezzar's dream in chapter 2 – we looked at these earlier. Most commentators agree that the four beasts and the four kingdoms represent the successive world powers of Babylon, Medo-Persia, Greece and Rome. Certainly, in Revelation, John describes the world power of his day – Rome – as having ten horns, like the fourth beast in Daniel's vision.

John is not alone in drawing upon the book of Daniel. Jesus, in the Olivet discourse, used the prophet Daniel to help prepare his disciples for the forthcoming destruction of the temple at Jerusalem. Jesus borrows Daniel's phrase, *'The abomination that causes desolation'*. We will later show how this refers to the idolatry that occurred in the temple, desecrating that holy place. The fact that Daniel is the only Old Testament prophet that Jesus specifically mentions in the Olivet discourse again highlights the importance of the book of Daniel in understanding eschatological events.

## Background to the seventy weeks

Now let us see how the 'seventy weeks' prophecy fits into the book as a whole. Part of the book of Daniel (chapters 1-6) records Daniel's life as an exile, first in the service of Nebuchadnezzar, then of

Belshazzar and finally of Darius, King of the Medes. Chapters 7-12 describe the revelations God gave to Daniel about the development of world powers, their conflict with the kingdom of God and the final victory of that kingdom over all hostile powers.

Daniel's revelations of the future were amazing. As we have seen, God showed him that four world empires would emerge, and Daniel's own life would span the first two of these. This unfolding scenario began with Judah's exile. The Old Testament explains that the people of Judah were taken into exile because they failed to live in line with the covenant that God had made with Moses. Their disobedience lost them God's blessing and provoked his judgment instead.

In addition, they paid scant attention to the prophets God sent to them, and soon their exile into the hands of a foreign king became inevitable, in line with the covenant's sanctions. God raised up the prophet Jeremiah to warn his people of imminent judgment. This would entail exile to Babylon and the destruction of Jerusalem and its temple. Daniel himself ended up in exile.

Chapter 9 of the book that bears his name records that Daniel, in Babylon, had been reading the word of the Lord given to Jeremiah that the desolation of Jerusalem would last seventy years. Aware that the seventy years had almost ended, he turned to God in prayer, making confession and asking that the desolation of Jerusalem and the sanctuary would finish, that the continuing wrath of God would be averted and that Jerusalem would once again be the place of God's habitation, instead of an object of scorn.

There was a reason why seventy years was the duration that God prescribed for the exile. Jerusalem would endure seventy years of desolation so that the land could enjoy its overdue Sabbath rests (2 Chronicles 36:21). This indicates that for 490 years prior to the exile the nation of Israel had failed to honour its covenantal obligation to observe the Sabbaths, which included not working the land on that day. Although its origins can be traced back to the creation account in Genesis 2, the keeping of the Sabbath became an integral part of the Mosaic covenant. The Israelites were permitted to work for six days but the seventh was to be a Sabbath rest when they were to do no work (Leviticus 23:3).

On entering Canaan the people of Israel were to ensure that the land itself also enjoyed a Sabbath rest – in terms of years as well as days. So, the fields could be worked for six years but the seventh was appointed a year of rest for the land (Leviticus 25:4). After seven cycles of Sabbath years, the 50th year was designated the Year of Jubilee, when debts were cancelled, slaves were released and liberty became the inheritance of every person.

## The 'seventy sevens'

Daniel had been confessing the failure of his people to keep the covenant commands, including observing the Sabbaths. His petition that God would restore the fortunes of Jerusalem was interrupted by the angel Gabriel, who declared to Daniel that as soon as he had begun to pray an answer had been given. That answer, Gabriel explained, involved '70 sevens' that God had decreed 'for your people and your holy city' (Daniel 9:24). Whereas Daniel had been contemplating the sad consequences of the *previous* 490 years of history, Gabriel announced events that would take place in the *following* 490 years.

Gabriel announced that there would be a total of 69 'weeks' of years until the coming of the Messiah, the prince. The mathematics proves to be spot on, taking us to the point at which Jesus began his earthly ministry.

In the middle of the final week (that is, after $3^{1}/_{2}$ years) he will put an end to sacrifice and offering (Daniel 9:27). Following this, Gabriel concludes his explanation of future events by stating: 'And on the wing of abominations shall come one who makes desolate, until the decreed end is poured out on the desolator' (Daniel 9:27 ESV).

We shall see in a moment what that means. In the meantime we can note that the 70 'sevens' (490 years) represent ten jubilee eras, ending in the ultimate Year of Jubilee, the dawning of the Messianic age. In line with this, Jesus made the following announcement in the synagogue at Nazareth at the start of his ministry:

> 'The Spirit of the Lord is on me, because he has anointed me to proclaim good news to the poor. He has sent me to proclaim freedom for the prisoners and recovery of sight for the blind, to set the oppressed free, to proclaim **the year of the Lord's favour**.' (Luke 4:18-19)

'The year of the Lord's favour' is a synonym for 'the Year of Jubilee.' So here Jesus announces the Year of Jubilee and affirms its arrival by concluding his reading with the statement, 'Today this scripture is fulfilled in your hearing'. The context of our passage in Daniel, then, is the expectation of the Messiah and the work he would accomplish. With that in mind, we can look at some of the other details.

According to Gabriel, the 70 'sevens' would witness the accomplishment of six clearly defined objectives. All of these, according to the New Testament writers, were fulfilled in the *first* coming of Jesus. Daniel 9:24 lists the six objectives:

## 1. 'To finish transgression'

According to the writer to the Hebrews, Jesus became the mediator of a new covenant by means of his death, in order to set people free from the transgressions committed under the first covenant (Hebrews 9:15). Before Jesus yielded up his spirit at the cross he proclaimed, 'It is finished'. He had done everything necessary to deal with transgression by his once and for all perfect sacrifice. He had atoned for sin, bringing reconciliation between God and sinners within reach. The sacrifice at Calvary broke sin's power over people's lives forever.

## 2. 'To put an end to sin'

This, too, Jesus has already done. John the Baptist announced the Messiah with the words, 'Look, the Lamb of God, who *takes away the sin* of the world!' (John 1:29). The New Testament writers confirm this: 'But now he has appeared once for all at the end of the ages *to do away with sin* by the sacrifice of himself… so Christ was sacrificed once *to take away the sins* of many people' (Hebrews 9:26, 28). The apostle Peter agrees, saying, 'For Christ also suffered once for sins, the righteous for the unrighteous, to bring you to God' (1 Peter 3:18).

## 3. 'To atone for wickedness'

Christ's death was an atoning death. The writer to the Hebrews takes up Jeremiah's promise of the new covenant and applies it to that atoning death and the inauguration of the New Covenant: 'For I will forgive their wickedness and will remember their sins no more. By calling this covenant "new" he has made the first one obsolete; and what is obsolete and outdated will soon disappear' (Hebrews 8:12-13). Christ's atoning death was comprehensive and universal in its scope. It made redundant any requirement for the offering of inferior animal sacrifices, of the kind prescribed by the Old Covenant.

Note that the Old Covenant is now 'obsolete' and about to 'disappear'. There is strong evidence that the book of Hebrews was written before AD 70, the year the temple at Jerusalem was destroyed. The expectation of the writer to the Hebrews that the Old Covenant sacrifices would soon disappear could therefore well have included the anticipation of the temple's demise, since it was there that the animal sacrifices took place.

## 4. 'To bring in everlasting righteousness'

To be justified by faith in Jesus is to be declared *righteous*. In Romans 5 Paul contrasts the lives of two individuals, Adam and Christ. He compares the terrible consequences of Adam's sin with the blessings achieved by Christ's sacrifice. He demonstrates how that sacrifice eradicates the consequences of Adam's sin, enabling believers to reign in life as a result of God's abundant provision of grace and his gift of righteousness (verse 17).

Paul summarises his conviction with the statement, 'For just as through the disobedience of the one man (Adam) the many were made sinners, so also through the obedience of the one man (Christ) the many will be *made righteous*' (Romans 5:19). An exchange occurred at the cross. Paul explains to the Corinthians that 'God made him who had no sin to be sin for us, so that in him we might become the righteousness of God' (2 Corinthians 5:21). In Paul's mind there is no doubt that Christ's first coming brought in everlasting righteousness.

## 5. 'To seal up vision and prophecy'

The purpose of a seal, usually stamped in wax by a person of authority, is to establish the authenticity of a document. Jesus Christ stamped his seal of approval on Old Testament prophecy by fulfilling all that was written there about himself. The apostle Peter certainly believed this: 'But this is how God fulfilled what he had foretold through all the prophets, saying that his Messiah would suffer… all the prophets who have spoken have foretold these days' (Acts 3:18, 24). Indeed Jesus has so thoroughly fulfilled the expectations of the Old Testament prophets that the apostle John summarises the situation by declaring that the Spirit of prophecy bears testimony to Jesus' (Revelation 19:10).

## 6. 'To anoint the most holy'

Daniel does not specify if 'the most holy' is a place or a person. Certainly he wanted the city of Jerusalem and its temple to be restored after its destruction by Nebuchadnezzar. But the angel Gabriel did not promise a restoration of the most holy place. John the Baptist suggests that it may instead refer to a person, or people. He said, 'I baptise you with water for repentance. But after me comes One who is more powerful than I...He will baptise you with the Holy Spirit and fire' (Matthew 3:11).

Here, John prophetically announced that Jesus would be characterised by a ministry of immersing believers in the Holy Spirit. Together, these constitute 'a chosen people, a royal priesthood, a holy nation, God's special possession' (1 Peter 2:9). Through his sanctifying work, Jesus' followers become a holy people. It is these whom he anoints by immersing them in his Spirit, thus empowering them to continue his own life and ministry in the world. John declares, 'You have an anointing from the Holy One' (1 John 2:20), indicating that Jesus, the ultimate Holy and Anointed One, imparts these same qualities to all who put their trust in him.

It's not that a holy temple does not exist under the new covenant. Paul says that this temple does not consist of stones like those of the Jerusalem temple under the Old Covenant. Instead, the holy temple now being built under the New Covenant is none other than a multitude of people who have become heirs of grace and members of God's household (Ephesians 2:19). It is this temple that is 'the most holy' and to which Jesus imparts his anointing.

We can see, then, how the work of Jesus at his *first* coming more than adequately fulfilled all six items in Gabriel's prediction.

## The final 'week'

The angel Gabriel divides the 70 'sevens' into sections. At first there will be 7 'sevens', followed by 62 'sevens' and then finally there will be 1 'seven'.

He makes the puzzling statement that after the 69th 'seven' (that is, after the 7 'sevens' and 62 'sevens' have run their course) 'the Anointed One will be put to death and will have nothing.' Clearly, if this is to take place after the 69th 'seven', the cutting off must take place during the last 'seven', the 70th 'seven'.

Isaiah had already prophesied this cutting off of the Messiah. He said of the 'suffering servant', 'he was *cut off* from the land of the living' (Isaiah 53:8) – a reference to Christ's death.

Following the cutting off of the Messiah, 'The people of the ruler who will come will destroy the city and the sanctuary' (Daniel 9:26). The onslaught will be overwhelming: 'The end will come like a flood: War will continue until the end, and desolations have been decreed' against the city. This aspect of the prophecy was fulfilled in history by the Roman commander Titus and his armies, who completely destroyed Jerusalem in AD 70.

Besides being 'cut off' in the 70th 'seven', the Messiah will also 'confirm a covenant with many' and 'in the middle of the seven' he will 'put an end to sacrifice and offering.'

Jesus affirmed his fulfilment of the first aspect when he took the cup during the Last Supper with his disciples. He announced, 'Drink from it, all of you. This is *my blood of the covenant,* which is poured out for many for the forgiveness of sins' (Matthew 26:27-28). The second aspect is also clear: Jesus put an end to the sacrifice and offering required under the Old Covenant by his self-sacrifice, which inaugurated a better covenant, causing the first one to become obsolete.

Gabriel concluded by prophesying the setting up of 'an abomination that causes desolation.' We know what this means, as Jesus made it clear in his Olivet discourse that this was the desecration of the temple by the besieging Roman army. Gabriel also indicated that desolation would, in due course, be poured out upon the desolator. Did this happen? Yes. History records that the Roman Empire was itself overthrown in the 5th Century AD.

Commentators are not unanimous in their interpretation of the 70 'sevens', or 'heptads', as they are sometimes called. Some see them as referring to literal years, thereby establishing a clear time-frame from when the order to rebuild Jerusalem was given to the start of Jesus' public ministry, as for example, in *The Seventy Weeks Prophecy* by Kevin J Conner.[1] Other commentators advocate that the 'sevens' should be interpreted in a symbolic fashion.[2]

Whichever interpretation one holds, the reading of the time frames in Daniel 9 strongly supports the view that the years or 'heptads' are normal, consecutive and continuous. We know from history that there was no break in the seventy-year exile of the Jewish nation, so we should expect no hiatus either in the future 70 'sevens' promised by the angel Gabriel, who gave no hint that these would be either interrupted or non-consecutive.

In the 19th century, dispensationalists began to propose a gap between the 69th and 70th 'heptad'. Their reason for this was their curious belief that the church age is not mentioned by the Old Testament prophets! The dispensational view at that time was that the rejection of Jesus by the Jewish nation caused them to forfeit the chance to receive and establish God's kingdom on earth. Accordingly the gospel came to the Gentiles and the church emerged as a kind of parenthesis to God's main purpose. That purpose, dispensationalism teaches, is still for the Jewish nation to inherit the kingdom of God. On this view, the 69 'sevens' have now lasted for 2000 years!

Dispensationalists take a different view of other aspects of this passage. For example, they interpret the 'he' who confirms a covenant with many as the antichrist rather than Jesus Christ. Also the 'most holy' that is to be 'anointed' does not refer, they say, to the Holy Spirit poured out on God's people but to a future anointing of the temple in Jerusalem – one that has yet to be rebuilt. According to Scofield, the antichrist will covenant with the Jews to restore their temple sacrifices for 'one week'. In the middle of that week he will break the covenant. The last $3^1/_2$ years of the seven are viewed as the time of the Great Tribulation.[3]

## Conclusion

There are two main alternatives to interpreting the '70 weeks' passage of Daniel chapter 9. The historic (partial preterist) view is that the weeks are consecutive and continuous, culminating in the 'cutting off' of the messiah, and the anointing of the body of Christ, his living temple. The dispensationalist view is that the 70th 'seven' is still future and as yet unfulfilled. This remains incompatible with the fact that the six objectives to be accomplished within the scope of the 70 'sevens' were fulfilled long ago, through Jesus' ministry at his first coming. To impose a 2000-year gap between the 69th and 70th 'weeks' cannot be warranted from anything Gabriel said and to do so appears arbitrary and contrived.

Peter teaches us that the prophets who spoke under the Old Covenant predicted the sufferings of Christ and the glories that would follow (1 Peter 1:10-11). There is no need for this Old Testament prophecy to be fulfilled in any way other than in Christ, his ministry and the glorious achievements of his death, resurrection and exaltation. This is the focus of Old Testament prophetic expectation, and we should allow nothing and no-one to divert our gaze from its glory.

## End notes

1. Kevin J Conner, *The Seventy Weeks Prophecy*, KJC Publications
2. Joyce Baldwin, *Commentary on Daniel*, IVP
3. Scofield Bible, p 915

# Chapter 5

# The Olivet discourse

We come now to perhaps the most important chapter of all, where we find out what Jesus himself had to say concerning the future – the Olivet discourse.

Towards the end of his earthly ministry, Jesus visited the temple at Jerusalem with his disciples. The grandeur of the temple made such an impact on the Twelve that they engaged Jesus in discussion about the magnificent structure as they walked to the Mount of Olives. Rather than sharing their enthusiasm over the beautiful stonework and the carved decorations of the temple walls, Jesus astounded them by predicting that a time was soon coming when 'one stone would not be left upon another'.

This left the disciples bewildered, and by the time they had reached the Mount of Olives – from where the entire temple could be viewed in all its splendour – they could contain their curiosity no longer. Jesus' response to their questions has become known as the 'Olivet discourse' and is recorded in all three synoptic gospels, in Matthew chapters 24 and 25, in Mark chapter 13 and in Luke chapter 21. It is the most extensive account of Jesus' teaching on future events.

At that time, the temple was still being built. Historians call this the 'second temple' to distinguish it from the original one built by Solomon, which Nebuchadnezzar and his Babylonian army had destroyed in 586 BC. The book of Ezra documents the rebuilding of this second temple under the leadership of Zerubbabel.

Initially it was a simple structure, lacking the grandeur of the earlier temple. In 20 BC, Herod the Great, Rome's delegated authority in Palestine, started a substantial building programme at the temple site, transforming it into a much larger and more ornate structure. The building programme continued after Herod's death and once, when Jesus visited the temple, the Jews mentioned that the project had already taken 46 years (John 2:20). Work on the temple was not actually completed until AD 64. In AD 70 the army of Imperial Rome razed it to the ground, following a siege that inflicted terrible suffering on the citizens of Jerusalem.

The siege of Jerusalem and the destruction of the temple are not recorded in the Scriptures themselves, but there is ample historical evidence of what took place in the writings of the Jewish historian, Josephus, dating from the middle period of the 1st century. Two of his works, *The Jewish Wars* and *The Jewish Antiquities*, provide a rich source of historical information on these events. It was this destruction of the temple that Jesus predicted some 40 years before it happened. No wonder the disciples had questions, and no wonder his reply in the Olivet discourse was a lengthy one!

## Two ways of interpreting the Olivet discourse

Matthew 24 is a crucial proof-text for dispensationalists, who interpret it in a completely *futurist* way. With its prediction of wars, famines and earthquakes, and dramatic references to the sun being darkened and stars falling from the skies, it is believed to refer to the end of the world and the return of Christ. Sadly, such a viewpoint is based largely on ignorance of first-century history and faulty methods of interpretation, and has only added to the climate of pessimism and fear among large sections of the church today.

By contrast, there is a long tradition of interpreting the Olivet discourse in its historical context with the conclusion that much of Jesus' teaching was fulfilled during the 1st century. This position is called *preterism*, and it comes in two forms: *partial* and *full preterism*. Full preterists hold that all of the predictions in the Olivet discourse were fulfilled in the 1st century AD. This is an extreme position that leaves nothing for the future at all – not even a future resurrection of the dead. A more balanced view is that of 'partial' or 'orthodox preterism'[1]. Partial preterists view the majority of the Olivet discourse (to verse 35) as having been fulfilled in the 1st century AD, with the remainder (from verse 36) to be fulfilled at the second coming of Christ. We shall return to the subject of preterism when we examine the book of Revelation.

One of the most influential of recent partial preterists was J. Marcellus Kik. In 1948 he published a book entitled *Matthew 24*. This was later incorporated in a longer work entitled *An Eschatology of Victory*, published in 1971. We recommend this work for its thorough exegesis of Matthew 24 from a partial preterist position. Other notable works have followed including those of R T France and N T Wright. These have been influential in our understanding of the Olivet discourse.

Now let's look at the text of the first part of the Olivet discourse, as far as Matthew 24:35. To help put it in context we will include the final section of the preceding chapter, beginning at Matthew 23:33, where Jesus condemns the Jewish religious leaders. Please resist the temptation to skip this important passage!

> *"You snakes! You brood of vipers! How will you escape being condemned to hell? Therefore I am sending you prophets and wise men and teachers. Some of them you will kill and crucify; others you will flog in your synagogues and pursue from town to town. And so upon you will come all the righteous blood that has been shed on earth, from the blood of righteous Abel to the blood of Zechariah son of Berekiah, whom you murdered between the temple and the altar. I tell you the truth, all this will come upon this generation."*
>
> *"O Jerusalem, Jerusalem, you who kill the prophets and stone those sent to you, how often I have longed to gather your children together, as a hen gathers her chicks under her wings, but you were not willing. Look, your house is left to you desolate. For I tell you, you will not see me again until you say, 'Blessed is he who comes in the name of the Lord.'"*
>
> *Jesus left the temple and was walking away when his disciples came up to him to call his attention to its buildings. 'Do you see all these things?' he asked. 'I tell you the truth, not one stone here will be left on another; every one will be thrown down.'*
>
> *As Jesus was sitting on the Mount of Olives, the disciples came to him privately. 'Tell us', they said, 'when will this happen, and what will be the sign of your coming and of the end of the age?' Jesus answered:*
>
> *"Watch out that no one deceives you. For many will come in my name, claiming, 'I am the Christ', and will deceive many. You will hear of wars and rumours of wars, but see to it that you are not alarmed. Such things must happen, but the end is still to come. Nation will rise against nation and kingdom against kingdom. There will be famines and earthquakes in various places. All these are the beginning of birth pains.*
>
> *Then you will be handed over to be persecuted and put to death, and you will be hated by all nations because of me. At that time*

*many will turn away from the faith and will betray and hate each other, and many false prophets will appear and deceive many people. Because of the increase of wickedness, the love of most will grow cold, but he who stands firm to the end will be saved. And this gospel of the kingdom will be preached in the whole world as a testimony to all nations, and then the end will come.*

*So when you see standing in the holy place 'the abomination that causes desolation,' spoken of through the prophet Daniel — let the reader understand — then let those who are in Judea flee to the mountains. Let no one on the roof of his house go down to take anything out of the house. Let no one in the field go back to get his cloak. How dreadful it will be in those days for pregnant women and nursing mothers! Pray that your flight will not take place in winter or on the Sabbath. For then there will be great distress, unequalled from the beginning of the world until now — and never to be equalled again. If those days had not been cut short, no one would survive, but for the sake of the elect those days will be shortened. At that time if anyone says to you, 'Look, here is the Christ!' or, 'There he is!' do not believe it. For false Christs and false prophets will appear and perform great signs and miracles to deceive even the elect – if that were possible. See, I have told you ahead of time.*

*So if anyone tells you, 'There he is, out in the desert,' do not go out; or, 'Here he is, in the inner rooms,' do not believe it. For as lightning that comes from the east is visible even in the west, so will be the coming of the Son of Man. Wherever there is a carcass, there the vultures will gather.*

*Immediately after the distress of those days 'the sun will be darkened, and the moon will not give its light; the stars will fall from the sky, and the heavenly bodies will be shaken.'*

*At that time the sign of the Son of Man will appear in the sky, and all the nations of the earth will mourn. They will see the Son of Man coming on the clouds of the sky, with power and great glory. And he will send his angels with a loud trumpet call, and they will gather his elect from the four winds, from one end of the heavens to the other.*

*Now learn this lesson from the fig tree: As soon as its twigs get tender and its leaves come out, you know that summer is near. Even so, when you see all these things, you know that it is near, right at the door. I tell you the truth, this generation will certainly not pass away until all these things have happened. Heaven and earth will pass away, but my words will never pass away."*

Jesus' teaching on the Mount of Olives resulted from two questions posed by the disciples. These questions had in turn been provoked by Jesus' statement that, 'the time will come when not one stone [of the temple] will be left on another; every one of them will be thrown down' (Luke 21:6). The Mark and Luke accounts record the disciples as asking:

1. When will these things happen?
2. What will be the sign that they are about to take place?

In Matthew's account the second question becomes a double one: 'What will be the sign of your coming and of the end of the age?' As typical Jews, the disciples expected the temple to be destroyed 'at the end of the age', which they identified with Jesus' return to usher in the age to come. They could not conceive that the temple might fall before then. All three of the synoptic gospel accounts of the Olivet discourse are Jesus' answer to these two questions.

## What is 'this generation'?

The key to understanding this passage is in verse 34, where Jesus asserts, 'I tell you the truth, this generation will certainly not pass away until all these things have happened.' The obvious meaning of this is that the events just described would all take place within the lifetime of that generation of Jews.

In biblical thinking, a generation is a period of 40 years. The Psalmist declares, for instance, that 'For forty years I was angry with that generation' (Psalm 95:10). Such a view does not work for dispensationalists, who have therefore argued for a different meaning of 'generation', namely the Jewish race. To grasp the meaning of 'this generation' let us observe how Matthew uses it throughout his gospel – which he does a further three times.

### 1. Matthew 11:16-19

*"To what can I compare this generation? They are like children sitting in the market places and calling out to others: 'We played the flute for you, and you did not dance; we sang a dirge, and you did not mourn.' For John came neither eating nor drinking, and they say, 'He has a demon.' The Son of Man came eating and drinking, and they say, 'Here is a glutton and a drunkard, a friend of tax collectors and sinners.'"*

The context here relates 'this generation' to the people living at the time of Jesus and John the Baptist. Jesus was pointing out that, although he and John had different emphases in their ministries, the people passed negative judgments on them both, resulting in both of them being largely rejected by their contemporaries.

### 2. Matthew 12:38-42

> *"Then some of the Pharisees and teachers of the law said to him, 'Teacher, we want to see a miraculous sign from you.' He answered, 'A wicked and adulterous generation asks for a sign! But none will be given it except the sign of the prophet Jonah. For as Jonah was three days and three nights in the belly of a huge fish, so the Son of Man will be three days and three nights in the heart of the earth. The men of Nineveh will stand up at the judgment with this generation and condemn it; for they repented at the preaching of Jonah, and now one greater than Jonah is here. The Queen of the South will rise at the judgment with this generation and condemn it; for she came from the ends of the earth to listen to Solomon's wisdom, and now one greater than Solomon is here.'"*

Once again Jesus used the phrase 'this generation' to refer to the people who were alive at that time. The one who was 'greater than Jonah' and the one who was 'greater than Solomon' was Jesus himself, living among them.

### 3. Matthew 23:35-36

> *"And so upon you will come all the righteous blood that has been shed on earth, from the blood of righteous Abel to the blood of Zechariah son of Berekiah, whom you murdered between the temple and the altar. I tell you the truth, all this will come upon this generation."*

'This generation' once again most obviously means those who actually rejected Jesus as prophet and Messiah. He had lived righteously before them and they would kill him, just as Abel and Zechariah had been murdered long before.

In Matthew's gospel, then, as well as in the accounts of Mark and Luke, 'this generation' only has one meaning: the contemporaries of Jesus, alive at that time. There is no evidence to suggest that 'this generation' should carry a different meaning from any other occurrence of it in the gospels. If this is true, then everything predicted by Jesus prior to verse 35 in the Olivet discourse was to be fulfilled during the lifetime of that generation. If we calculate a generation as about 40 years, this takes us up to AD 70.

## Two methods of interpreting the Olivet Discourse

**The disciples' questions:**

When will this happen?

What will be the sign of your coming and of the end of the age?

| | | |
|---|---|---|
| **Jesus' answer:** | *Dispensationalist view:* | |
| | Verses 1-51 | Events leading up to the return of Christ (Answering both questions) |
| | *Partial preterist view:* | |
| | Verses 1-35 | Events leading up to AD 70 (Answering the question: 'When will this happen?') |
| | Verses 36-51 | Events leading up to the return of Christ (Answering the question: 'What will be the sign of your coming and of the end of the age?') |

We will now examine the passage itself section by section, beginning with the sometimes baffling references to signs.

## Verses 24:4-14: Don't be misled by some signs

Jesus begins answering the disciples' questions by warning against deception and misleading signs. These signs fall into two categories: signs in the world and signs in the church.

### *Signs in the world – Matthew 24:4-8*

#### 1. The appearance of false Christs (Messiahs)

The Jewish historian Josephus notes many instances where impostors in Palestine claimed to be the Christ. One such incident is also recorded in the book of Acts when Peter and John went to Samaria. There they met a man named Simon who was described by the citizens as 'the divine power known as the great power' (Acts 8:10). Irenaeus, one of the early church fathers of the 2nd century AD, describes how Simon claimed to be the Son of God and the creator of angels, thus claiming divinity for himself.

#### 2. News of wars and rumours of wars

Although Palestine was relatively peaceful during Jesus' earthly ministry, shortly after his death the nation experienced turbulent times. One event that caused widespread anxiety was the order of the Emperor Caligula, whose reign began in AD 37, that a statue of himself should be placed in the temple at Jerusalem. The Jewish authorities refused to comply with Rome's edict and as a result lived in perpetual fear that the Roman army might be dispatched to enforce the imperial command.

Another instance of the instability of the times was a battle between Syrians and Jews in the northern port of Caesarea, resulting in the death of some 20,000 Jews. The fighting between the two ethnic communities divided many villages and caused neighbours to take up arms against one another, resulting in a constant state of agitation.

### 3. The occurrence of natural disasters

Jesus prophesied that famines and earthquakes would occur in various places. One such famine is foretold in Acts 11:27-28 by the prophet Agabus. It occurred a little later during the reign of Claudius (AD 41-54). Earthquakes, too, were prevalent in the Roman Empire prior to AD 70. Acts 16:26 records a violent earthquake that shook the prison at Philippi where Paul and Silas were incarcerated. The earthquake was so severe that the foundations were shaken, all the prison doors flew open and the prisoners' chains were loosened.

Many such earthquakes were recorded throughout the Mediterranean area, including Judea, Colossae and Laodicea. A severe one badly damaged the city of Pompeii in AD 63. Because Pompeii was close to the capital, Rome, this earthquake was extensively reported in contemporary records. Jesus describes these various events as 'the beginning of birth pains' and warns the disciples not to construe them as signs that the end itself had already come.

### Signs in the Church – Matthew 24:9-14

### 1. Persecutions and martyrdom

Jesus prophesied that his followers would be hated by all nations because of him, that the authorities would hand them over to be persecuted, and that some would be martyred. This certainly took place. Acts 8:1 records that 'On that day a great persecution broke out against the church at Jerusalem'. This resulted in most of the Christian community being scattered throughout Judea and Samaria. The persecution was incited further by the pharisaic zealot named Saul of Tarsus, who continued to issue murderous threats against Christ's disciples and sought to imprison in Jerusalem those whom he apprehended. Acts also records the murder of the apostle James, who was put to death with the sword following his arrest by King Herod (Acts 12:1-2).

## 2. Apostasy among the followers of Jesus

The turning away from the faith that Jesus indicated would take place is referred to in the later epistles of the New Testament. Shortly before his death, Paul wrote to Timothy to say that all the believers in the Roman province of Asia had deserted him. The province of Asia comprised the western part of modern Turkey, including the city of Ephesus. Paul had worked extensively in this area and had lived there for three years. The persecution of believers had become so intense in that locality that even some of Paul's well-known fellow-workers like Phygelus and Hermogenes had deserted him (2 Timothy 1:15).

In addition to the persecution, Jesus prophesied that many false prophets would appear in order to deceive many people. The apostle John, in his first epistle, confirmed that Jesus' prediction had by that time become a reality. He warned his fellow-believers against believing every spirit but instead encouraged people to 'test the spirits to see whether they are from God, because many false prophets have gone out into the world' (1 John 4:1).

A further consequence of the apostasy, Jesus predicted, would be that the love of most Christians would grow cold. Indifference would replace a passionate and wholehearted loyalty to Christ. The writer to the Hebrews was evidently aware of such a trend, admonishing his readers to 'pay more careful attention, therefore, to what we have heard, so that we do not drift away' (Hebrews 2:1).

## 3. The Gospel preached in the whole world

When we allow Scripture to interpret Scripture we understand that Jesus' prediction that the gospel would be preached in the whole world in that generation found a glorious fulfilment during the Apostle Paul's lifetime. Paul states: 'All over the world this gospel is bearing fruit and growing' (Colossians 1:6). And again in the same letter: 'The gospel that you heard … has been proclaimed to every creature under heaven' (Colossians 1:23).

All of the above signs in the church, like the ones in the world, are described by Jesus as the beginning of birth pains and not the end itself. He affirmed that only when all of them had been accomplished would 'the end' he spoke of be fulfilled. Remember, the end that is in view here is when 'one stone will not be left upon another'.

## Verse 15: the final authenticating sign

In Matthew 24:15, Jesus reveals the one sign that will authentically demonstrate that the end has come: it is 'the abomination that causes desolation'. The parallel passage in Luke sheds light on what Jesus meant when it quotes him as saying, 'When you see *Jerusalem being surrounded by armies,* you will know that its desolation is near. Then let those who are in Judea flee to the mountains, let those in the city get out, and let those in the country not enter the city' (Luke 21:20-21).

So the 'abomination that causes desolation' is the surrounding of Jerusalem by the Roman armies. These armies carried ensigns displaying eagles and images of the Emperor, to which veneration was given. The abomination was the idolatrous worship offered up by the Roman armies to something other than the one true God.

Roman armies besieging Jerusalem were the sign to the Christians, according to Jesus, that the time had come to leave the city. It is estimated that during the siege and sacking of Jerusalem around one million Jews lost their lives. But the Christian community took Christ's words literally and escaped the massacre. According to Eusebius, writing in the 4th century AD, the Christians who fled Jerusalem gained safety by crossing the Jordan River and settling as refugees in Pella, in the present-day nation of Jordan.

## Verses 16-22: the Great Tribulation

The historical account of events leading to the destruction of Jerusalem in AD 70 is described by R.T. France in his commentary on Matthew's gospel.

> The Jewish revolt began in AD 66, and during 67-68 the Roman commander Vespasian conquered most of Palestine. The Roman civil war in 68-69 led to a suspension of military operations in the East, but during that period Jerusalem was torn apart by its own civil war, as different Jewish parties battled for control, with the temple (the inner courts controlled by the Zealots under Eleazar and the outer court by John of

Gischala) at the centre of the fighting. When eventually the Roman attack was resumed in 69, Jerusalem was already in a weakened and demoralized state. The rest of Judea was quickly reduced (apart from the strongholds of Herodium and Masada), and when Vespasian returned to Rome to take up his new office as emperor, his son Titus put Jerusalem under siege for five terrible months until the temple and much of the city were destroyed in the fall of AD 70.[2]

The citizens of Jerusalem who endured the siege were starved of food and resources. The situation inside the city was made far worse by the factional fighting between three political groups within the Jewish community. Barbarity was exercised not only by the Romans on the Jews but also by Jewish elements upon one another. In the latter part of the siege food was either scarce or non-existent, and rumours of its presence in a household often led to vicious attacks on these dwellings by armed gangs.

Matthew describes the days of the siege as times of 'great distress' (Matthew 24:21, NIV). Other Bible versions render these words as 'great tribulation', for example the NKJV and NASB. Luke further describes these times as 'days of vengeance' (Luke 21:22 NKJV, NASB), indicating divine judgment.

The dire conditions inside the besieged city were documented by the contemporary Jewish historian Josephus in his book *The Wars of the Jews*. His descriptions of the suffering, famine, violence and wickedness that existed among Jews in the city provide a horrific account of life there even before the Roman assault began. Among the horrors were the dead being left unburied, their bodies putrefying in the streets. People resorted to cannibalism and the collapse of moral values is highlighted by Josephus' observations that people executed pernicious actions upon each other 'without mercy and omitted no method of torment or of barbarity.'[3]

The fact that over a million Jews perished authenticates the prophecy of Jesus that the distress of that time would be 'unequalled from the beginning of the world until now – and never to be equalled again' (Matthew 24:21). It is undeniable that, much later in history, about six million Jews perished under the persecuting regime of Nazism, but the severity of human suffering and distress experienced by the inhabitants of Jerusalem during the siege was of a greater intensity than the events in World War II. In Luke's account Jesus describes how the people of Jerusalem would 'fall by the sword and... be taken as prisoners to all the nations' (Luke 21:24).

The forcible capture and exile of the people of Jerusalem is displayed to this day in the dramatic carved illustrations on the Arch of Titus in Rome. This monument was erected in honour of Titus, his military conquest of the Jewish people and the capture of their capital, Jerusalem. The carvings depict the Jewish leaders being led to Rome bound and manacled by their triumphant captors.

So these were days of 'great tribulation' indeed. Jesus asserted that 'If those days had not been cut short, no one would survive, but for the sake of the elect those days will be shortened' (Matthew 24:22). In this regard, Kik quotes the Roman commander Titus speaking after Jerusalem had been captured: 'We have certainly had God for our assistant in this war and it was no other than God who ejected the Jews out of the fortifications, for what could the hands of men, or any machines, do toward overthrowing these towers?'[4]

## Verses 23-29: Warnings about the time of Christ's coming

Jesus indicated that, at that time, rumours would abound that the Christ had already come, and that false Christs and false prophets would appear, attempting to deceive the followers of the true Christ (Matthew 24:23-24). He urged them to ignore every such rumour. His coming again, he made clear, would not be a secret event, hidden from the masses, but public and highly visible, as widely seen as a flash of lightning (Matthew 24:26-27). From these instructions the disciples of Jesus were assured that his coming again would not take place during the siege that produced the destruction of the temple.

Jesus then graphically described the temple as a carcass, in other words a structure with no internal life. He had already prophesied that the house would be left desolate, abandoned by God, who is himself Eternal Life. God vividly signalled his abandonment of the temple by ripping open the temple veil at the moment Jesus yielded up his spirit on the cross (Matthew 27:50-51). According to Jesus a carcass attracts vultures. The Greek word for 'vulture' here can equally be translated 'eagle', which points again to the besieging Roman armies with their eagle ensigns.

Jesus continued his discourse and prophetic pronouncements with the phrase, 'Immediately after the distress [or 'tribulation' – NKJV, NASB] of those days...' (Matthew 24:29). The word 'immediately' means 'at once, instantly, without any intervening time or space'.[5] What Jesus was about to describe, then, is not to be attributed to a still-future time. Rather, these events were to closely follow the siege and collapse of Jerusalem in AD 70.

You could be forgiven for wondering how some of them could be said to have happened at the time. The imagery is very graphic and can therefore seem to be applicable only to Christ's ultimate return in glory. But here is where our principles of Bible interpretation can help us, including the need to read the New Testament in the light of the Old Testament that preceded it.

The prophetic and apocalyptic imagery of this passage echoes similar Old Testament imagery. We have no need to refer it to some alleged future event prior to the Lord's return. Indeed, Jesus explicitly intended to prevent such an interpretation by introducing the word 'immediately', thereby connecting his statements to the events in AD 70.

In particular, the descriptions of the sun being darkened, the moon not giving its light, the stars falling from the sky and the heavenly bodies being shaken, can appear to be images appropriate only to the end of the world. But the Old Testament shows them clearly to refer, not to the end of the world, but to *the overthrow and downfall of nations*:

- Isaiah prophesied God's judgment on Babylon by declaring, 'The stars of heaven and their constellations will not show their light. The rising sun will be darkened and the moon will not give its light' (Isaiah 13:10). It did not happen literally but Babylon certainly fell.
- Again, Isaiah described God's judgment on Edom as the displacement of heavenly bodies: 'All the stars of the heavens will be dissolved and the sky rolled up like a scroll; all the starry host will fall like withered leaves from the vine, like shrivelled figs from the fig tree'(Isaiah 34:4).
- Ezekiel used similar imagery to describe the destruction of Pharaoh: 'When I snuff you out, I will cover the heavens and darken their stars; I will cover the sun with a cloud, and the moon will not give its light. All the shining lights in the heavens I will darken over you; I will bring darkness over your land, declares the Sovereign Lord' (Ezekiel 32:7-8).
- Jeremiah did the same when foretelling the judgment on Judah at the hand of the Babylonians: 'The earth will mourn and the heavens above grow dark' (Jeremiah 4:28).

These great nations and their kings were the 'stars' of their era. How appropriate, then, for the prophets to use stellar language to describe their collapse! Whenever the Old Testament prophets referred to darkened heavens and heavenly bodies no longer giving light, they meant the ending of the glory of nations and their rulers because of God's judgments on them. In the same way, Jesus' use of 'darkened heavens' imagery refers to God's judgment on the nation and leaders of Israel, and the extinguishing of their glory.

## Verses 30-31: the sign of the Son of Man

Jesus introduced his next sentence with 'At that time...' So he continued to refer to first-century events. What he said, though, is a little surprising: 'At that time the sign of the Son of Man will appear in the sky' (Matthew 24:30). Surely, we imagine, this can only refer to Christ's second coming? How, then, can we see it as taking place 'at that time'?

We understand that a sign points to a reality, but is not the reality itself. For example, the sign that the Queen of England is in residence at Buckingham Palace is the Royal Ensign being flown from the flagpole on top of the building. She herself does not appear on the palace ramparts but the presence of the flag indicates that she is inside the building.

In the same way, in the first century the sign that the Son of Man was in heaven was not the appearance of Jesus in the sky. The sign that he was in heaven, enthroned with all authority, was the pile of rubble that existed in the place of the former impressive temple. He had said the temple would be destroyed; now he tells us that this would be a sign to all that the old covenant system had become obsolete and that he now reigned as King of Kings and Lord of Lords from heaven, to where he had ascended.

Jesus added that the destroyed temple would be a cause of mourning by 'all the nations of the earth' (Matthew 24:30). But surely it would just be Jews, not all nations, who would mourn the loss of the temple? The word translated in the NIV as 'nations' is the Greek *phulai*. This word is used one other time in Matthew (19:28) where the NIV translates it 'tribes'. The NKJV and NASB both correctly use the word 'tribes'. Elsewhere in Matthew 24 the word 'nation' translates the Greek word *ethnos* (verses 7 and 9). The use of 'nations' in verse 30 is therefore inconsistent, and the word 'tribes' is more appropriate – referring to the tribes of Israel making up the Jewish nation.

Next, the NIV translators have chosen the word 'earth' to translate the Greek *gï*. Just as in English 'earth' may mean either soil or the planet itself, so in Greek the word *gï* has more than one meaning. It too can refer to the planet (Matthew 28:18) and to soil (Matthew 13:8). But it can also mean 'land' in the sense of the territory of a country or region. Joseph, for instance, was instructed to return from Egypt to the land (*gï*) of Israel (Matthew 2:20-21).

In the light of all this the phrase 'the nations of the earth' employed by the NIV translators could be better and more legitimately rendered 'the tribes of the land'. That the tribes of the land of Israel were in mourning is completely understandable since their beloved temple, which had stood for almost 600 years, was now reduced to ruins.

In Matthew 24:30, then, there are three things that Jesus said would occur 'at that time': the sign of the Son of Man in heaven, the tribes of the land mourning – and 'the Son of Man coming on the clouds of the sky.' This third item has understandably been applied by many to the second coming of the Lord. But this is a mistake and, again, the Old Testament prophets can help our understanding of this imagery.

In a vision, Daniel saw before him 'one like a son of man, coming with the clouds of heaven. He approached the Ancient of Days and was led into his presence. He was given authority, glory and sovereign power; all peoples, nations and men of every language worshipped him' (Daniel 7:13-14).

In this prophetic vision the Son of Man coming with the clouds of heaven does not refer to Jesus coming to earth. The Son of Man is coming instead to 'the Ancient of Days' – to God himself. The passage describes Christ's ascension to heaven with great power, glory and majesty after his victory at the cross. In this context the 'clouds' speak – as they so often do – of the divine presence, majesty, deity, power and glory. A typical example is Isaiah's vision of the Lord coming with clouds:

> *See, the Lord rides on a swift cloud and is coming to Egypt. The idols of Egypt tremble before him, and the hearts of the Egyptians melt within them. I will stir up Egyptian against Egyptian – brother will fight against brother, neighbour against neighbour, city against city, kingdom against kingdom.* (Isaiah 19:1-2)

Isaiah saw the Lord riding on a cloud, but we know there was no personal manifestation of his presence to the Egyptians. Rather, the cloud imagery speaks of God's judgment on the Egyptians by stirring up brother to fight against brother without the Lord making any personal appearance.

David, using similar language, speaks of how God delivered him from his enemies. He declares that God 'parted the heavens and came down; dark clouds were under his feet' (Psalm 18:9). Once again clouds represent judgment and deliverance without any sense of God personally visiting David.

In the light of these Old Testament examples we need not look for a personal appearance of Jesus to fulfil the phrase 'coming on the clouds of the sky' in Matthew 24. The imagery is simply saying that God would bring deliverance to his people by judging their enemies and at the same time advancing his purposes. The next phrase that Jesus uses confirms this: 'He will send his angels with a loud trumpet call, and they will gather his elect from the four winds, from one end of the heavens to the other' (Matthew 24:31).

The word 'angels' immediately brings to mind those spirit messengers who, throughout Scripture, help and strengthen God's people. But the English word 'angel' translates the Greek *angelos*, which simply means 'messenger'. A messenger could be sent by God, by man or by Satan. Messengers may indeed be spirit beings but they could just as easily be human beings. For example, John the Baptist was a 'messenger' (*angelos*) who prepared the way for Jesus (Matthew 11:10). Then John's disciples, whom he sent to Jesus, are also called 'messengers' (*angelos*, Luke 7:24). Later, the disciples whom Jesus sent ahead of him into a Samaritan village, were 'messengers' (*angelos*, Luke 9:52). We believe the word in Matthew 24 also refers to humans. Jesus sent out his messengers when he entrusted his disciples with the Great Commission to go and make disciples of all nations.

The phrase 'with a loud trumpet call' is a literal expression in much of the Old Testament, such as when the trumpet was sounded on the Day of Atonement. But the term, can also have a figurative sense, as when the Apostle John heard the voice of Jesus speaking to him like a trumpet (Revelation 1:10).

At the time of the destruction of the temple, Jesus' messengers again heard the 'trumpet call' of his command to faithfully proclaim the good news of the gospel to all people everywhere. The gospel, now freed definitively from its exclusively Jewish ties by the destruction of the temple and its worship, could range freely throughout the earth – as God had always intended. To his messengers he gave the privilege of gathering his elect from all over the earth, represented by the four winds. Mark's account describes this reaping as occurring 'from the ends of the earth to the ends of the heavens' (Mark 13:27), signifying the worldwide response to the message of the gospel. Note that the disciples would gather the *nations* to Jesus. Earlier, Jesus had expressed his longing to gather the *nation of Israel* to himself, but Israel's unwillingness to respond prevented this from happening, resulting instead in judgment on their house (Matthew 23:37-38).

## Verses 32-35: the lesson of the fig tree

Jesus summarised his response to the disciples' question about the destruction of the temple by drawing their attention to the behaviour of the fig tree. The approach of summer is signalled by the condition of the fig tree. The sprouting of tender twigs and the appearance of foliage indicate that summer is near. In the same way, the signs that Jesus had just described pointed to the fact that the time when not one stone of the temple would be left upon another was not far off.

Jesus, as we have seen, went into considerable detail about these signs. He did so because he didn't want his disciples to be taken by surprise by the cataclysmic events leading up to the temple's destruction. He affirmed this by saying, 'This generation will certainly not pass away until all these things have happened'. He went on to emphasise this statement by asserting that even if heaven and earth passed away his words would remain for ever.

Our studies so far have brought us to the end of the first part of the Olivet discourse. Now we must turn to the second part, which marks a change of direction.

## Verses 36-45: the day of the Lord

Verse 36 is the hinge-verse of Matthew 24. It starts with the word 'But', indicating a contrast between what has gone before and what will now follow – and that contrast is startling, with a complete change of tone.

Following Jesus' astounding statement that the people of his generation would live to witness not one stone of the temple left upon another, he continued to answer the disciples' questions by saying, 'But of *that* day and hour no one knows, not even the angels of heaven, but My Father only' (Matthew 24:36 NKJV). He is addressing the issue of his coming at the end of the age.[6]

The sense of contrast between verse 36 and Jesus' earlier words is certainly striking. Before verse 36 Jesus was specific and detailed about the signs that would precede the destruction of the temple. He clearly identified events that could be understood and interpreted without misconception. It was that clarity that led the Christians in Jerusalem, for example, to flee Jerusalem, thereby escaping its awful fate.

By contrast, verse 36 introduces statements that are as vague and unspecific in their nature as the earlier ones were clear and specific. Jesus admits that, concerning '*that* day and hour', no one knows, not even the Son himself! '*That* day and hour' is, of course, in contrast to the time around the destruction of Jerusalem already described.

There has been a change of subject. Jesus has now moved forward in time to his ultimate return. Instead of giving signs that would signal the time when the Son of Man would come again, Jesus simply described the period before his return as being like the days before Noah entered the Ark.

In Noah's day there were no signs at all: the people had no forewarning of the deluge that was about to engulf them. God had spoken personally to Noah, commanding him to prepare an Ark for the salvation of his family and representatives of all living creatures, but his contemporaries had no warning from prior signs. They continued with life as normal – described by Jesus as 'eating and drinking, marrying and giving in marriage, up to the day Noah entered the Ark' (Matthew 24:38). Although Noah is described as 'a preacher of righteousness' (2 Peter 2:5), the people of his day were impervious to his message, and the onset of the flood caught them completely unawares.

The suddenness and surprise associated with Christ's second coming, without any prior signs or warnings, are further illustrated in Jesus' description of the normality of life that will precede the time of his arrival: 'Two men will be in the field; one will be taken and the other left. Two women will be grinding with a hand mill; one will be taken and the other left' (Matthew 24:40-41).

Who are the people that will be taken and who are those who will be left? The Old Testament account of Noah leaves no doubt as to their identity. It was righteous Noah and his family who was saved and as a result was 'left' on earth. And it was the wicked of Noah's generation who were 'taken' in judgment. David saw the same outcome for the righteous and the wicked and prophetically described their different futures:

> A little while, and the wicked will be no more; though you look for them, they will not be found. But the meek will inherit the land and enjoy great peace. (Psalm 37:10-11)

Jesus himself, in the Sermon on the Mount, describes the future of the righteous with the statement, 'Blessed are the meek, for they will inherit the earth', (Matthew 5:5). That is how God rewards the righteous. The wicked, however, can claim no part in the future 'home of righteousness' that God has planned. Whereas his first coming focused on dealing with sin (Hebrews 9:28), his second coming will inaugurate a time of judgment that will entirely consume his adversaries (Hebrews 10:27). So it is the wicked who are taken and the righteous who are left.

Because Jesus' second coming will have no signs announcing its approach, the command to his followers is, 'Keep watch, because *you do not know* on what day your Lord will come' (Matthew 24:42) Followers of Christ are to stay awake and cultivate alertness so as to anticipate and eagerly await the coming of the Master. We are to be prepared so that we will not be ashamed at his appearing (1 John 2:28).

Jesus' coming, he says, will be like a thief in the night. This picture further demonstrates that his arrival will be without warning and unannounced. Thieves do not distribute calling cards in a neighbourhood they intend to burgle. If they did, householders would stay awake and not allow their homes to be broken into. Jesus then pressed home the importance of being vigilant regarding his coming again by telling three parables. All three carry the same meaning and application.

### The faithful and wise servant (Matthew 24:45-51)

The master, going away for a while, entrusts to his household overseer the task of ensuring that his fellow-servants are cared for and well fed. If, on his return, the master finds that the overseer has been fulfilling his responsibilities, he will reward him by entrusting *all* his possessions to him. But should the servant act wickedly by getting drunk and failing in his responsibilities, the master will remove all his privileges and exclude him from the household.

### The ten virgins (Matthew 25:1-13)

Ten virgins are assigned to meet the bridegroom with lamps to illuminate his journey. Five are described as 'wise' and take spare oil with them. Five are 'foolish', failing to take any oil. Because the bridegroom takes a long time to make his appearance, all the virgins become tired and fall asleep. At midnight the ten virgins are woken by cries that the bridegroom is now ready. The foolish virgins with no oil are unprepared and need to rush off and try to purchase oil for their lamps.

In the meantime, the bridegroom arrives, and only the five wise virgins, who had already obtained their oil, are allowed to escort him to the wedding banquet. The foolish virgins are denied access to the meal and festivities because they missed the bridegroom's arrival. By their failure to keep watch they forfeit access to the wedding festivities.

### The parable of the talents (Matthew 25:14-30)

A man embarking on a journey entrusts his property to his servants. To one he gives five talents of money, to another two talents, and to another one talent. The last servant hides his master's money in the ground, whereas the other two put the money to work. After a long time the master returns. He honours the two servants who have gainfully used what they had been given but chastises the one who failed to put the resource to use.

The three parables share common features. Firstly, the appearance of the master or bridegroom is delayed. The phrase 'a long time' occurs in each of the parables (Matthew 24:48, 25:5, 19). Secondly, when the master or bridegroom does appear he arrives unexpectedly and without prior warning. Finally, in each parable the faithful are rewarded for their faithfulness, whereas the unfaithful suffer loss because of their disobedience.

Since Jesus offers no signs to signal his second coming, his primary command to his followers is to be faithful in the work he has given each one of us to do. Jesus himself said he did not know the timing of his return. He was evidently not able to provide us with any detailed information about his second coming. But, in his grace he sent the Holy Spirit, after his ascension, to be a guide and comfort to each of his disciples. His promise was that the Spirit of Truth would guide us into all truth and, also, would tell us what is yet to come (John 16:13).

We may not know the timing of Jesus' return, but we can know the joy of being empowered by the Holy Spirit to perform the tasks he has allocated to us. In addition, the Holy Spirit within us heightens our desire for and anticipation of the Lord's return. Living in fellowship with the Spirit and obeying his promptings will ensure that God's people will not be taken by surprise at their Lord's coming again. Instead we can look forward to the joy of seeing him again and experiencing the blessing of the rewards that he will bestow upon all who have faithfully pursued their calling.

## The final judgment (Matthew 25:31-46)

Jesus concludes his teaching at the Mount of Olives by telling a parable about the judgment that will occur at his return. The parable of the sheep and the goats describes how Jesus will separate one type of person from another, just as surely as a shepherd is able to separate sheep from goats. The sheep are ushered to his right hand – the place of blessing and reward. Conversely, the goats are placed on his left and do not inherit the blessings bestowed on the sheep. The sheep are invited to partake of their inheritance, experiencing the fullness of the kingdom prepared for them since creation.

The sheep receive their inheritance because of their righteous deeds. Jesus honours them for giving him food when he was hungry, something to drink when he was thirsty, an invitation to their home when he was a stranger, providing him with clothing when he needed clothes, caring for him when he was sick, and visiting him when he was in prison. The sheep are puzzled, unaware of having performed these tasks. They ask Jesus, 'When did these events occur?' He explains that to perform these righteous actions for the benefit of his brothers, is to serve him personally.

In the same way the goats are unaware that they have failed to serve Christ by neglecting to serve Christ's brothers when they had opportunity to do so. Their failure to demonstrate kindness in practical deeds results in their exclusion from the kingdom and their consignment to eternal punishment. Knowing that Jesus will return should focus our lives on displaying good deeds and kindness to all, and especially to those who are spiritual brothers and sisters. In this way the church will shine like light in the darkness, demonstrate the reality of our relationship with Jesus and win people to him.

## Conclusion

Matthew chapter 24 has proved to be very fertile ground for prophecy teachers and end-time experts who believe it should be read as a catalogue of apocalyptic terrors leading up to the return of Christ. We have sought to show that this is in fact a violation of the passage. The Olivet discourse falls naturally into two parts. Up to verse 35 Jesus concerns himself with warning his disciples about the events leading up to the destruction of Jerusalem in AD 70. Historical records show that every detail of Jesus' warnings was fulfilled in that great event.

From verse 36 however, Jesus is speaking of his final return. There are no lurid descriptions of the end of the world, simply the exhortation to be about our heavenly Father's business until he comes. Viewed in this way, the passage makes perfect sense.

## End notes

1. For an excellent discussion on the two preterist schools of thought we recommend Professor Jay E Adams's book *Preterism: Orthodox or Unorthodox*, published by Timeless Texts
2. *Commentary on Matthew's Gospel*, R T France
3. Josephus, *The Wars of the Jews*
4. Kik, *An Eschatology of Victory*
5. *Oxford Dictionary*
6. Unfortunately, the original NIV took liberties with the Greek text by omitting the word 'but' that begins the sentence. Most other versions include 'but' or 'however'. Interestingly, the NIV 2010 edition restores it.

Chapter 6

# The Book of Revelation

Philip, a zealous young disciple of Christ, was in the midst of a powerful move of God. The entire city of Samaria had turned to the Lord as they saw the miracles performed at his hands. Then in the full flow of the revival, an angel of God instructed him to head down to the desert of Gaza in order to help just one individual.

There Philip found a richly dressed man, a high-ranking official of the Ethiopian queen Candace, sitting in his chariot and reading from the scroll of the prophet Isaiah. Seizing the opportunity, Philip approached the official and asked, 'Do you understand what you are reading?' to which the Ethiopian replied, 'How can I unless someone guides me?' (Acts 8:31). It was an honest answer to a question we all face – how to understand the Bible.

Depending on which book of the Bible we are reading, the task of understanding varies in difficulty. But nothing really prepares us for our encounter with the book of Revelation! Many books of the Bible are at least written in a form familiar to the modern reader. The final book of the New Testament, however, the book of Revelation, seems to be the most enigmatic and impenetrable of all.

The first five books of the New Testament – the four gospels and the book of Acts – are stories about Jesus and the early church respectively, written in a narrative style that we are all used to. The following twenty-one books are all letters written by various authors to individuals or church communities in the first century AD, letters we can all handle.

But the book of Revelation is quite different. Neither purely narrative nor simply a letter, it is a form of literature unfamiliar to the modern reader. It introduces dragons and beasts, angelic inter-ventions and devastating judgments in a way that leaves us reeling with questions as to the meaning and implications of the text.

Even Bible translators themselves have remarked how different the book of Revelation is from the other writings. J.B. Phillips, for example, makes the following observations in the preface to his translation of the book of Revelation:

> The most obvious and striking feature of the book at first sight is the oddness of the Greek in which it is written ....... Revelation piles word upon word remorselessly, mixes cases and tenses without apparent scruple, and shows at times a complete disregard for normal syntax and grammar.[1]

## Literary style

If the book of Revelation is to be profitable, we must appreciate it for the kind of literature it is. The first few verses of the book come to our assistance here because they immediately show what we are dealing with.

### Revelation is an apocalypse

The opening three words of the book of Revelation in the original Greek are *Apokalypsis Iesou Christou*, which means in English 'the revelation of Jesus Christ'. The purpose of an apocalypse – as we saw in chapter 4 – is to *reveal* something. Revelation is a revealing of one specific subject: the person of Jesus Christ. Whatever else this book includes, John is communicating to his readers a revelation of Jesus Christ: who he is and the work he has accomplished and will accomplish in the future.

Apocalyptic literature was written during times of persecution or oppression and carried the hope of eventual victory of good over evil. It was common among Jewish and Christian communities between 250 BC and AD 150, but the book of Revelation is the only example we have of such literature in the New Testament.

An apocalypse uses an unfolding story to convey revelatory information. In every apocalypse this information is communicated through an 'other worldly' being to a human recipient. In Revelation, John receives the information from an angel (Revelation 1:1).

The book of Revelation, however, is distinct from every other apocalypse in one respect: in all other such writings the author remains anonymous or uses a pseudonym, but in the book of Revelation the apostle John reveals himself as the author (Revelation 1:9).

An apocalypse conveys its message by the use of symbols, visions, images, dreams and cryptic language, all of which contain hidden meanings. Sometimes in Revelation the meaning of the symbols is made clear. At the end of chapter 1, for example, we are told that the seven stars that John saw in the right hand of Jesus represent the angels of seven churches, and that the seven golden lamp stands, among which John saw Jesus standing, are seven churches. Later, in chapter 12, a creature called the great dragon appears. He is described as 'that ancient serpent who is called the devil and Satan, the deceiver of the whole world' (Revelation 12:9). In keeping with sound principles of Bible interpretation, we should attribute no meaning to the symbol other than the one given in the text – this is Satan.

All apocalyptic literature views the present in the light of the future, and the earthly realm and its activities in the light of heaven and its activities. Revelation fits this pattern with statements like, 'The one who conquers' [present tense] 'will be granted to sit with Christ on his throne' [future tense] (13:21). Again, at the beginning of chapter 4 John sees a door open in heaven and is invited to enter the heavenly realms from which perspective he not only sees heavenly activities but understands how those activities are outworked in the earthly realm. So Revelation is a classical case of apocalyptic literature.

### Revelation is a prophecy

Revelation 1:3 introduces the book as a prophecy: 'Blessed is the one who reads aloud the words of *this prophecy*, and blessed are those who hear, and who keep what is written in it, for the time is near'.

The purpose of the book, then is not to surprise, alarm or confuse but to produce readers who are 'blessed', that is, who as a result of their reading will experience a sense of wellbeing. In this respect the book of Revelation fits the purpose of prophecy as described by Paul, who said: 'Everyone who prophesies speaks to men for their strengthening, encouragement and comfort' (1 Corinthians 14:3). Prophecy is given to build up, stir up and cheer up those who receive the prophetic word. We can be sure, then, that any interpretation of the book of Revelation that causes the reader to be depressed, discouraged or demoralized is the opposite of what John intended.

### Revelation is a letter

Letters have a form and structure of their own. They usually have a stylised beginning and ending. Contemporary letters begin with 'Dear....' and end with 'Yours....' The letters recorded in the New Testament also display stylised beginnings and endings – but the ones normal in that era. Each of Paul's letters, for example, begins by identifying Paul as the author, the person or community to whom the letter is being sent ('all those in Rome'; 'the churches of Galatia'; 'Timothy', etc.), and a greeting of grace to the recipients. In the same way, each epistle ends by proclaiming the grace of the Lord Jesus Christ to the recipients.

The book of Revelation displays the literary characteristics of a letter with its stylised beginning and ending. It opens with 'John, to the seven churches that are in Asia: Grace and peace to you' (1:4), and ends with 'The grace of the Lord Jesus be with you all. Amen' (22:21).

As to their literary form, letters are classified as occasional documents, that is, the author writes in the context of certain circumstances and speaks to a specific situation. If we are to understand a letter we must determine the historic context and circumstances of the writer and its recipient. Any attempt to apply the message of a letter to ourselves without first understanding its original context is bound to lead to error.

With the book of Revelation the literary characteristics of apocalypse, prophecy and letter must be honoured and appreciated together. Only then will we avoid the trap of forcing narrow and dogmatic interpretations onto the text.

## Important issues to consider

Christians often read the book of Revelation expecting to find ready answers to the myriad questions it poses. But Revelation, let us remember, is chiefly an apocalypse, a genre largely unfamiliar to us, and cannot be read through the interpretive lenses we usually apply to other literature. A better approach is to allow the book itself to impress upon us its own priorities and urgencies. Numerous New Testament scholars have adopted this approach, including Professor Richard Bauckham, whose book *The Theology of the Book of Revelation* will provide you with excellent study material if you are interested in pursuing this further.[2]

We have identified some of the issues that appear to be important to the author, John, and will hopefully help you, as a contemporary reader, to approach the book with greater objectivity.

### *The theology of Revelation is Christ-centred*

We have noted that the book of Revelation is primarily an unveiling of Jesus Christ. This is clear from the book's opening sentence. Then just a few verses later John describes his personal encounter with the risen Christ:

> *I was in the Spirit on the Lord's Day, and I heard behind me a loud voice like a trumpet saying, "Write what you see in a book and send it to the seven churches, to Ephesus and to Smyrna and to Pergamum and to Thyatira and to Sardis and to Philadelphia and to Laodicea."* (Revelation 1:10-11)

As John turns around to identify the person speaking to him he is greeted by the resurrected Christ and is so overwhelmed by the majesty of his appearance that he falls at his feet as if he were dead. This profound encounter with Christ sets the stage for everything that unfolds through the rest of the book.

For John, this awesome revelation of the ascended Christ – who now has the title of 'Ruler of the kings of the Earth' – provides the backdrop and framework for everything that follows. At no time does the introduction of figures like the beast, the false prophet or the harlot Babylon detract from the supremacy of Jesus Christ as the ever-living and ever-ruling one.

This revelation of Christ's supremacy is completely in line with the Christology of the other New Testament writers. Paul, for instance, describes Christ as:

> *... the image of the invisible God, the firstborn over all creation.... He is before all things and in him all things go together. And he is the head of the body, the Church...so that in everything he might have the supremacy.* (Colossians 1:15-18)

In the same way Peter announces to the assembled crowd on the day of Pentecost, 'Let all Israel be assured of this: God has made this Jesus, whom you crucified, both Lord and Christ' (Acts 2:36).

In establishing the supremacy of Christ at the very beginning of the book of Revelation John not only concurs with the other New Testament writers about Jesus' status, but also rejects permission for any interpretation of his book other than the one that views Christ's universal rule as central.

### Revelation frequently alludes to Old Testament prophecy

Although there are no formal quotations from the Old Testament prophetic scriptures anywhere in the book in Revelation, it is saturated with verbal and pictorial allusions to them. John is himself a prophet (Revelation 22:9) – and he draws upon the vast wealth and imagery of the Old Testament prophets to express his revelation to the first century church. For instance, Revelation 18:1 - 19:8 is an oracle against Babylon that echoes every one of the oracles against Babylon prophesied by Isaiah and Jeremiah.

This example illustrates how an understanding of the Old Testament prophetic writings is foundational to appreciating how John applies his message to first century readers. Babylon was the besieger and destroyer of historical Jerusalem. Now Rome and its armies are doing the same thing in the first century AD. The latter is an echo and fulfilment of the former.

### Numbers in Revelation are symbolic

In Revelation numbers are highly symbolic, in keeping with the nature of the apocalyptic genre. Any attempt to read the numbers in a literal manner will inevitably lead to confusion. Only when we understand the non-literal nature of the numbers can we appreciate their symbolic significance.

For example, the number seven symbolises completeness and perfection. This is so even from the earliest chapters of the Old Testament, where God rested on the seventh day after completing the work of creation (Genesis 2:2). In Revelation, Jesus gives personal messages to seven churches, symbolising his word to the whole church (Revelation 2 and 3). Seven is the number of seals on the scroll of the future (Revelation 5 and 6). Seven angels blow seven trumpets (Revelation 8, 9 and 11) and seven angels pour out seven golden bowls full of the wrath of God (Revelation 15 and 16). In addition there are seven beatitudes promising blessing to those who read, hear and keep the prophecy (Revelation 1:3; 14:13; 16:13; 19:9; 20:6; 22:7, 14). Finally, the seven spirits of God (Revelation 4:5) represent the fullness of the one Holy Spirit.

The number four is mentioned three times in one verse: 'I saw four angels standing at the four corners of the earth, holding back the four winds of the earth' (Revelation 7:1). Four thus symbolises the earthly realms. Three, on the other hand, symbolises God and the heavenly realms: 'Holy, holy, holy is the Lord God Almighty who was and is and is to come' (Revelation 4:8). The threefold use of 'holy' points in that direction, as does the threefold phrase 'who was and is and is to come', which is used three times – in Revelation 1:4, 8; 4:8.

Finally, the number twelve, echoing the twelve tribes of Israel, is a reference to the people of God. The New Jerusalem is portrayed as having twelve gates, with twelve angels present at the gates, and inscribed on those gates are the names of the twelve tribes of the sons of Israel (Revelation 21:12). Multiples of twelve are used to describe the vast measurements of the city. Its length and breadth measure 12,000 stadia and the city wall is 144 (12x12) cubits thick (Revelation 21:16-17). The walls of the city have twelve foundations and on them are written the twelve names of the twelve apostles of the Lamb.

The number twelve is also used to identify those who have the name of God and the Lamb written on their foreheads – 144,000 in total (12x12x1000) representing a vast (but not literal) number of people. Lastly, the woman clothed with the sun – who appears in Chapter 12 and gives birth to a male child who is to rule all the nations – has a crown of twelve stars on her head, indicating that the Messiah will come forth from the people of God.

### The Lamb has conquered and his followers, too, are to conquer

At the centre of heaven's celebrations is the one who sits on the throne, and also the Lamb (Revelation 5:13). The Lamb has conquered through shedding his blood and in the process has purchased people for God from every tribe and language, people and nation. Because the Lamb has overcome, he has received the honour of sitting with his Father on his throne.

But the conquering Lamb is not to remain alone in his victories. The overcoming Christ encourages every believer in the seven churches to believe that they can emulate their Lord in overcoming the hostilities they face as they pursue the interests of Christ and the establishing of his kingdom. The prize for those who overcome is the honour of sitting with Christ on his throne, just as he was honoured to sit on his Father's throne. And how do the saints overcome? It is 'by the blood of the Lamb and by the word of their testimony' (Revelation 12:11). Overcoming also involves loving Christ more than one's own life and being willing to embrace martyrdom if faced with the prospect.

## *There is an unfolding of a divine romance*

Revelation paints an epic love story between the groom, Jesus and his bride, the church. This beautiful love relationship is seen to take place as a contrast to another partnership which by comparison is utterly grotesque – the doomed love affair between the beast and the garish prostitute Babylon.

The thread of the divine romance is first seen in the address to the seven churches of Asia. Ephesus in particular is highlighted as having forsaken her first love. Smyrna on the other hand is commended for her refusal to yield in the face of affliction and persecution. She receives commendation from the Lord and encouragement to remain faithful. Other churches are encouraged to remain faithful by holding fast to what is already theirs. Each of these statements reflects the Lord's desire that his bride remains faithful to him alone and retains a purity of devotion even in the midst of severe opposition.

The picture of the bride and the groom carries with it powerful echoes from the Old Testament prophets, who saw God's people in a bridal relationship with Jehovah (for example, Ezekiel 16). Whereas the people of Israel had been unfaithful to the Lord and indulged in spiritual adultery by worshipping foreign gods, the bride of Christ is applauded for making herself ready for the wedding celebration with the Lamb (Revelation 19:7). She appears in her glorious beauty towards the end of Revelation's narrative (21:2) to conclude the ultimate 'happy ever after' story.

Jesus and his bride dwell together in eternal bliss with the trauma of her sufferings having been consigned firmly to the past. Eternal fruitfulness and blessings flow as the product of divine romance, represented by the tree of life yielding fruit every month and its leaves providing healing for all nations.

## Revelation compared to Daniel

The Old Testament book most similar to Revelation is Daniel. Both authors were prophets who received revelation from God in the context of the oppression of God's people. Both prophets received graphic images from heaven and both experienced angelic encounters in the process. God permitted Daniel to see visions of the future which included the rise and fall of several world empires. At the end of his revelation, Daniel was told that what he had received was to be closed up and sealed until the time of the end. In other words, it would not be Daniel's contemporaries who would understand and benefit from his prophetic images.

With John it was to be the complete opposite, for he was told, 'Do *not* seal up the words of the prophecy of this book, because the time is near' (Revelation 22:10). The contents of Revelation, then, were applicable to the believers in the first century AD and the book has remained unsealed since its writing so that all who read it, in every generation, may benefit from the words of the prophecy.

## Four traditional schools of interpreting Revelation

In our appendix on Bible interpretation we identify four main schools of thought with regard to understanding the book of Revelation. We are going to look at these more closely now.

### Historicist

The historicist sees the book of Revelation as a commentary on the course of history from the first century until the present time. Inevitably, there are differing viewpoints about the meaning of the images and symbols as they apply in history. It is hard to avoid confusion when trying to identify pointers in Revelation with historical events and figures like the Black Death that caused devastation in Europe in the mid 14th century, or Napoleon's military conquests at the beginning of the 19th century.

The historicist viewpoint appealed to Protestant theologians at the time of the Reformation. Many saw the Roman Catholic Church as the Beast, a view that helped stir up Protestant communities against the Papal system and its injustices. More recently the historicist position has experienced a dramatic decline in popularity due to the difficulty of applying the symbols and pictures in Revelation to more recent history.

### Idealist

This view holds that no actual events of history, either past or future, are depicted in the book of Revelation. Instead it regards the symbols as displaying spiritual realities and timeless principles.

111

Viewed through this interpretive lens, for example, John's vision of the Lamb on the throne demonstrates that Jesus is always in control, whatever the temporal circumstances on earth.

The idealist contends that the great themes of Revelation are played out without any necessary reference to single historical events. These themes would include the triumph of good over evil, of Christ over Satan and the vindication of the martyrs in light of diabolical oppression. While these themes undoubtedly are a message for each generation, the fact that Revelation is a letter must root the symbols and their meaning into the context of first-century Middle Eastern Christianity. Failure to do so undermines the concept of the book as a letter with immediate application. This is why the idealist viewpoint by itself will always fail to reflect the fullness that exists within this remarkable book. One of the best treatments of Revelation from an idealist point of view is Tony Ling's *The Lion and the Lamb*.[3]

## Futurist

Futurists believe that the book of Revelation refers primarily to events yet to occur. They concede that the letters to the seven churches in Chapters 2 and 3 were written to first-century church communities, but they hold that the beginning of Chapter 4, where John is taken up to heaven, signals a cut-off point. Everything after that point, they say, describes the days leading up to and surrounding the return of Christ. Today a majority of believers probably take a futurist view of Revelation – in many cases because they are unaware of the alternatives.

Dispensationalists hold to a particular futurist viewpoint. They believe that everything in chapters 4 to 19 will occur within a literal seven-year period between the alleged secret rapture and the second coming of Christ. During this time the Great Tribulation is supposed to occur. And immediately following the seven-year period comes a literal thousand-year reign of Christ on earth.

We maintain, however, that the book of Revelation displays a marvellous unity, offering no evidence at all that a break of two thousand years should be inserted at the end of chapter 3. The whole book is a letter written by John and, what is more, the themes introduced in the first three chapters are reintroduced in later chapters with additional themes added to them – and no hint of a hiatus anywhere along the line.

## Preterist

We met preterism in our study of the Olivet discourse. Partial preterism is the position taken by the authors of this book when approaching Matthew 24 and the book of Revelation.

The word 'preterist' is derived from the Latin word *praeteritus*, which means 'gone by'. The preterist interprets the greater part of the book of Revelation as having been already fulfilled in the first century. John starts his book by telling us that the things which God has shown him 'must soon take place' (1:1). A couple of verses later he states that 'the time is near'. Preterists take these words at face value, believing they indicate that Revelation relates primarily to John's own day.

Crucial, therefore, to the preterist position is the need to date the book of Revelation around the mid AD 60s, prior to AD 70 and the destruction of Jerusalem. Although there is a long tradition of placing Revelation in this time-frame, the most popular view today holds that John wrote it in the mid 90s AD, so forcing the contents of the book beyond the first century AD. Placing Revelation in the mid 60s AD makes natural sense of the warnings and encouragements to believers living in that period of persecution under the Emperor Nero, and with the Jewish temple still intact.[4]

All Christians, of course, maintain a preterist view of many Old Testament prophecies, since they believe that in his first coming Jesus fulfilled them literally and accurately. In his gospel, Matthew in particular repeatedly affirms that the coming of Jesus fulfilled the Old Testament prophets by using the phrase, 'This was to fulfil what was spoken by the prophet' (Matthew 1:15; 4:14; 8:17; 12:17; etc.). Jewish people, on the other hand, do not view Jesus Christ as fulfilling any of these prophecies, so they anticipate, instead, the coming of their Messiah in the future. In the same way, preterists see Revelation as mostly already fulfilled, while futurists await its fulfilment in a period still to come.

As we saw when examining the Olivet discourse, not all preterists are the same. There are full preterists and partial preterists. Partial preterists believe that *much* of the book of Revelation was outworked in the first century AD. Because Revelation is a letter, they see it as having an immediate relevance to the seven churches to which it was sent. They identify the beast of Chapter 13 as the Roman Empire, which at that time was implacably opposed to the message of Christ and persecuted Christians for their allegiance to the Lord

Jesus rather than to Caesar. Partial Preterists also regard the destruction of Jerusalem in AD 70 as 'the day of the Lord', a time of God's judgment and the coming of Christ in judgment on Jerusalem for refusing to respond to her Messiah. They see the events of AD 70 as prefiguring the *final* Day of the Lord, the time of judgement and the *parousia* of Christ that is yet to come.

It is virtually impossible to view the consigning of the devil to the lake of burning sulphur in chapter 20 as having been fulfilled in the first century. But remember that one of the purposes of apocalyptic writing is to describe the events of the present in the light of the future. Therefore John is here describing the ultimate fate of Satan even though in John's first-century period the devil appears to have been powerful enough to give the Beast (the Roman Empire and its military power) such great authority (Revelation 13:2).

Full preterists, on the other hand, view AD 70 and the destruction of the temple with its Judaic religious practices as itself the promised *parousia* of Christ, the day of the Lord with its associated judgment, the end of that present age and the inauguration of the age to come. By so doing, full preterists deny a future resurrection of the dead. These two positions are quite different and care must be taken not to attribute to partial preterists the errors of full preterism!

## Evaluating the four perspectives

We have already described the difficulties of attempting to interpret the book of Revelation from a historicist position. It is therefore no surprise that most Bible scholars today hold that viewing it as a record of unfolding history no longer carries any credibility.

The historicist tradition fell into disrepute because of lack of agreement in relating actual historic events to the visions depicted in Revelation. The futurist school faces similar difficulties in that it cannot, in advance, provide consistent and accurate interpretations of future events. This is obviously true of dispensationalists like Hal Lindsey, whose timescale of predictions made in the early 1970s has been shown to be completely inaccurate as actual historical events have unfolded.

Jesus indicated in the Olivet discourse that the period before his return would be characterised by the normality of everyday living, 'eating and drinking, marrying and giving in marriage' (Matthew 24:38). According to Jesus there will be *no* special signs leading up to his second coming. Any attempt, therefore, to find such signs in Revelation is a futile exercise in the light of Jesus' teaching.

For these reasons, we believe that the book of Revelation was not written as 'history in advance' in the way that both the historicist and futurist schools claim. Rather, it is written in the form of a letter, to be received and understood by the Christians in the middle part of the first century AD. As a result we wish to affirm the validity of the partial preterist method of interpretation.

'Partial' is a key word. Since John was instructed to ensure that the book of Revelation remained unsealed, its contents must also be applicable to subsequent generations. The fact that the Holy Spirit has incorporated the book into the Christian Scriptures means it must be beneficial, along with the rest of the New Testament writings, for the teaching and equipping of Christians throughout the church age. Such a conviction is in keeping with the idealist viewpoint that Revelation contains timeless principles and lessons applicable to all believers in every age.

We pointed out earlier that Revelation consists of three literary genres: letter, prophecy, and apocalypse. Any interpretative method must give due weight to each of these genres. It is our conviction that, between them, the partial preterist and idealist viewpoints do this best and therefore provide us with the most useful means of interpreting the book's contents.

## Reading Revelation in the light of the Olivet discourse

The revelation of Jesus Christ received by John on the island of Patmos was communicated to him by an angel. This messenger must have been a truly glorious being, for twice John desires to worship him. On both occasions the angel forbids this, explaining that he also is a fellow-servant (Revelation 19:10; 22:8-9). The angel deflects John's attention from himself to the Lord on each occasion with a statement. On the second occasion he says, 'Worship God', and on the first, 'The testimony of Jesus is the spirit of prophecy'.

According to Bauckham, this latter phrase 'must mean that the witness Jesus bore is the content of Spirit-inspired prophecy'.[5] The words Jesus spoke are therefore crucially important in shaping a right understanding of the prophetic Scriptures, especially the book of Revelation. We must pay careful attention to phrases that Jesus had previously used in the Olivet discourse to describe future events. There are two such phrases in Revelation spoken earlier by Jesus and recorded in Matthew 24.

1. **Revelation 1:7** *Look, he is coming with the clouds, and every eye will see him, even those who pierced him...*

We saw that Jesus' coming with the clouds in Matthew 24:30 is linked to Daniel's vision of the Son of Man approaching the Ancient of Days (Daniel 7:13). The phrase 'coming with the clouds', we concluded, speaks of Jesus approaching the Father on his ascension into heaven and not of his return at the *parousia*.

'Every eye will see him, even those who pierced him', does not mean that those who crucified Jesus would still be alive to witness his second coming. The word 'see' is used figuratively to mean 'perceive' as when they say, 'Ah, I see!' When the temple of Jerusalem was destroyed those who pierced him would perceive that Jesus' words regarding the temple had been fulfilled. This in turn would indicate that Jesus was now in heaven with authority, glory and sovereignty.

Jesus said something similar when addressing the high priest at his trial. Having affirmed to the assembled Sanhedrin that he was the Christ, Jesus declared, 'But I say to all of you: In the future you will see the Son of Man sitting at the right hand of the Mighty One and coming on the clouds of heaven' (Matthew 26:64). Jesus was not suggesting that this company of rulers would be alive to witness his parousia, but rather that unfolding events in Jerusalem would cause them to perceive that Jesus was indeed the ascended Christ, received back into glory – the meaning of 'coming on the clouds of heaven' – and permitted to sit at God's right hand.

2. **Revelation 7:14** *These are they who have come out of the great tribulation*

The phrase 'great tribulation' appears, as we saw, in Matthew 24:21. There, Jesus was describing events that would follow the appearance of 'the abomination that causes desolation'. That abomination, we noted, referred to the practice of idol worship in the temple area associated with the besieging Roman army, who gave divine honour to effigies of their emperor and carried them as ensigns. The dreadful conditions for the inhabitants of Jerusalem trapped by the prolonged siege were described by Jesus as 'great tribulation'. That time of distress, he said, would be unique to that day: 'unequalled from the beginning of the world until now and never to be equalled again' (Matthew 24:21).

The phrase 'great tribulation', therefore, applies uniquely to the events leading up to the destruction of Jerusalem in AD 70. Those whom John saw around God's throne, dressed in white robes and serving him day and night, are identified by the angel as those who are coming out of this one great tribulation.

By allowing 'the testimony of Jesus' to interpret these two passages in Revelation we learn that they relate to events that took place in the first century. Honouring the testimony of Jesus this way requires us to consistently apply his interpretation of these phrases into their first-century context and not to suggest that they refer to future events. We cannot use the phrase 'coming with the clouds' to describe his future second coming. Similarly, because the great tribulation has already been fulfilled in history, we should no longer anticipate it as a future catastrophic event.

## Conclusion

The book of Revelation is part and parcel of the Bible – Holy Spirit-inspired Scriptures. Due to the nature of its particular genre it has been endlessly exploited as a source of exotic and speculative teaching on the end times and the future return of Christ. We have sought, instead, to demonstrate an alternative approach to this marvellous book that accords with sound principles of interpretation and makes sense to the reader here and now.

The book of Revelation is all about Christ, from beginning to end: his decisive victory over Satan the dragon, and his continued victory in his church, over every enemy ranged against her. It will continue to be a source of encouragement and comfort for all who are engaged in battle against the evil one until our final victory.

## End notes

1. JB Philips, *The Book of Revelation* 1957 Geoffrey Bles Preface pp xi and xii
2. Richard Bauckham, *The Theology of the book of Revelation*, Cambridge University Press, 1993
3. Tony Ling, *The Lion and The Lamb*, Destiny Image,

4. Kenneth Gentry has devoted a whole book to reviewing the evidence concerning the time in which Revelation was written. In *Before Jerusalem Fell – dating the book of Revelation* Gentry reaches the conclusion that 'A date in either AD65 or early AD 66 would seem most suitable', p336

5. Richard Bauckham, *The Climax of Prophecy*

# Chapter 7

# The millennium muddle

Like many of the other topics we are covering in this book, the millennium has been the cause of much debate and controversy over the centuries. The word 'millennium' comes from the Latin word *mille,* meaning 'thousand' and *ennium* meaning 'years'. It is used with reference to only one passage in Scripture, Revelation 20:1-10, where it describes a 1000-year reign of Christ. That much is without dispute!

The crux of the debate lies in how we interpret this passage. Is it referring to a literal period of 1000 years or a symbolic one? What is the nature of this rule of Christ and where does it figure in the course of history?

We quote the passage below in full from the New International Version:

> *And I saw an angel coming down out of heaven, having the key to the Abyss and holding in his hand a great chain. He seized the dragon, that ancient serpent, who is the devil, or Satan, and bound him for a thousand years. He threw him into the Abyss, and locked and sealed it over him, to keep him from deceiving the nations anymore until the thousand years were ended. After that, he must be set free for a short time.*
>
> *I saw thrones on which were seated those who had been given authority to judge. And I saw the souls of those who had been beheaded because of their testimony for Jesus and because of the word of God. They had not worshipped the beast or his image and had not received his mark on their foreheads or their hands. They came to life and reigned with Christ a thousand years. (The rest of the dead did not come to life until the thousand years were ended.) This is the first resurrection. Blessed and holy are those who have part in the first resurrection. The second death has no power over them, but they will be priests of God and of Christ and will reign with him for a thousand years.*

> *When the thousand years are over, Satan will be released from his prison and will go out to deceive the nations in the four corners of the earth – Gog and Magog – to gather them for battle. In number they are like the sand on the seashore. They marched across the breadth of the earth and surrounded the camp of God's people, the city he loves. But fire came down from heaven and devoured them, and the devil, who deceived them, was thrown into the lake of burning sulphur, where the beast and the false prophet had been thrown. They will be tormented day and night for ever and ever.*

All agree that the passage divides into three sections as follows:

Verse 1-3    Satan is bound for 1000 years to keep him from deceiving the nations.

Verses 4-6    The saints reign with Christ for 1000 years.

Verses 7-10    Satan is released after the 1000 years and attempts to deceive the nations again, but is defeated and punished by being thrown into the lake of burning sulphur, indicating his final destruction.

Before proceeding further with our study, here is an outline of the main positions that Christians have taken over the centuries as to its meaning.

## Classic premillennialism

This view holds that Jesus will return *before* (pre) the millennium. It was the predominant view held by the early church fathers, a natural extension of the Jewish and early Christian hope that Messiah would return to set up his earthly kingdom.

Classic premillennialists believe there will be two resurrections, one for believers at the beginning of the millennium and another for the unsaved at the end of it. The literal 1000-year reign of Christ, they believe, is the ultimate fulfilment of Christ's reign in heaven extending into the earth. Jesus will reign on the earth through his people, the church, after he returns.

The Greek translation of the Latin *mille* is *chilioi* and classic premillennialism is also sometimes known as 'chiliasm'.

## Dispensational premillennialism

This is the more recent variety of premillennialism that formed part of the belief system devised by Irving and Darby in the 1800s. It is distinct from classical premillennialism. In dispensational pre-millennialism, the 1000-year reign of Christ on earth is Jewish in nature. Jesus will reign through a restored Jewish nation from a rebuilt temple in Jerusalem. The Old Testament feasts and sacrificial system will also be restored as a memorial to the work of Christ.

Furthermore, dispensationalists believe the millennium will be preceded by the secret rapture of the church. This will occur seven years before the coming of Christ in glory to establish his millennial kingdom. Classic premillennialists believe no such things.

## Postmillennialism

According to postmillennialists, Jesus will return *after* (post) a 1000-year reign. Postmillennialists believe the growth and expansion of Christianity in history will result in a largely 'Christianised' world in which Satan will be effectively bound and a golden age of 1000 years ushered in. Rather than taking it literally, most postmillennialists see it as indicating a very prolonged period.

The 'first resurrection' of Revelation 20:5 is seen as the regeneration of believers through the new birth (John 5:24). As a result, believers are now reigning with Christ (Romans 5:17) and, although they may die physically, the 'second death' has no power over them. At the end Christ will return to wind up human affairs and establish the eternal state.

## Amillennialism

This view holds that there is no (hence the negative prefix 'a') literal millennium. Instead the term should be viewed as signifying the whole period between the first and second comings of Jesus when good and evil exist side-by-side.

The binding of Satan has taken place as the result of Christ's victory at Calvary, his resurrection and the outpouring of the Spirit. Satan can no longer prevent the nations responding to the message of the gospel. This period will culminate in a brief satanic backlash – the loosing of Satan – before Christ returns to judge the world and banish Satan to the lake of fire.

Amillennialists view all the promises made to Israel in the Old Testament as fulfilled in Christ and the church in the present age.

Each viewpoint has its own strengths and weaknesses. We will try to assess them fairly and, because we are dealing with events and dates still in the future, aim to avoid dogmatism. Most of our comments will address the dispensational position which has come to dominate the Christian landscape today.

While respecting the classical premillennial position we are of the view that Revelation 20 does not refer to a literal future reign of Christ based in Jerusalem. Equally we find some difficulty with postmillennialism, which tends to be unrealistically optimistic.

Instead we are going to demonstrate why we believe the amillennial interpretation of Revelation 20 best accords with the hermeneutical principles we are applying throughout this book as explained in the Appendix. That being said, we acknowledge that the passage isn't easy to interpret from any position! Our only other reservation is that amillennialism sometimes takes an unnecessarily pessimistic outlook. It tends to view the future as an evenly matched battle between good and evil until Christ comes to complete his kingdom. We are really 'victorious amillennialists', believing that through the church the kingdom of God will outshine the kingdom of darkness before Christ returns. Despite this objection we are sticking with the 'amillennial' label for the sake of simplicity.

The millennium debate is delicate to say the least! Greater minds than ours have grappled with Revelation 20 through the centuries and still the questions remain. It is a shame that at times the debate has degenerated into open warfare between believers who all share the same 'blessed hope of the coming of our Lord and Saviour'. Let us take a look at how the various views developed.

## A brief history of millennium teaching

Early Christian ideas of the return of Christ were doubtless coloured by traditional Jewish Messianic expectations. Jews held that Messiah would come to judge evil, rescue his chosen people and establish his kingdom on the earth for 1000 years, based in Jerusalem.

The early Christian believers viewed the millennial hope was as material salvation to come. It would provide relief from persecution and the promise of escape from the sufferings of this life. Linked to it was the hope of the physical resurrection of the dead. Many of those who opposed the idea of the millennium did so because they denied a physical resurrection. The two were tied together. To believe one was to believe the other – a view that is largely irrelevant today.

Some of Jesus' own sayings were interpreted literally to support the idea of a future physical reign of Christ on earth. Among these were Matthew 5:5, 26:29 and Luke 19:17-19. Then the specific mention of the 1000-year reign by John in Revelation 20 gave further credence to these beliefs. The great mass of Christians saw the coming of Christ to set up his earthly kingdom as imminent.

Premillennialism continued as the predominant viewpoint for the first three centuries. Many of the early church fathers (though by no means all) held this position, including Papias, Irenaeus, Justin Martyr, Tertullian, Hippolytus, Methodius, Commodianus and Lactantius. But as we have already noted, nothing in any of the writings of the church fathers suggests belief in a separate rapture. Although dispensationalists are fond of quoting the works of the church fathers to support secret-rapture teaching, this notion was in fact unknown before the 1800s.

It was Augustine (AD 354-430) who, taking ideas pioneered by the 4th century Donatist monk Tyconias, rejected premillennialism in favour of a symbolic interpretation of Revelation 20. For him the age of the church was the millennial reign of Christ and the 1000 years represented the entire period from the cross to Christ's return. This is, as we have seen, the amillennial approach. It was these ideas, set forth in Augustine's work *The City of God*, which went on to dominate Western church thinking throughout the medieval period. Premillennialism was marginalised, though not completely without its adherents, during this long period.

The Protestant reformers of the 16th century on the whole continued with the amillennial position. They did so partly, perhaps, because of the excesses of some Anabaptists – groups of Reformation believers operating outside of the established churches of the time and holding to premillennial ideas.

In the 1600s postmillennialism began to make its mark, spurred on by the work of Daniel Whitby (1638-1726). According to his view, the world would be converted to Christ, the Jews restored to their land and Catholicism defeated. This would usher in a literal 1000 years of universal peace and prosperity.

Postmillennialism – though of a less rigid kind – was behind the great missionary movement of the 18th and 19th centuries. The expectation that the world really could be won to Christ spurred thousands to take the gospel to every corner of the globe and seek to Christianise the nations to whom they went.

We have already seen how premillennialism underwent a revival of interest in the 1800s through Irving and Darby. Their particular brand of teaching, however, was quite distinct from the classic premillennialism that had been taught previously and that remains to this day as one of the respected mainstream positions.

The dispensational line of premillennialism gained ground in the 19th century through the likes of W. E. Blackstone, James Hall Brooks, G. Campbell Morgan, H. A. Ironside, A. C. Gaebelein and, of course, in the 20th century through C. I. Scofield and his *Reference Bible*.

Today dispensationalism is the dominant view within the premillennialist fold. A literal, future reign of Christ from Jerusalem for 1000 years forms a key component of the complex dispensationalist system of doctrine despite the fact that it is based only on one Bible passage. A consideration of the hermeneutical principles outlined elsewhere in this book would immediately warn us away from such a pitfall.

Having formed an overview of millennial views it is time for us to look more closely at Revelation 20, from which the teaching has been formed.

## Examining Revelation chapter 20

There are really only two main options as to how we interpret this passage: literally or symbolically. This can be illustrated as follows:

| the literal approach | Classic Premillennialism: future reign of Christ through the church |
|---|---|
| | Dispensationalism: future reign of Christ through the Jewish nation |
| | Postmillennialism: future reign of Christ in a Christianised world |
| the symbolic approach | Amillennialism: Christ reigning now in this church age |

For the sake of clarity we have presented the dispensational position next to the amillennial position in a side-by-side commentary on the passage.

| Revelation 20:1-10 | Literal dispensational interpretation | Symbolic amillennial interpretation |
|---|---|---|
| And I saw an angel coming down out of heaven, having the key to the Abyss and holding in his hand a great chain. He seized the dragon, that ancient serpent, who is the devil, or Satan, and bound him for a thousand years. He threw him into the Abyss, locked and sealed it over him, to keep him from deceiving the nations anymore until the thousand years were ended. After that, he must be set free for a short time (verses 1-3). | A secret rapture of the church will be followed 7 years later by the return of Christ, at which time Satan will be bound for a literal 1000-year period. During this time Jesus will reign over the world through the Jewish nation from a re-built temple in Jerusalem. At the end of this period, Satan will be released and will stir up a revolt against this earthly reign of Christ among a sizeable percentage of the earth's population. | Satan was bound at the cross, defeated but not yet destroyed. Jesus said, *'Now is the time for judgment on this world; now the prince of this world will be driven out. And I, when I am lifted up from the earth, will draw all people to myself'* (John 12:31-32). Christ rules now over all things, not just the church. Christians willingly bow the knee, but Jesus is 'head over all things' – even those who are ignorant of it or resent it. A brief period of intense satanic opposition to the church will precede Jesus' return. |
| I saw thrones on which were seated those who had been given authority to judge. And I saw the souls of those who had been beheaded because of their testimony for Jesus and because of the word of God. They had not worshipped the beast or his image and had not received his mark on their foreheads or their hands. They came to life and reigned with Christ a thousand years. (The rest of the dead did not come to life until the thousand years were ended). This is the first resurrection. Blessed and holy are those who have part in the first resurrection. The second death has no power over them, but they will be priests of God and of Christ and will reign with him for a thousand years. (verses 4-6) | Between the rapture and the return of Christ, God will be pouring out his wrath on the world (this is what dispensationalists understand as the 'great tribulation'). But people will still turn to Christ and some of them will be martyred. At Christ's return, these martyred saints will be physically raised from the dead and reign with Christ in his millennial kingdom along with the Jews. There are therefore two resurrections. The rest of the dead have to wait until the end of the millennium for their resurrection. | John is describing all Christians who have remained faithful to Christ in a hostile world. Some of them are indeed martyred. They are secure with the Lord. The first resurrection is simply our new birth at conversion. Paul said, *'He made us alive with Christ even when we were dead in transgressions'* (Ephesians 2:5). We reign in life with Christ now (Romans 5:17). This is how the 1000 years should be understood. Those who have been born again (the first resurrection) are free from their sentence to hell (the second death). They are priests to God now and reign with him now. |

| Revelation 20:1-10 | Literal dispensational interpretation | Symbolic amillennial interpretation |
|---|---|---|
| When the thousand years are over, Satan will be released from his prison and will go out to deceive the nations in the four corners of the earth – Gog and Magog – to gather them for battle. In number they are like the sand on the seashore. They marched across the breadth of the earth and surrounded the camp of God's people, the city he loves. But fire came down from heaven and devoured them. And the devil, who deceived them, was thrown into the lake of burning sulphur, where the beast and the false prophet had been thrown. They will be tormented day and night for ever and ever. (verses 7-10) | At the end of the millennial reign of Christ, Satan will be loosed and will stir up a rebellion in the earth against the rule of Christ. Hordes of people will march against Jerusalem in defiance. But God will send fire down from heaven and destroy them. Satan will then be thrown into hell where his two stooges, the beast and the false prophet, have already been thrown. | Before the return of Christ, persecution will come to a head when Satan is loosed to stir up wicked people against the church. They will come against the church (the camp of God's people) but this will be brought to a swift end when Jesus returns in power to judge the world. Satan and all who follow him will be cast into the lake of fire (hell). |

The dispensationalist position could be summarised as follows:

> *The Bible should be taken at face value and believed for what it says. If Revelation chapter 20 states there will be a 1000-year reign of Christ on the earth, surely it means it. Anything less is 'spiritualising' the truth away. God still has a plan for the Jews – after all they are his ancient people, aren't they? Jesus is going to come back and reign from a rebuilt temple in Jerusalem and fulfil all the prophecies in the Old Testament that speak of a golden age to come. Then he will confront the devil and destroy him once and for all along with all those who didn't really submit to him in their hearts during the millennium. Then will follow the judgment and the age to come.*

## Explaining the amillennial position

Having summarised the amillennial and dispensationalist views side-by-side we are going to examine the passage in detail showing why we believe the figurative amillennial interpretation represents, on balance, the best approach.

The 1000-year millennium, while not literal in terms of time, is entirely real. It must be understood as the age we are now in, when Satan has been bound and people are turning to Christ. In biblical numerology the number 10 signifies completion. For example, the 10 plagues on Egypt signified the complete judgment of God. The 10 commandments signified the complete summation of the law. John's gospel records Jesus making 10 'I am' statements and performing 10 miraculous signs. The number 1000, which is 10 X 10 X 10, should be understood as a complete age, or entire span of time – and a long one at that.

Jesus' future kingdom should not be limited to a 1000-year earthly reign prior to the judgment and eternal state. His kingdom is advancing in the earth now through the church, overthrowing the powers of darkness and liberating men and women from Satan's dominion.

All accept that one's view of the millennium depends entirely on how this passage in Revelation is interpreted, in particular verses 4 and 5, which lie at the heart of the matter. All accept, too, that there are challenges whichever way one interprets the passage. Let us now turn to it.

> And I saw an angel coming down out of heaven, having the key to the Abyss and holding in his hand a great chain. He seized the dragon, that ancient serpent, who is the devil, or Satan, and bound him for a thousand years. He threw him into the Abyss, and locked and sealed it over him, to keep him from deceiving the nations anymore until the thousand years were ended. After that he must be set free for a short time. (Revelation 20:1-3)

Fortunately the identity of the 'dragon' is without dispute! Satan is described here as being bound for 1000 years so as not to deceive the nations any longer. Here is a telling description of what happened at the cross. Satan's power was broken and the Holy Spirit released to bring the nations to Christ through the witness of the church. Jesus described this when he said, 'how can anyone enter a strong man's house and carry off his possessions unless he first ties up the strong man? Then he can plunder his house.' (Matthew 12:29). He was of course referring to his work at the cross of which he said 'Now is the time for judgment on this world; now the prince of this world be driven out. And I, when I am lifted up from the earth, will draw all people to myself' (John 12:31-32).

From the time of Jesus' death and resurrection the veil of spiritual deception has been lifted from the nations and the gospel is going forth liberating men and women from spiritual darkness. Satan has been bound in that he has been unable to prevent this. In China, for example, communism has been unable to prevent the rapid spread of the gospel. Similarly in India, Hinduism and Sikhism have been no match for the growth of the Christian church.

> *I saw thrones on which were seated those who had been given authority to judge. And I saw the souls of those who had been beheaded because of their testimony about Jesus and because of the word of God. They had not worshipped the beast or its image and had not received its mark on their foreheads or their hands. They came to life and reigned with Christ a thousand years. (The rest of the dead did not come to life until the thousand years were ended.) This is the first resurrection. Blessed and holy are those who share in the first resurrection. The second death has no power over them, but they will be priests of God and of Christ and will reign with him a thousand years.* (Revelation 20:4-6)

John describes a group of people sitting on thrones followed by a description of the souls of those martyred for the testimony of Jesus and the word of God. Are these two groups of people one and the same? The words, 'also I saw…', suggest not. The second part of verse 4 can also be rendered, 'and such as worshipped not the beast, neither his image' (ASV). In other words a second group of people are in view here, the faithful saints who are still alive.

What is meant by 'they came to life and reigned with Christ for a thousand years'? The expression 'came to life' uses the Greek word, *zao*. It is frequently used of physical resurrection (e.g. Matthew 9:18, John 4:50) but is also used in the New Testament to describe spiritual regeneration. We believe this is what John is speaking of here: these people 'came alive' spiritually. Two New Testament passages use *zao* in reference to spiritual regeneration:

> *Very truly I tell you, a time is coming and has now come when the dead will hear the voice of the Son of God and those who hear will live [zao]. For as the Father has life in himself, so he has granted the Son also to have life in himself. And he has given him authority to execute judgment, because he is the Son of Man.* (John 5:25-27)

The expression, 'and has now come', is a clear reference to spiritual resurrection, or new birth, and contrasts with the physical resurrection that Jesus goes on to speak of in verses 28-29.

> *But because of his great love for us, God who is rich in mercy, made us alive [a form of* zao*] with Christ even when we were dead in transgressions – it is by grace you have been saved. And God raised us up with Christ and seated us with him in the heavenly realms in Christ Jesus, in order that in the coming ages he might show the incomparable riches of his grace, expressed in his kindness to us in Christ Jesus.* (Ephesians 2:4-7)

In verse 4 John is therefore describing two groups of believers in the church age: those who have been martyred and those who are alive. Both have the status of being spiritually regenerate. In verse 6 he refers again to these believers in the phrase, 'They will be priests of God and of Christ and will reign with him for a thousand years'. Again this is exactly the position of those who have been brought to spiritual life in Christ: they are all priests, with direct access to God, and they all reign in life.

Verse 5, by contrast, describes the unsaved who will be raised to life in the last day to face judgment: 'The rest of the dead did not come to life until the thousand years were ended'. This refers to the one physical resurrection of all at the last day. The reason John does not refer to the regenerate here is because they have already come out from under judgment through their spiritual resurrection.

Dispensationalists claim that the passage should be interpreted literally, which requires us to believe that there are two physical resurrections separated by a literal 1000 years. But if we follow our principles of Bible interpretation we will build our doctrine of the resurrection by first examining passages that offer clear and explicit teaching on the resurrection and then interpret Revelation 20 in the light of those passages. This is what we have done here.

The Old Testament contains prophetic anticipation and the book of Revelation presents prophetic fulfilment. Between these two sit the clear statements of the New Testament such as John 5 and Ephesians 2. Revelation 20 should be interpreted in the light of what is clear and unambiguous, like these scriptures.

There is another problem with the 'two separate resurrections' view. If the passage is speaking of two physical resurrections separated by 1000 years, surely there would be other biblical evidence for this view apart from the passage in front of us? Yet this is not the case. On the contrary the Bible repeatedly teaches that there is only one physical resurrection, comprising both the just and the unjust who are raised at the same moment. For example Jesus' own words in John's gospel:

> Do not be amazed at this, for a time is coming when all who are in their graves will hear his voice and come out – those who have done what is good will rise to live, and those who have done what is evil will rise to be condemned. (John 5:28-29)[1]

The timing of this one resurrection and judgment is frequently referred to as taking place on 'the last day' (John 6:39; 11:24; 12:48; Romans 2:16). There are not two last days but one – when Jesus will return to accomplish everything he has purposed. Notice, too, that the final judgment described in verses 11-15 comes *after* the millennial reign described in verses 4-6. Throughout Scripture this final judgment is always placed immediately after the return of Christ, for example 2 Thessalonians 2:1-10. Therefore the dispensationalists' millennium could not take place between the return of Christ and the final judgment as they would propose.

Finally, from verse 7 we have a description of Satan being released to 'deceive the nations' for a brief time. Following the principle of interpreting what is obscure in the light of what is clear, and of respecting the literary style of the book of Revelation, we take this section as meaning that there will be a brief period of satanic opposition to the church just prior to the return of Christ. This confrontation will trigger God's intervention in judgment against Satan and those allied with him. The passage therefore closes with Satan being thrown into the lake of fire and humanity appearing before the throne of God for final judgment.

## Dilemmas with a premillennial kingdom

Before concluding this chapter, there is one further aspect to consider, namely, the nature of the Jerusalem-based millennial kingdom that dispensationalism presents.

Let's try to visualise it for a moment. The ascended and exalted Christ allegedly returns to earth in all his glory only to confine himself to a stone temple in Jerusalem. If 2000 years ago Paul said, 'The God who made the world and everything in it is the Lord of heaven and earth and does not live in temples built by human hands' (Acts 17:24), how much more true will this be when Jesus appears from heaven? How could the glorified Christ, living in a rebuilt temple in Jerusalem, possibly represent progress for the kingdom of God? How can we sensibly expect to revert to a physical temple, priesthood, animal sacrifices and Jewish festivals, when the New Testament says all these things have been done away with in the light of the New Covenant realities that we are now enjoying? As Hebrews 8:13 affirms, 'What is obsolete and outdated will soon disappear.' It has vanished for good! The New Testament writers speak of Christ ushering in a new heaven and a new earth, not a return to Old Testament symbols and rituals.

The kingdom inherited by the church is advancing by the power of the Holy Spirit to wrest men and women from Satan's dominion and infuse them with eternal life. The coming kingdom of the premillennialist is a strange step back from this to an earthly theocracy populated by a mixture of saints in resurrected bodies living side by side with un-resurrected mortals. Premillennialists cannot escape this odd prospect. To quote one respected dispensationalist: 'Therefore the wicked or rebellious in the kingdom, as that period progresses, are the unbelieving children of believing parents. This alone can harmonise all that scripture says on the matter'.[2] In other words, the premillennialist has to accept the notion that the millennial kingdom actually degenerates in the course of time! Christ's reign in the lives of his subjects grows weaker and weaker to the point where a vast multitude of them rebel against him!

This is a strange kingdom indeed, which cannot maintain itself during the most glorious manifestation of Christ ever known to humanity! It does not culminate in peace but in conflict. For after a period of 1000 years Satan is allegedly able to muster multitudes of rebellious souls possessed with the idea that they can throw off Christ's rule and march to Jerusalem against him. No scripture anywhere describes such an unthinkable prospect except the premillennial interpretation of Revelation 20.

In the light of these observations on the premillennial kingdom of the dispensationalists one has to ask, what purpose would it achieve? It certainly cannot be a vindication of Christ's authority, for it culminates in rebellion!

Some may ask, 'Does any of this matter? No-one knows for certain anyway!' The fact is it matters intensely, because what we believe becomes our hope and our hope governs our manner of life here and now.

Dispensationalists view the world as beyond help and growing worse. To quote Hal Lindsey, we live on the 'late great planet Earth'. Jesus is coming to rescue the beleaguered church from its enemies only in order to establish his rule from Jerusalem. Their hope is for Christ to call a halt to evil and sin by setting up his kingdom on the earth – a kingdom that, as we have seen, rules over a strange mixture of subjects and declines as the 1000 years roll by. Not a great deal to inspire there!

The hope held out to us throughout the Bible is for the kingdom of God to be manifest in the world now through the church reigning with Christ in the power of the Spirit, until the world is filled with the knowledge of the glory of God and Jesus returns for his perfected bride.

If I believe that the world is about to end and that Jesus is coming to rescue me, it will produce a radically different life than if I believe that the kingdom of God is coming in power and that the church is in the process of being restored to her intended glory and grace. The more I know who I am in Christ, the less I will be looking to escape. Yes, it matters!

## End notes

1. See also Daniel 12:2-3; Acts 24:15; Matthew 25:31-46
2. Paul D. Feinberg, *Three Views on the Rapture*, p 77

# Chapter 8

# The rapture riddle

Without warning and at precisely the same moment, road networks the world over come to a standstill as drivers mysteriously disappear from their vehicles. Cars plough into each other with no-one at the wheel. Buses hurtle off roads killing and injuring tens of thousands of passengers. Trucks and lorries jack-knife and spin over, causing mayhem and carnage. Passengers and pedestrians alike are killed in their multitudes. And the chaos is not confined to the road system alone for trains, airplanes and ships all find themselves missing crew members and indeed numbers of passengers.

Meanwhile across every continent the same phenomenon is occurring: factory and office workers, school children, shopkeepers, civil servants, hospital patients – people from every stratum of life simply vanish without a trace. In some parts of the globe whole communities of people disappear while in other places, just ones and twos. No nation of the world is unaffected by this extraordinary occurrence.

If the popular rapture teaching is to be believed, this is the scenario the world is soon going to experience as Christians are 'evacuated' to heaven by an act of God in order to escape a global meltdown of human warfare and divine judgment. Where is this teaching based in Scripture? We are going to investigate.

The teaching of a secret rapture of believers prior to the full return of Christ is built around 1 Thessalonians 4:16-17, which uses an expression from which the term 'rapture' has been coined. The passage reads as follows:

> For the Lord himself will descend from heaven, with a loud command, with the voice of the archangel and with the trumpet call of God, and the dead in Christ will rise first. After that, we who are still alive and are left will be caught up together with them in the clouds to meet the Lord in the air. And so we will be with the Lord forever.

The key phrase is 'caught up'. It translates from the Greek word *harpazo*, which means to seize, take by force or snatch away. In the Latin Vulgate version of the Bible *harpazo* is translated using the word *rapio*. It is from this Latin word that the English word 'rapture' is derived.

So the word itself is biblical – not so the elaborate scheme of future events that dispensationalists have constructed around it. They anticipate the church being removed from the earth ushering in a period of tribulation and bringing the Jews once more onto the centre stage of history.

It is important to realise that dispensationalism, as popularised today, falls into question as a system if its teaching on the two-stage return of Christ is undermined. If there is no rapture what happens to the case for a distinct role for the Jewish nation, a tribulation period and colourful end-time characters like the beast and the antichrist? It is immediately weakened.

## Variations in rapture teaching

The idea that the church will be secretly raptured away from the earth at the beginning of a seven-year period of tribulation is referred to as the 'pre-tribulation rapture' position. It is the most dominant view on the timing of the rapture within dispensationalism, but not the only one. During the last 150 years two other variations in rapture teaching have emerged:

### Post-tribulation rapture

This view holds that the church will be raptured at the *end* of the seven-year tribulation period, not before it, to be followed immediately by the return of Christ in glory to the earth with the believers.

Until the 1890s this position was common among early dispensationalists. It is of course, similar to the position held by classical premillennialism, except that classical premillennialists believe the return of Christ ushers in a 1000-year millennial reign of Christ on earth for redeemed Jews and Gentiles. They do not hold to the view that the church disappears from the earth or that there is a distinct role for Israel.

It was the famous Niagara Bible Conferences of the 1880s and 1890s that prompted the change. Heated arguments and vitriolic writings gradually saw post-tribulationists marginalised by those who held to the pre-tribulation position. The death knell was the publication in 1909 of the Scofield Reference Bible, whose notes were entirely pre-tribulationist.

From around this time, dispensationalism came to be associated in full with a pre-tribulation position for the rapture. It was also increasingly incorporated into the doctrinal statements of seminaries and denominations serving only to increase the divisive nature of the debate. The post-tribulation position was gradually squeezed out until more recently, when it has seen some resurgence. Notable recent post-tribulationists include Robert H. Gundry, George Eldon Ladd and more recently still, Douglas J. Moo.

## Mid-tribulation rapture

Mid-tribulationists believe that the rapture of the church occurs mid-way through the seven-year period of tribulation. It was Norman B Harrison who first proposed this variation in his book, *The End: Rethinking the Revelation*, published in 1941. This view is also called the *'mid-seventieth week rapture'*, after the reference to the prophetic timetable prophesied in Daniel 9:27. It has remained a minority viewpoint in the premillennial scheme of things.[1]

The notion that Christians will suddenly be removed from the earth in a secret rapture, leaving unbelievers behind, has invited wild and fearful ideas of the future. Books like the *Left Behind* series written by Jenkins and LaHaye have served only to heighten such a pre-occupation among impressionable sections of the church. These novels present a lurid description of a world plunged into chaos as the church makes its exit and leaves everyone else to suffer.

The 1970s film, *Thief in the night*, was effective in scaring teenagers witless at youth outreaches, softening them up before an eager evangelist presented his gospel appeal. This sure-fire approach to evangelism would always result in decisions for Christ, many based on questionable motives.

How has it been possible to deduce from the passage in 1 Thessalonians that Paul is teaching a secret removal of the church from the earth before the actual coming of the Lord Jesus? This belief is the lynch-pin of all that is held dear by dispensationalists and we need to examine it from a number of directions.

## The passage itself

Dispensationalists believe that 1 Thessalonians 4 refers to the rapture of the church (or as they like to express it, the Lord's coming *for* the saints) and that chapter 5 refers to a different event altogether – the return of Christ (the Lord's coming *with* the saints). In their thinking, this approach to the two chapters warrants a two-part return of Christ. But was Paul in fact teaching the Thessalonian church such ideas? There are just too many problems with this approach.

Firstly, chapter 5 is a seamless continuation of chapter 4. The Bible's chapter divisions are not Spirit-inspired, and there is no indication anyway that Paul has moved on to discuss an event removed seven years into the future. Dispensationalists point to the transitional particle 'now', Greek *de*, in 5:1 to support the idea that a contrasting subject is being introduced. The word *de*, however, as well as denoting mild contrast is also frequently used 'as a transitional particle pure and simple without any contrast intended'.[2] There is nothing at all in the passage to indicate that Paul is doing anything but continuing his description of the one return of Christ in its various facets.

Secondly, in chapter 5 Paul encourages the Thessalonians by saying they are 'not in darkness so that *this day* should surprise you like a thief' (verse 4). In the light of this fact he then exhorts them:

> So then, let us not be like others who are asleep, but let us be awake and sober…But since we belong to the day, let us be sober, putting on faith and love as a breastplate, and the hope of salvation as a helmet (verses 6, 8).

Paul is clearly still referring to the event he has described in chapter 4. If, however, believers had been raptured away in chapter 4, as dispensationalists insist, such words to believers would be irrelevant. How can Paul exhort them to prepare for what they will be absent from?

Thirdly, although Paul uses a variety of expressions in 1 and 2 Thessalonians to describe the return of Jesus, it becomes obvious on examination that they all describe the same event. This extends into the way the same words and expressions are used throughout the New Testament. In order to bolster the argument that Scripture teaches a two-stage return of Christ, dispensationalists have had to teach that some of these terms refer to the rapture and some to the return of Christ in glory.

Let's look at them in more depth beginning with three that we have already examined in an earlier chapter:

## Parousia

Paul's first letter to the Thessalonians was written to allay the concern of the believers regarding those of their number who had already died. Since Christ had not returned, they wondered, would they now miss his coming altogether? Paul writes to inform the church of his teaching, thus correcting any misguided thinking on their part. He encourages them concerning their departed friends, assuring them that the deceased will certainly not miss out on the Lord's second coming.

In order to remove any doubt about his meaning in 4:17, Paul uses two particular words, the first of which is *parousia*. We saw in chapter 6 how it referred to the coming of a king with his retinue to visit one of his cities. The gates would open and the people would come out to meet the king before bringing him back with them into the city. This is a very telling description of the coming of Jesus. *Parousia* not only appears in 1 Thessalonians 4:15, 'we who are left until the *coming* of the Lord', a passage supposedly referring to the rapture, but also in 1 Thessalonians 5:23, 'be kept blameless at the *coming* of our Lord Jesus', which supposedly does not![3]

*Parousia* then, appears in passages that dispensationalists claim refer in some cases to the rapture and in some other cases to the return of Christ. It is far simpler to accept that all refer to the same single event: the return of Christ to accomplish all he intends to do on that one glorious day. There is in fact, only one coming, not two. The meaning of *parousia* does not accord with something hidden but open and manifest, quite the opposite to the dispensational view of a secret rapture.[4]

Paul reinforces the point by his use of a related word *apantesis*: 'Then we who are alive, who are left, will be caught up together with them in the clouds to meet (*apantesis*) the Lord in the air, and so we will always be with the Lord.' *Apantesis*, like *parousia*, was used in connection with the visit to a city of an eminent dignitary such as the emperor. F. F. Bruce explains the meaning of the word:

> When a dignitary paid an official visit (parousia) to a city in Hellenistic times, the actions of the leading citizens in going out to meet him and escort him back on the final stage of his journey was called the **apantesis**.[5]

Paul's readers would immediately understand that being 'caught up' to meet Jesus described their joyful encounter with him as they eagerly welcomed the return of their Lord to the earth. Nowhere is there any suggestion that Jesus would do a U-turn and return to heaven – and even less evidence that believers would follow him there!

### Epiphaneia

The second word we must examine is 'appearance', translated from the Greek *epiphaneia*, from which we get the word 'epiphany'. It literally means 'a shining forth':

> And then the lawless one will be revealed, whom the Lord Jesus will kill with the breath of his mouth and bring to nothing by the **appearance** of his coming. (2 Thessalonians 2:8, ESV)

Here is a text that according to dispensationalists describes the second phase of Christ's return, seven years after believers have been raptured away. But, embarrassingly, *epiphaneia* also appears in texts that clearly anticipate the presence of believers:

> In the sight of God, who gives life to everything, and of Christ Jesus, who while testifying before Pontius Pilate made the good confession, I charge you to keep this command without spot or blame until the **appearing** of our Lord Jesus Christ, which God will bring about in his own time... (1 Timothy 6:13-15)

> Now there is in store for me the crown of righteousness, which the Lord, the righteous Judge, will award to me on that day – and not only to me, but also to all who have longed for his **appearing**. (2 Timothy 4:1-8)

> ...while we wait for the blessed hope – the **appearing** of the glory of our great God and Saviour, Jesus Christ, who gave himself for us to redeem us from all wickedness and to purify for himself a people that are his very own, eager to do what is good. (Titus 2:13-14)

The conclusion is that all these scriptures refer to one and the same event, the single return of Christ.

### Apokalypsis

We will now revisit the word 'revelation', translated from the Greek *apokalypsis*. It means an uncovering or unveiling and appears in 2

Thessalonians 1:7: 'This will happen when the Lord Jesus is *revealed* from heaven in blazing fire with his powerful angels'.

According to dispensational teaching, this passage relates to the alleged second phase of Jesus' coming: his return in glory. However this same word *apokalypsis* is used in the following passages that dispensationalists claim refer to the initial rapture of the church. And that, according to them, is a secret snatching away of the church, anything but the glorious revealing of Christ that *apokalypsis* suggests. First, note what Paul says in 1 Corinthians 1:7:

> ... *so that you are not lacking any gift, awaiting eagerly the* **revelation** *of our Lord Jesus Christ, who will also confirm you to the end, blameless in the day of our Lord Jesus Christ.* (1 Corinthians 1:7-8, NASB)

> *These have come so that the proven genuineness of your faith – of greater worth than gold, which perishes even though refined by fire – may result in praise, glory and honour when Jesus is* **revealed.** *Though you have not seen him, you love him; and even though you do not see him now, you believe in him and are filled with an inexpressible and glorious joy, for you are receiving the end result of your faith, the salvation of your souls.* (1 Peter 1:7-9)[6]

Finally, Jesus himself refers to his own coming as a revelation in Luke 17:30. But with that, he includes a warning to watch and prepare, something that would be irrelevant if the believers had been removed already.

> *It will be just like this on the day the Son of Man is* **revealed**. *On that day no one who is on the housetop, with possessions inside, should go down to get them. Likewise, no one in the field should go back for anything. Remember Lot's wife! Whoever tries to keep their life will lose it, and whoever loses their life will preserve it.* (Luke 17:30-33)

### The day of the Lord

Another significant expression referring to Christ's return is 'the day of the Lord'. This is common Old Testament prophetic language describing the coming of Jehovah to judge the earth and his people.[7]

It also appears frequently in the New Testament, including 1 Thessalonians 5:2: 'You know very well that *the day of the Lord* will come like a thief in the night', and 2 Thessalonians 2:2: 'saying that *the day of the Lord* has already come.'[8] Dispensationalists claim that 'the day of the Lord' refers exclusively to the coming of Christ to judge the world and therefore requires the church to have been previously removed by the rapture. The weight of New Testament teaching, however, is that believers are going to participate fully in that day, something that would not be possible if they had been raptured away! Consider Paul's words to the Corinthians: 'He will also keep you firm to the end, so that you will be blameless on *the day of our Lord Jesus Christ*' (1 Corinthians 1:8).[9]

Neither is the 'day of the Lord' exclusively one of judgment; it is also one of deliverance. This is precisely what the return of Christ will be, judgment for God's enemies and, at the same time, deliverance for his people as he rescues them from the wrath of God through his coming, just as 2 Thessalonians 1:5-10 describes.

Then there is the matter of the resurrection of the dead. Dispensationalists claim that, at least for the righteous, this takes place at the rapture, when 'the dead in Christ will rise first' (1 Thessalonians 4:16). But Scripture clearly teaches that the resurrection is part and parcel of the coming of Christ in glory – something dispensationalists relegate to seven years later. Five times in John's gospel Jesus proclaims that he will raise up 'at the last day' those who believe in him (6:39; 40; 44; 54; 11:54). The resurrection must therefore constitute part of that day.

From all this the conclusion is inescapable: the word 'rapture', found in 1 Thessalonians 4:17, describes one aspect of the single-event return of Christ. There is nothing explicit in 1 Thessalonians chapters 4 and 5 to warrant the belief in a two-stage return of Christ. The most that can be done in claiming support for such views is to overlay onto the text the already accepted belief in a separate rapture.

## The collective interpretation of supporting Scriptures

Extracting the doctrine of the rapture from 1 Thessalonians depends on interpreting a number of other key scriptures through a dispensational lens. Taken on their own, none of them explicitly refers to the rapture of the church. Only by first accepting the possibility of the rapture can these scriptures be bundled together to support such an idea.

This point has not been lost on prominent dispensationalists themselves. John Walvoord accepted that 'neither post-tribulationism nor pre-tribulationism is an explicit teaching of Scripture',[10] and George Eldon Ladd said that pre-tribulationism was 'an assumption in the light of which the scriptures are interpreted'.[11] So what are the key scriptures adduced in support of dispensationalism? Let's examine them one by one.

### Daniel 9:27

Daniel 9:24-27, as we have observed earlier, describes a period of 'seventy weeks' of years and is speaking prophetically of the history of Israel leading up to the first coming of the Messiah. Since we have examined this passage in some depth previously, we will summarise the main issue here briefly. The key verse is verse 27, which speaks of the final week:

> *He will confirm a covenant with many for one 'seven.' In the middle*
> *of the 'seven' he will put an end to sacrifice and offering.*

Fundamental to the dispensational position is to interpret this week of seven years as disjointed from the previous 'weeks' by a period of at least 2000 years, thrusting it into the modern day and fitting it into a futurist interpretation of Daniel's prophecy.

Most Bible scholars, whatever their persuasion, view the first 69 weeks of years (483 years) as taking us to AD 27 – the time of the commencement of Jesus' ministry. Placing the seventieth week immediately after the preceding 69 weeks views the first three and a half days of the final week as the period of Jesus' earthly ministry. Then in his death at the cross he put an end to (Old Testament) sacrifices and offerings. The second three-and-a-half-day period covers the time from Christ's resurrection to the destruction of the Jewish temple.

Placing this week at the end of 2000 years of history, as dispensationalists do, views the 'he' of verse 27 as antichrist rather than Jesus. They believe that after the rapture of the church the antichrist will make a covenant of peace with the Jews. But after three and a half years he will break this covenant. This will trigger intense tribulation.

There is absolutely nothing in the passage itself to suggest that the seventieth week should be placed at the end of history. It is only possible if it is pre-supposed and the text violated to support such a view.

### 1 Corinthians 15:51-54

*Listen, I tell you a mystery: We will not all sleep, but we will all be changed – in a flash, in the twinkling of an eye, at the last trumpet. For the trumpet will sound, the dead will be raised imperishable, and we will be changed. For the perishable must clothe itself with the imperishable, and the mortal with immortality. When the perishable has been clothed with the imperishable, and the mortal with immortality, then the saying that is written will come true: "Death has been swallowed up in victory".*

It is incredible that anyone could use this passage to argue a case for the rapture teaching and yet many do so. The case is made however completely on the basis of silence. The argument goes like this:

'Because there is no mention here of a tribulation, the passage must refer to the rapture rather than the post-tribulation return of Christ in glory.

'Because there is no mention of Christ returning in a blaze of glory or setting up a millennial kingdom, it must refer to the rapture.'

A straightforward reading of Paul's words in this passage does nothing to contribute to the idea of a rapture of the church before the return of Christ. The verses simply state that at the return of Christ believers will receive their immortal bodies. Such a truth is without dispute and does not need a second event to support its merits.

### Revelation 3:10

*Since you have kept my command to endure patiently, I will also keep you from the hour of trial that is going to come on the whole world to test the inhabitants of the earth.*

This Scripture has been used for many decades to support the idea that Jesus will rapture the church away before a brief but ferocious tribulation period. According to this view the Philadelphian believers addressed in this verse are promised that they will be kept (by being raptured) from the trial (7-year tribulation period) that the whole world will shortly experience. Dispensationalists claim that Jesus' words in verse 11 that he is 'coming soon' reinforce this point.

Much of the debate has revolved around the precise meaning of the expression, 'I will keep you from'. Does it mean 'taken out of the way' or simply 'protected from but still in the middle of'? The arguments wage back and forth, ironically most of the time between pre-tribulationist and post-tribulationist dispensationalists. In fact the expression can take either meaning and therefore doesn't prove any particular position.

Of course the reader who approaches this passage already believing in a pre-tribulation rapture will see it as an important proof text despite the fact that it teaches nothing explicit about a rapture at all.

The better thing would be to allow the passage to speak for itself in the context of the whole book of Revelation. Jesus was speaking to a real church experiencing suffering and persecution in the first century AD. He was encouraging and strengthening them in their adversity. The 'hour of trial' refers most likely to the impending stress felt throughout the Roman Empire at that time. Jesus is promising to protect them in the midst of their trials just as he did to the disciples in John 17:15 when he prayed, 'My prayer is not that you take them out of the world but that you protect them from the evil one'.

To reinforce this point he exhorts them to 'hold fast what you have, that no one may take your crown' – words that are hardly relevant if the church is to be removed from the testing![12]

## The meaning of 'imminence'

Much of the controversy and debate over the rapture has revolved around 'imminence' – the idea that Jesus could return at any moment and we simply do not know when. Dispensationalists draw heavily upon certain words of Jesus for this notion, for instance:

*As it was in the days of Noah, so it will be at the coming of the Son of Man. For in the days before the flood, people were eating and drinking, marrying and giving in marriage, up to the day Noah entered the ark; and they knew nothing about what would happen until the flood came and took them all away. That is how it will be at the coming of the Son of Man. Two men will be in the field; one will be taken and the other left. Two women will be grinding with a hand mill; one will be taken and the other left. Therefore keep watch, because you do not know on what day your Lord will come. But understand this: if the owner of the house had known at what time of night the thief was coming, he would have kept watch and would not have let his house be broken into. So you also must be ready, because the Son of Man will come at an hour when you do not expect him.*
(Matthew 24:37-44)

See also Luke 12:35-40 which concludes, 'You also must be ready because the Son of Man will come at an hour when you do not expect him' (verse 40), and Matthew 25:1-13 which concludes, 'Therefore keep watch, because you do not know the day or the hour' (verse 13).

By the early 1900s, the imminence of the rapture had become crucial in the teaching of dispensationalism. John F. Walvoord maintained that this pre-tribulation understanding of imminence was 'the central feature of pre-tribulationism'.[13] Because of their belief in it, dispensationalists cannot reasonably expect anything definite to take place before the rapture. For them such a thought fatally undermines the unexpected nature of Christ's return for his church and should therefore be rejected as unscriptural.

This was expressed as long ago as 1895 by A. T. Pierson when he said, 'The imminence of the Lord's coming is destroyed the moment you locate between the first and second coming...any period of time whatsoever that is a definite period, whether 10, 100 or 1,000 years. I cannot look for a thing as an imminent event which I know is not going to take place for 10 years to come...'[14]

Sadly this same belief that the rapture could happen at any moment contributed to the escapist mentality that infected large parts of the evangelical church in the West during the 20th century. Instead of viewing the world as the arena for the invasion of God's kingdom, Christians saw it as an alien and hostile place from which the church will narrowly escape!

This escapist mindset had a deep and damaging effect on the way the 20th century church viewed its position in the world, contributing to its withdrawal from redemptive activity in society. Note the words of Robert G. Clouse in 1977:

> *Many evangelicals, heavily influenced by pre-millennialism, do not wish to see social change which would improve the lot of their fellow men. Despite the clear teaching of the Bible that believers are to love their neighbours and help them physically and spiritually, far too many Christians narrow their mission to an attempt to win souls for Christ.*[15]

Fortunately there are encouraging signs that this attitude is being reversed as the church rediscovers its mandate to invade the world with the works of the kingdom and realises that God has an agenda for the church to fulfil in the earth before the return of Christ. Dispensationalists understandably find it impossible to hold these two concepts in tension. Either you believe the coming of the Lord (for them, the rapture) is possible any moment, or you don't!

So how are we to understand the 'imminence issue' and why did Jesus warn his followers about the unexpected nature of his return?

First it should be noted that the passages warning us of Jesus' sudden return are actually exhortations to be ready so that we are not taken by surprise: the point being that surprise is not inevitable. Again and again Scripture makes it clear that for those who are watching and ready, that day will *not* catch them out as a thief. Paul could not be clearer:

> But you, brothers and sisters, are not in darkness so that this day should surprise you like a thief. You are all children of the light and children of the day. We do not belong to the night or to the darkness. (1 Thessalonians 5:4-5)

For those living in darkness – unbelievers – that day will indeed come without warning, but for the bride who is prepared and ready it will not! We may not know the precise day or hour, but there will be a sense that everything is in place for his return. In other words this is a call to personal preparation and readiness, not a doctrinal statement on the timing of the *parousia*.

Secondly, in speaking about his return, Jesus explicitly mentioned a delay. Indeed, that delay would be the main reason some of his followers would risk losing their alertness:

> Who then is the faithful and wise servant, whom the master has put in charge of the servants in his household to give them their food at the proper time? It will be good for that servant whose master finds him doing so when he returns. Truly I tell you, he will put him in charge of all his possessions. But suppose that servant is wicked and says to himself, 'My master is staying away **a long time**,' and he then begins to beat his fellow servants and to eat and drink with drunkards. The master of that servant will come on a day when he does not expect him and at an hour he is not aware of. (Matthew 24:45-50)

The parable of the ten virgins makes the point that 'the bridegroom was a long time in coming' (Matthew 25:5), and the parable of the talents that '*after a long time* the master of those servants returned' (Matthew 25:19). One of the clearest exhortations in this respect comes from the letter of James:

*Be patient, then, brothers and sisters, until the Lord's coming* [parousia]. *See how the farmer waits for the land to yield its valuable crop, patiently waiting for the autumn and spring rains.* (James 5:7)

In line with this 'long delay', which has already reached 2,000 years, God is evidently working out his cosmic purpose that will, in the fullness of time, culminate in the return of Christ in glory and the inauguration of the age to come. Jesus will 'see the fruit of the travail of his soul and be satisfied' (Isaiah 53:11, AMP) – but not before his agenda is accomplished.

## End notes

1. An even more obscure position is that of the *partial rapture*. This view holds that the rapture will be reserved only for believers who are eagerly watching and waiting for the Lord's coming. Less vigilant believers will be left behind to endure the tribulation period. The rapture is therefore a reward for some believers only. It has remained a marginal view throughout the last 180 years.
2. Quoted by Douglas Moo in *Three Views on the Rapture*, page 183
3. See also 2 Thessalonians 2:1; 1 Corinthians 15:23; James 5:7-8; 2 Peter 3:4; Matthew 24:3, 27, 37 and 1 John 2:28.
4. As *Kittel's Theological Dictionary* states, 'The parousia is the definitive manifestation of what has been effected already as an eschatological reality...It is the point where history is mastered by God's eternal rule.' (Volume 5, page 870)
5. 1 and 2 Thessalonians, *New Bible Commentary*
6. See also 1 Peter 1:13; 4:13, which reinforce the point
7. See for instance, Isaiah 2:5-21; Joel 2:1-32; Amos 5:18-20; Zephaniah 1:14-2:3
8. Other New Testament references to the 'day of the Lord' include 2 Peter 3:12; Romans 2:5,16; 1 Corinthians 1:8; Philippians 1:6,10,2:16; 1 Peter 2:12.
9. Notice also the reference to 'the day of our Lord Jesus Christ', mentioned here in 1 Corinthians 1:7, to reinforce the case that Paul is speaking of none other than the complete return of Jesus.
10. Walvoord, *The Rapture Question*, p 148
11. *The Blessed Hope*, p 88

12. One further scripture is worth mentioning, that of John 14:1-4: *Do not let your hearts be troubled. Trust in God; trust also in me. In my Father's house are many rooms; if it were not so, I would have told you. I am going there to prepare a place for you. And if I go and prepare a place for you, I will come back and take you to be with me that you also may be where I am. You know the way to the place I am going.* This passage has been traditionally held to refer to the one return of Christ at the end of the age. But dispensationalists have claimed it as a proof text for teaching the rapture, insisting that Jesus' words in verses 2 and 3 refer to his 'coming *for* the saints' in a secret rapture as distinct from his subsequent return in glory. Supposing for a minute that Jesus is indeed speaking of his end-time return, one would never conclude on the basis of this passage that he is advocating a rapture teaching. It is no more than a statement of fact that the return of Jesus involves, among other things, the receiving of believers by Jesus in the air to meet him. Reading a two-part return of Christ into this passage is only possible by viewing it through the lens of dispensationalism. But upon closer inspection, there is good reason to believe that these verses do not refer to the return of Christ at all, but rather the coming of the Holy Spirit at Pentecost. Why would that be so? Firstly, the word Jesus uses for 'come' is *erchomai*, not the word *parousia* that is normally associated with the return of Christ. *Erchomai* is never used by the New Testament writers to refer to Jesus' return. It would be a strange choice of word. Secondly, we need to consider these verses in the context of the whole section of John's Gospel in which it appears, which is a discourse by Jesus on the coming of the Holy Spirit. In verse 18 of chapter 14 Jesus says, 'I will not leave you as orphans; I will *come* to you'. In verse 23 Jesus says that for those who love him, he and the Father 'will *come* and make our home with him'. Again in verse 28 he says, 'You heard me say, "I am going away and I am *coming* back to you"'. It is almost without dispute that on every occasion Jesus is referring to the sending of the Holy Spirit and on every occasion he uses the same word for 'come' as he did in verse 3, namely *erchomai.* It is far more likely, therefore, that 'the Father's house' is our present enjoyment of God's presence in our lives as our heavenly Father rather than a reference to our future destination. This understanding of John 14:1-4 has strong support from Craig S Keener in his *Commentary on John.* He says,

'the eschatological language that may be present should be construed in this instance (not everywhere in John) as focussing on Jesus' coming after the resurrection to impart the Spirit who will continue his presence' (page 938). Bultmann (*Theology* 2:57), and Dodd (*Interpretation*, 395) also accord with this view.

13. Walvoord, op cit p 99
14. *The Coming of the Lord – the Practical Centre of the Bible,* address delivered at the Prophetic Conference, Allegheny, 1895
15. *The Meaning of the Millennium,* p 210

# Chapter 9

# Wrath and tribulation: there is a difference!

One of the strangest features of the American-led invasion of Iraq in 2003 was the sheer number of Allied soldiers who died or were wounded by 'friendly fire'. The notion that any fire can be friendly is ironic. But we understand what the expression means: soldiers coming under fire from their own side because of accidental exposure or mistaken identity.

This concept is at the root of dispensationalist arguments surrounding the 'great tribulation'. It is the debate over whether believers might be caught in the blast zone of God's wrath poured out on the wicked world just before Jesus returns, or whether they will escape in the rapture. Where you stand depends on your understanding of two expressions, 'the wrath of God' and 'the great tribulation', and their respective timing.

The concept of the great tribulation is one of the pillars of the dispensationalist belief system, one that has deeply affected Christian thought and culture in recent generations. 'Don't get left behind' – the song of Christian rock musician Larry Norman in the early 1970s – had the whole church singing the questionable eschatology that Hal Lindsey's *Late Great Planet Earth* was preaching:

A man and wife asleep in bed,
She hears a noise and turns her head, he's gone,
I wish we'd all been ready.
There's no time to change your mind,
The Son has come and you've been left behind.

'Are you ready? Jesus could come at any moment, and woe betide anyone who does not escape in the rapture before the great tribulation!' This was the line of countless evangelists appealing for people to respond before it was too late.

Let's briefly recap what that teaching is all about before we show that there is in fact a difference between wrath and tribulation – and that we should fear neither!

## Popular tribulation teaching

We have observed that, according to dispensational teaching, the return of Jesus is separated into two events. First of all the secret rapture will occur, when believers will be snatched away from the earth. The full coming of the Lord will take place seven years later. It is during the second half of this seven-year period that God will supposedly unleash his terrifying wrath on those who remain on the earth – the great tribulation.

The Jewish people will allegedly turn to Christ in large numbers in this seven-year period, but because this takes place *after* the rapture they will have to endure the tribulation. There are also some non-Jews who will repent and turn to Christ during this period. They are often given the nickname 'tribulation saints' because, as a consequence of being left behind, they too will suffer the wrath of God in the great tribulation. So we have at least two categories within God's family who get caught in friendly fire!

The notion that our loving heavenly Father could direct his wrath at rebellious man knowing that some of his children will also suffer is in itself a perverse idea. But now let's add another ingredient to this scenario: the teaching in some circles that believers today can lose their salvation in a time of backsliding. Such a teaching breeds a deep insecurity. 'Am I saved? How can I be sure I will not be left behind?' The motivation for repenting and following Christ in such a culture is reduced to fear and the threat of suffering.

Particularly in the USA, evangelistic 'altar calls' often address two separate groups: first-timers and backsliders. Many of the latter fear they have lost their salvation and need to find it again. As a consequence in many Christian circles the expectation of Christ's coming is not a comfort but a source of dread and a means of browbeating the flock into line. Just the idea of having to endure the great tribulation is enough to get people to the altar!

Such popular views of the great tribulation have their roots firmly in the theology of dispensationalism. For example Charles C. Ryrie in his book *Basic Theology* views this period in the following terms:

...the Tribulation will be unique because of the way men act.
In one of the early judgments, men will hide themselves in the

dens and caves of the mountains and say, "Fall on us and hide us from the face of Him who sits on the throne and from the wrath of the Lamb!" (Revelation 6:16). When the Great Tribulation comes, men will act as if they think the world is coming to an end.[1]

The truth of Christ's return is actually meant to kindle optimism and faith in the hearts of believers. After Paul speaks about it to the Thessalonian church, he finishes by saying, 'Therefore encourage one another with these words' (1 Thessalonians 4:18), a far cry from the situation today.

The dispensational scheme of the end times depends on three assumptions:

- That 'tribulation' means God's end-time wrath.
- That such a period will occur before Christ returns in glory.
- That Christians will be raptured away before this takes place.

Like the three legs of a stool, these suppositions all work together. Throw any one of them into question and the stool falls over.

We dealt with the subject of the rapture in the previous chapter. Here we want to examine the other two legs of the stool: does tribulation mean the wrath of God, and does the Bible teach the idea of an end-time great tribulation preceding the coming of Christ in glory?

## The good news, Christ is coming!

The Bible presents us with an overwhelmingly positive picture of the coming of the Lord for those who own his name. Firstly, the return of Christ should be eagerly anticipated by all who belong to him since they will be with him and enjoy his personal presence for ever. The apostle Paul describes this prospect as 'the blessed hope' (Titus 2:13) because it will usher in an age where death, mourning, crying and pain will have all passed away.

Hope, not dread or fear, is frequently linked to the return of Christ. Peter says 'he has given new birth into a living hope through the resurrection of Jesus Christ from the dead' (1 Peter 1:3). He says that, despite our present sufferings, this prospect causes overwhelming joy (verse 6).

Secondly, the return of Christ is the culmination of a global invasion of God's kingdom. God is working out a plan and his people, the church, are the instrument he is using. Our understanding of God's purpose in the world will have a deep impact on our feelings toward it. More than ever the church is recognising its role as agent of the kingdom of heaven to transform society, as Jesus explained (Matthew 6:10), rather than to escape the earth in a rapture.

Finally, Christ will return for a glorious church. Jesus will come for his bride 'as a radiant church, without stain or wrinkle or any other blemish, but holy and blameless' (Ephesians 5:27), not furtive and shameful like a person caught off guard. Paul spoke of this to the Thessalonian church: 'For what is our hope, our joy, or the crown in which we will glory in the presence of our Lord Jesus when he comes? Is it not you? (1 Thessalonians 2:19). He fully expected the church to be ready for the coming of the Lord, 'blameless and holy in the presence of our God and Father when our Lord Jesus comes with all his holy ones.' (1 Thessalonians 3:13).

The preoccupation of dispensationalism is whether believers will have to endure the great tribulation. Because they believe that this tribulation is the wrath of God, and that believers are promised they will escape such wrath, they overlay these beliefs onto their end-time scheme of events and conclude that most of the church will escape the world in the rapture prior to such tribulation. This is the appeal of the *Left Behind* fictional series. Who in their right mind would want to be left behind to face three and a half years of disease, famine, warfare and deprivation, particularly when you believe God is the author of it all?

Not that we should be complacent; the prospect of Christ's return should be a great motivation to sober living and watchfulness. Although we contend that God has a global agenda that is working from one generation to the next, none of us know when our days will end. My life *could* be over at any time and while planning for the next 500 years, I should live as though today could be my last day! We will now take a closer look at the theme of God's wrath.

## A biblical perspective of the wrath of God

The Old Testament prophets spoke of a coming 'day of the Lord' that would usher in the age to come. Because of their foreshortened perspective they anticipated this to be a single event but, as we have already established, we have the advantage of seeing the coming of Christ in two phases. Jesus came first 2000 years ago to inaugurate the kingdom and take away sin, and he will come a second time to consummate the kingdom, to bring salvation in its totality to his people and to judge everyone according to their deeds.

The prophet Zephaniah anticipated the Lord's coming with the following description:

> *The great day of the Lord is near – near and coming quickly.*
> *The cry on the day of the Lord is bitter;*
> *The Mighty Warrior shouts his battle cry.*
> *That day will be a day of wrath …*
> *Neither their silver nor their gold will be able to save them*
> *on the day of the Lord's wrath.*
> *In the fire of his jealousy the whole earth will be consumed,*
> *for he will make a sudden end of all who live on the earth.*
> (Zephaniah 1:14-15, 18)

The concern of the prophets like Zephaniah was to warn people that the Lord intended to demonstrate wrath at his coming. Similarly, when John the Baptist came as a prophet to prepare the way for the Christ he called for the people of his day to 'Repent for the kingdom of heaven has come near' (Matthew 3:2). The Pharisees and Sadducees, intrigued by his message and the manner of his ministry, stood at a distance and observed John's activities. His statement to them was, 'You brood of vipers! Who warned you to flee from the coming wrath?' (Matthew 3:7).

The question is, towards which group of people will God's wrath be directed? The apostle John answers this question in his gospel, leaving us in no doubt: 'Whoever believes in the Son has eternal life, but whoever rejects the Son will not see life, for *God's wrath remains on them'* (John 3:36).

The wrath of God is reserved exclusively for those who reject Christ. Those who believe in the Son and accept Christ look forward to a happier prospect: eternal life. In the time of Jesus the gospel writers indicated which categories of people deliberately chose to reject Christ. Jesus himself said to his disciples: 'The Son of Man must suffer many things and be rejected by the elders, the chief priests and the teachers of the law, and he must be killed and on the third day be raised to life' (Luke 9:22).

Later, Jesus affirmed that this rejection extended to the Jewish nation of his day in general: 'But first he (the Son of Man) must suffer many things and be rejected by this generation' (Luke 17:25).

The fearful consequence of the Jews' rejection of Jesus was to come under the wrath of God. In the Olivet discourse, Jesus prophesied that the generation who refused to believe in him would experience the wrath of God in what Jesus described as 'days of vengeance' (Luke 21:22 NKJV). This would be fulfilled in the destruction of the temple at Jerusalem and anguish experienced by the whole nation of Israel: 'There will be great distress in the land and wrath against this people' (Luke 21:23).

John's statement that the wrath of God remains on those who reject the Son applies not only to the contemporaries of Jesus but to every subsequent generation. All who refuse to be gathered to Christ and choose to live outside of God's protective, fatherly love remain exposed to his wrath. This has been the condition of every believer before they responded to Christ's offer of salvation.

Paul describes that condition as being 'dead in your transgressions and sins .... we were by nature deserving of wrath' (Ephesians 2:1, 3). But now that we have been reconciled to Christ and are joined to him we are completely delivered from God's wrath. We have become the inheritors of eternal life and as a result no longer need to live in fear of that wrath.

Paul is clear about our salvation and secure position in Christ. In his letter to the Romans he states, 'Since we have now been justified by his blood, how much more shall we be *saved from God's wrath* through him!' (Romans 5:9). And to the Thessalonians: 'you turned to God from idols to serve the living and true God, and to wait for his Son from heaven, whom he raised from the dead – Jesus, *who rescues us from the coming wrath*' (1 Thessalonians 1:9-10). And as if to remove any lingering doubts: 'God did *not appoint us to suffer wrath* but to receive salvation through our Lord Jesus Christ' (1 Thessalonians 5:9).

It could hardly be clearer: those who have responded to Christ's offer of salvation and have entered into the riches of his great grace are now completely protected from any future wrath associated with the Lord's second coming. By contrast, those outside of Christ and his salvation remain dangerously exposed to God's wrath. In fact they are already experiencing a measure of God's judgment. 'The wrath of God is being revealed from heaven against all the godlessness and wickedness of people, who suppress the truth by their wickedness' (Romans 1:18).

As long as people reject God's provision of salvation through Jesus Christ, condemnation remains on them, whether they are Jew or Gentile. Paul's assessment of his own countrymen, the Jews, was:

*They displease God and are hostile to everyone in their effort to keep us from speaking to the Gentiles so that they may be saved. In this way they always heap up their sins to the limit. The wrath of God has come upon them at last.* (1 Thessalonians 2:15-16)

In the light of the biblical evidence we may rest assured that, as believers in Christ, we have been rescued from the coming wrath, reserved exclusively for rebels and unbelievers. Our inheritance in Christ is the enjoyment of eternal life in the present and the joyful anticipation of rewards for obedience. No believer will be caught up in an outpouring of God's wrath prior to the return of Christ.

## What does the Bible mean by tribulation?

The English word 'tribulation' translates the Greek word *thlipsis*, which can also be rendered by the English words affliction, distress, anguish, persecution and trouble. The word originally means a 'pressing, pressure or anything which oppresses the spirit'. It denotes, by extension, the suffering that ensues due to pressure of circumstances or antagonism from people.

Believers have inherited the kingdom of God but still live in a fallen world; it is inevitable that we will experience opposition from those still influenced by the kingdom of darkness. The apostle Peter wrote to his contemporaries, 'Dear friends, do not be surprised at *the fiery ordeal that has come on you to test you,* as though something strange were happening to you. But rejoice in as much as you participate in the sufferings of Christ, so that you may be overjoyed when his glory is revealed' (1 Peter 4:12-13).

Jesus explained that, although we live in the world, we are born from above and no longer share the nature of this world. The consequence of being in the world but not of the world is that we will experience the same attitudes from society that Jesus himself encountered. Towards the end of his life he bluntly told his disciples, 'In this world you will have trouble (*thlipsis*)'. He quickly added however, that this should not cause his followers to be despondent: 'take heart! I have overcome the world' (John 16:33).[2]

The New Testament clearly teaches that trouble (*thlipsis*) will accompany those who choose Christ-like living. For example, Paul warns the young believers in Galatia that 'we must go through many hardships [*thlipsis*] to enter the kingdom of God' (Acts 14:22). He also assures those justified through faith that peace with God is now our experience and that we can rejoice in the hope of the glory of God. Then he continues by stating that our rejoicing is not limited to times of favourable circumstances but can also encompass adverse ones – times of suffering (*thlipsis*). Indeed, right attitudes during times of adversity produce perseverance and godly character (Romans 5:1-4).

In view of the eternal weight of glory that Paul confidently expected for himself, his current troubles (*thlipsis*), he said, were light and momentary. Even though these included imprisonment, flogging, beating with rods, stoning and shipwrecks, his confidence in his future inheritance enabled him to endure (2 Corinthians 4:17).

The church at Thessalonica also suffered. They received the message of the gospel from Paul and his companions and imitated their lives of faith in spite of enduring severe suffering (*thlipsis*) from their fellow-citizens. Though not immune from such *tribulation* they were deeply aware that they had been rescued from the coming *wrath* (1 Thessalonians 1:6, 10). In his second letter to them he says:

> *we boast about your perseverance and faith in all the persecutions and trials* [thlipsis] *you are enduring. All this is evidence that God's judgment is right, and as a result you will be counted worthy of the kingdom of God, for which you are suffering. God is just: He will pay back trouble* [thlipsis] *to those who trouble* [thlipsis] *you.* (2 Thessalonians 1:4-6)

The book of Acts concurs with Paul's words, using *thlipsis* to describe persecution. Luke says in Acts 11:19, 'Now those who had been scattered by the persecution *[thlipsis]* that broke out when Stephen …' Luke also records Paul as saying in Acts 20:23, 'I only know that in every city the Holy Spirit warns me that prison and hardships *[thlipsis]* are facing me.'

These early disciples were triumphant in their tribulation, knowing that whatever the devil or the world might throw at them, God was for them and nothing could separate them from his love.

In summary, the Bible assures us that tribulation and wrath are not synonymous. Tribulation is the opposition of a hostile world; it is the enemy's antagonism toward the church and can be expected as normal. The wrath of God, however, is something that those who belong to Christ will never have to endure. There is no biblical evidence of believers being at the receiving end of such wrath, and any attempt to burden a Christian with the threat of impending wrath should be rejected.

## The great tribulation

We need to begin this section by saying that the expression 'great tribulation' is indeed biblical, appearing in some of the older translations. Jesus himself used it in the Olivet discourse as he described the conditions that would lead up to the destruction of the temple in AD 70. Hostility towards the citizens of Jerusalem would be so severe that Jesus could say of those events: 'Then there will be *great tribulation* unequalled from the beginning of the world until now - and never to be equalled again' (Matthew 24:21, KJV).

The accounts written by Josephus, a Jewish eye-witness to these horrors, indicate that over one million people died in the few years that culminated in the sacking of Jerusalem in AD 70. The extent of the tribulation and massacre of the inhabitants of Jerusalem was so great and severe that Jesus said its intensity would never again be equalled in the history of the world.

There are several other occasions in the New Testament where the Greek words for 'great tribulation' (*thlipsis megas*) are used. The famine that struck Egypt when Joseph was ruler of that nation is identified as a time of great tribulation (Acts 7:11). The same Greek words are used to describe the terrible persecution suffered by the church in Jerusalem following the martyrdom of Stephen (Acts 8:1; 11:19). Those in the city of Thyatira who had followed the false prophet Jezebel and her teaching were to suffer judgment from the ascended Christ resulting in their experiencing 'great tribulation' (Revelation 2:22).

In the book of Revelation, John identifies the believers in heaven arrayed in white robes as having 'come out of the great tribulation' (Revelation 7:14). Commentators who interpret the book of Revelation from a preterist perspective view this 'great tribulation' as having already been accomplished. These believers became included into the Kingdom as a result of Judaism's decline associated with the destruction of Jerusalem's temple.

Those who interpret the apocalypse from a futurist viewpoint insist, to the contrary, that the great tribulation must be viewed as a still-future event. But will there be a period of great tribulation before the return of Christ? There is every possibility. If so, what will it look like? The answer is that it will almost certainly look like every other period of tribulation in history: the church will be on the receiving end of hostility, persecution and hatred by a God-rejecting society. What is certain, according to Jesus is that any future persecution will not exhibit the intense degree of pain and suffering endured by the inhabitants of Jerusalem prior to its fall.

It may surprise you to know that there is greater persecution against believers today than at any time in history. More martyrs die for Christ each year than ever before, church buildings are destroyed, the homes of pastors are set on fire, Christians are harassed and hounded. Yet none of this should be seen as disaster any more than when the early church experienced persecution. The early church believed they were privileged to be persecuted: 'The apostles left the Sanhedrin, rejoicing because they had been counted worthy of suffering disgrace for the Name' (Acts 5:41). Jesus had prepared the apostles for what would befall them and explained it was all part of the plan:

> Blessed are you when people hate you, when they exclude you and insult you and reject your name as evil, because of the Son of Man. Rejoice in that day and leap for joy, because great is your reward in heaven. (Luke 6:22-23)

Paul, who suffered more persecution than all his peers, was immovable in his conviction that God was with him and for him in all he suffered:

> Who shall separate us from the love of Christ? Shall trouble or hardship or persecution...no, in all these things we are more than conquerors... (Romans 8:35-37)

Such persecution is always likely to feature somewhere in the world until Jesus comes.

## Conclusion

Virtually all of the talk about the 'great tribulation' takes place within the circles of those who hold to a two-stage return of Christ, namely, a secret rapture followed by a public return seven years later. This questionable approach has allowed confusion and argument to continue and has perpetuated the idea that believers will escape a coming great tribulation because of the mistaken belief that the tribulation is the wrath of God.

By returning to the historic view that the return of Christ is one climactic and victorious event, the idea of a coming great tribulation is completely undermined. Instead of escaping the wrath of God we are here to redeem the world. Instead of fear we have faith. Instead of looking for the antichrist we are bringing in the kingdom of God!

We have attempted to show that references to a great tribulation in the New Testament are not pointing to a period of God's wrath poured out between a rapture and return of Christ. Instead, tribulation is the normal opposition that the church experiences from a hostile world – opposition that Jesus warned us of and over which we are more than conquerors through Christ who loved us.

## End notes
1. Charles C. Ryrie, *Basic Theology*
2. See also John 15:18-21; 16:1-4

Chapter 10

# The antichrist, beast and man of lawlessness

Tune into any Christian TV programme on the coming of Christ or read any book on the end times and you are almost sure to hear some teaching on a mysterious figure most often referred to as the antichrist.

It seems to have a mesmerizing effect on the Christian community. Indeed, many believers today seem more excited about the coming of the antichrist than of the Christ. They talk confidently about what this much-anticipated world ruler will do but are less certain when it comes to their expectations of the nations being won to Christ or society transformed.

Despite the best efforts of prophecy teachers to pin down this end-time character, it has proved to be an elusive task. His identity has been revised numerous times in the light of unfolding world events, each candidate falling from favour when predicted historical events have not worked out as anticipated.

'The antichrist' is just one of three titles given to this puzzling end-time character that features so prominently in the teaching of modern dispensationalists and prophecy teachers. The other two titles are 'the beast' and 'the man of lawlessness'. The titles are taken from separate passages of Scripture. But do they refer to one and the same person, as is claimed? And how did such feverish speculation come to be generated on the issue? We will examine each of the three titles in turn.

## The antichrist

Much of our concept of antichrist in the modern church comes from connecting disparate passages of Scripture with the few actual references to antichrist. As a consequence, the antichrist is identified with 'the ruler who will come' of Daniel 9, 'the man of lawlessness' of 2 Thessalonians, and 'the beast' of Revelation 13. By combining these scriptures, prophecy teachers have predicted a future ruler who will gain great political power in the world, opposing the interests of Christ and persecuting the church, resulting in a time of great tribulation.

Endless speculation around this belief is fanned into flame by the books of end time prophecy teachers. Recently it has been the turn of the *Left Behind* series of novels to stoke the fires of antichrist fever.

The Scriptures mention the actual word 'antichrist' on only four occasions and each reference is found in the epistles of John. The book of Revelation, also written by John, is frequently used as a source for teaching on an end-time antichrist figure, but John never uses the word 'antichrist' in his Apocalypse. An investigation of the four actual instances provides a much better understanding of what John meant when he used the term.

It is impossible to understand John's warnings about antichrist unless we first appreciate the significance of the word 'Christ'. Our English word 'Christ' is taken from the Greek word *Christos* which simply means 'anointed one', that is, the one anointed by God's Spirit. The Greek word is, in turn, a translation of the Hebrew word *mashiach* from which we get the English word 'messiah'.

The Messiah of the Old Testament is God's appointed and anointed deliverer of his people Israel. He is the one sent to save them from their enemies and oppressors. There were three anointed offices in the Old Testament: those of prophet, priest and king. The Messiah would come in fulfilment of all three. It was a title of divinity and royalty, unique in salvation history.

Anyone claiming the title Christ would be identifying themselves with the Messiah of the Jewish people prophesied in the Old Testament. Therefore as a title given to Jesus of Nazareth, *Christos* identified him as God's unique and long-anticipated Saviour. Acknowledgment of this among those claiming to be followers of Jesus was therefore crucially important. Jesus could be a prophet, teacher, healer or leader of a sect, but only the confession 'Jesus of Nazareth is the Christ' verified someone as an authentic believer.

This was Peter's confession when responding to Jesus' question, 'Who do you say that I am?' Peter replied, 'You are the Christ, the Son of the living God' (Matthew 16:16, NASB). It was the recognition of his divine nature. John emphasised this point at the end of his gospel:

> *These things are written so that you may believe that Jesus is the Christ, the Son of the living God; and that by believing you may have life in his name.* (John 20:31, NASB)

Denial that Jesus was the *Christos* of God was considered nothing less than heretical. It was the litmus test of your theology and faith. All of this helps us to understand the word 'antichrist', which is similarly a translation of the Greek *antichristos*. Bear in mind that 'anti' can mean either 'against' Christ or 'instead of' Christ and could well combine both ideas.

In the first century the debate over antichrist was more to do with one's belief than with a personality. John's concern was to protect the church from heresy. With this background in mind we can now approach John's four passages. In chronological order they are as follows:

> *Dear children, this is the last hour; and as you have heard that the* **antichrist** *is coming, even now many* **antichrists** *have come. This is how we know it is the last hour. They went out from us, but they did not really belong to us. For if they had belonged to us, they would have remained with us; but their going showed that none of them belonged to us.* (1 John 2:18-19)

We can deduce several truths from this opening statement of John regarding the antichrist. Firstly, there was not just one antichrist; there were many. Secondly, these antichrists already existed when John wrote his epistle because he describes them as having already come (verse 18). Finally, those identified as antichrists seem to have been people who had once belonged to the church but had now left. Although they had appeared to belong to the church community, their departure revealed that this had never really been the case.

> *Who is the liar? It is whoever denies that Jesus is the Christ. Such a person is the* **antichrist** *– denying the Father and the Son.* (1 John 2:22)

Antichrist is here identified as anyone who denies that Jesus is the Christ or Messiah. By denying that Jesus is actually God's Son that person, by the same token, denies the Father who sent the Son.

The denial of Jesus as the Christ stemmed from a theology that rejected his true identity. That belief system ran contrary to the revelation brought by the apostles of Christ and by rejecting apostolic teaching it showed itself to be heretical in nature.

Antichrist may describe the individuals holding such views, but also the heretical belief system they were embracing, which resulted in their withdrawal from the community of Christian believers.

> *Dear friends, do not believe every spirit, but test the spirits to see whether they are from God, because many false prophets have gone out into the world. This is how you can recognise the Spirit of God: Every spirit that acknowledges that Jesus Christ has come in the flesh is from God, but every spirit that does not acknowledge Jesus is not from God. This is the spirit of the **antichrist**, which you have heard is coming and even now is already in the world.* (1 John 4:1-3)

The spirit of antichrist – denial that Jesus had come from God – was a lying and deceiving spirit which John encouraged the Christian community to recognise and test. It was the influencer of many false prophets who had gone out into the world, each of whom denied that Jesus Christ had come in the flesh as the Messiah sent from God.

The Christian community had previously been warned that this spirit of antichrist was going to come into the world. Here John affirms that what he had warned of was now present and operating in the propagation of lies and half-truths about Jesus Christ.

> *Many deceivers, who do not acknowledge Jesus Christ as coming in the flesh, have gone out into the world. Any such person is the deceiver and the **antichrist**.* (2 John 1:7)

The deceivers of John's day, the deniers of Jesus Christ whom John identifies as the antichrist, were many in number. Church history records that heretical teaching was common in the first century, much of it revolving around the acceptance or denial of Jesus' true identity. Paul, John and Peter all tackled this issue, contending for the truth of the gospel in their epistles.

## Conclusion

In summary, from the descriptions provided by John in his epistles we can safely draw the following conclusions about 'antichrist':

The spirit of antichrist was at work in the world even in John's day. That same spirit, by its denial of Jesus Christ being God's Son, the Christ, and being born as a real man, perpetuates the same pernicious heresies to this day.

The spirit of antichrist spawns many antichrist figures who, in line with that spirit, oppose God's truth as revealed in the person of Jesus

Christ and the apostolic testimony of the New Testament writers. The church of Jesus Christ is in no way to be intimidated by this horde of opponents, because the eternal Spirit of God dwells bodily in all true believers.

John boldly affirms that 'the One who is in you is greater than the one who is in the world' (1 John 4:4). Because the Holy Spirit inhabiting us as believers is greater than the antichrist spirit prevalent in society, John encourages us to be confident that the demonic entities have already been overcome through the work of Christ at the cross. Just as our Lord himself overcame, so all believers have the ability through the indwelling Spirit to overcome every spirit that does not acknowledge Jesus Christ as Lord.

There are no grounds at all in John's epistles for the notion of an end-time world ruler emerging to control a one-world government in opposition to the church. Sound principles of Bible interpretation forbid us building a teaching from silence or conjecture. Neither can Bible passages legitimately be superimposed onto John's references to antichrist in order to create something he never intended.

## The beast, his mark and the seal of God

Ian's wife Marj received Jesus Christ into her life in the 1970s. Those early years of her Christian life were eye-opening and enthralling, as she began to appreciate the riches of God's word and the joy of sharing life with other believers. Most of the Christians she met were a great help to her in explaining and applying the truths of Scripture. One day, however, she was rather disturbed by a passing conversation with a lady in the church whom she did not really know. This lady informed Marj that she should not buy a certain brand of washing powder, for the packaging had a bar code imprinted on it and this represented 'the mark of the beast'. Marj related this story to her home group leaders, who sensibly told her to dismiss the idea and buy the washing powder without fear.

Misplaced teaching about the mark of the beast has been the cause of unwarranted fear and speculation among Christians for generations. Barcodes are just one of a number of suspect views that have run their course in the Christian community. Another favourite is magnetic strips on credit cards.

A more recent idea is that the mark of the beast will be a small microchip inserted into the right hand or forehead of every person.

A radio frequency identification system (RFID) will thus be able to track people's movements and activities, causing them to be unable to buy or sell without it, apparently fulfilling Revelation 13:17.

Since we have established that the book of Revelation is a letter, its contents must have been meaningful to those to whom John wrote. A letter is never written with the idea in mind that only people reading it 2000 years later will be able to make sense of its contents! We are therefore right to avoid fanciful interpretations of Revelation and the mark of the beast in particular.

In order to appreciate what John was seeking to communicate, let us look at the Scriptures in which the phrase 'the mark of the beast' occurs in context.

> *And the dragon stood on the shore of the sea. And I saw a beast coming out of the sea. He had ten horns and seven heads, with ten crowns on his horns, and on each head a blasphemous name. The beast I saw resembled a leopard, but had feet like those of a bear and a mouth like that of a lion. The dragon gave the beast his power and his throne and great authority. One of the heads of the beast seemed to have had a fatal wound, but the fatal wound had been healed. The whole world was astonished and followed the beast. Men worshipped the dragon because he had given authority to the beast, and they also worshipped the beast and asked, 'Who is like the beast? Who can make war against him?'* (Revelation 13:1-4)
>
> *Then I saw another beast, coming out of the earth. He had two horns like a lamb, but he spoke like a dragon. He exercised all the authority of the first beast on his behalf, and made the earth and its inhabitants worship the first beast, whose fatal wound had been healed. And he performed great and miraculous signs, even causing fire to come down from heaven to earth in full view of men. Because of the signs he was given power to do on behalf of the first beast, he deceived the inhabitants of the earth. He ordered them to set up an image in honour of the beast who was wounded by the sword and yet lived. He was given power to give breath to the image of the first beast, so that it could speak and cause all who refused to worship the image to be killed. He also forced everyone, small and great, rich and poor, free and slave, to receive a mark on his right hand or on his forehead, so that no one could buy or sell unless he had the mark, which is the name of the beast or the number of his name. This calls for wisdom. If anyone has insight, let him calculate the number of the*

*beast, for it is man's number. His number is 666. Then I looked, and there before me was the Lamb, standing on Mount Zion, and with him 144,000 who had his name and his Father's name written on their foreheads.* (Revelation 13:11-18)

These passages in Revelation identify an unholy trinity of characters who are a parody of the triune nature of the Father, Son and Holy Spirit. This ungodly threesome is the dragon, the beast that comes out of the sea, and the beast that comes out of the earth. The identity of the dragon is not a problem as he is revealed in Revelation 12:9 as 'that ancient serpent called the devil, or Satan, who leads the whole world astray'.

This passage also identifies two kinds of people: those with the mark of the beast on their right hand or forehead (Revelation 13:16-18), and those with the name of the Lamb and the name of the Father written on their foreheads (Revelation 14:1).

Before going any further we need to appreciate the significance of the hand or the forehead as a means of communicating allegiance. The Old Testament is helpful here. Deuteronomy 6:5-8 states:

*Love the Lord your God with all your heart and with all your soul and with all your strength. These commandments that I give you today are to be upon your hearts. Impress them on your children. Talk about them when you sit at home and when you walk along the road, when you lie down and when you get up. Tie them as symbols on your **hands** and bind them on your **foreheads**.*

The 'hand' represents our actions and the 'forehead' our thoughts and attitudes. To have someone's mark on one's hand and forehead is a way of saying one is dedicated to that person in both attitude and action.

The symbols on the hands and the foreheads spoken of in Deuteronomy 6 indicate allegiance and devotion, on behalf of the Jews, to Jehovah who had delivered them out of Egypt and brought them into the land of Canaan. In the same way, the marks on the hands and foreheads of the two communities in Revelation refer to the allegiance and devotion of those communities to the person whose marks they bear.

We can better understand the nature of these two communities by considering the other references in the book of Revelation to both the mark of the beast and the seal of God.

### The mark of the beast

> If anyone worships the beast and its image and receives its mark on
> their forehead or on their hand, they, too, will drink the wine of God's
> fury, which has been poured full strength into the cup of his wrath.
> They will be tormented with burning sulphur in the presence of the
> holy angels and of the Lamb. And the smoke of their torment will rise
> for ever and ever. There will be no rest day or night for those who
> worship the beast and its image, or for anyone who receives the mark
> of its name. (Revelation 14:9-11)

> The first angel went and poured out his bowl on the land, and ugly,
> festering sores broke out on the people who had the mark of the beast
> and worshipped its image. (Revelation 16:2)

> But the beast was captured, and with it the false prophet who had
> performed the signs on its behalf. With these signs he had deluded
> those who had received the mark of the beast and worshipped its
> image. The two of them were thrown alive into the fiery lake of
> burning sulphur. (Revelation 19:20)

> I saw thrones on which were seated those who had been given
> authority to judge. And I saw the souls of those who had been
> beheaded because of their testimony about Jesus and because of the
> word of God. They had not worshipped the beast or its image and had
> not received its mark on their foreheads or their hands. They came to
> life and reigned with Christ a thousand years. (Revelation 20:4)

Clearly those who had the mark of the beast were under judgment
and destined for God's wrath because their allegiance and devotion
had been to someone other than the Lamb, who was seated on the
throne as King of kings and Lord of lords.

Much of the fear generated in the Christian community over the
mark of the beast lies in the idea that believers will be forced against
their will to receive this mark but then face God's judgment for
having done so. Our reading of Scripture shows that this is
completely misplaced, for those receiving the beast's mark do so not
reluctantly, but in open rebellion against God.

The word for 'mark' in the original Greek is *charagma*, which
means 'stamp', 'brand', 'impress' or 'engraving'. The word *charagma*
is used exclusively with reference to the mark of the beast and this is
the only place in the New Testament that we find it.

## Seal of the living God

*Then I saw another angel coming up from the east, having the **seal** of the Living God. He called out in a loud voice to the four angels who had been given power to harm the land and sea: "Do not harm the land or the sea or the trees until we put a **seal** on the foreheads of the servants of our God." Then I heard the number of those who were **sealed**: 144,000 from all the tribes of Israel. (Revelation 7:2-4)*

*The fifth angel sounded his trumpet, and I saw a star that had fallen from the sky to the earth. The star was given the key to the shaft of the Abyss. When he opened the Abyss, smoke rose from it like the smoke from a gigantic furnace. The sun and sky were darkened by the smoke from the Abyss. And out of the smoke locusts came down on the earth and were given power like that of scorpions of the earth. They were told not to harm the grass of the earth or any plant or tree, but only those people who did not have the **seal** of God on their foreheads. They were not allowed to kill them but only to torture them for five months. And the agony they suffered was like that of the sting of a scorpion when it strikes. During those days people will seek death but will not find it; they will long to die, but death will elude them. (Revelation 9:1-6)*

The word *charagma*, used to describe the mark of the beast, is not used to distinguish those who carry the seal of the Living God. The word 'seal' is the Greek *sphragis*, which, in the context of Revelation 7, describes an 'emblem of ownership and security'.[1]

The people identified as carrying the seal of the Living God are described as servants of God, protected by him and able to see his face and reign with him forever. They do not carry the mark of the beast but are worshippers of God who are able to sing the song of Moses and the song of the Lamb (Revelation 15:2-3; 22:1-5).

In order to understand what the seal of God represents here in Revelation, we will look at other references in the New Testament to the act of sealing.

*Now it is God who makes both us and you stand firm in Christ. He anointed us, set his **seal** of ownership on us, and put his spirit in our hearts as a deposit, guaranteeing what is to come. (2 Corinthians 1:21-22)*

*And you also were included in Christ when you heard the message of truth, the gospel of your salvation. When you believed, you were* *marked in him with a **seal**, the promised Holy Spirit, who is a deposit guaranteeing our inheritance until the redemption of those who are God's possession – to the praise of his glory.* (Ephesians 1:13-14)

*And do not grieve the Holy Spirit of God, with whom you were **sealed** for the day of redemption.* (Ephesians 4:30)

In each of the above statements, Paul affirms that those who believe in Christ have been sealed with the person of the Holy Spirit. The anointing of the Spirit, then is the mark of ownership and authenticity that distinguishes believers in Jesus from every other person.

John records in his gospel that Jesus also had the seal of God on his life. When speaking of himself, Jesus confirmed that his heavenly Father had placed on him the seal of approval (John 6:27). The sealing on Jesus' life represents the person of the Holy Spirit. John the Baptist recognised Jesus because God had told him that, 'The man on whom you see the Spirit come down and remain is the one who will baptise with the Holy Spirit' (John 1:33).

We have seen that the word 'Christ' means 'Anointed One', and what Jesus accomplished in his earthly ministry he did by the anointing of the Spirit. The sealing of the Spirit that authenticated Jesus' life and ministry is now the down-payment given to all who have placed their faith in Christ. Little wonder, then, that the early believers were called 'Christians', expressing the life of their Master and demonstrating that their lives, too, were characterised by the sealing, presence and anointing of the Holy Spirit.

## Identifying the mark of the beast

Before attempting to determine the meaning of the beast's mark, it would be helpful to uncover the identity of the beast himself. John's description of the beast coming out of the sea with ten horns and seven heads is clearly rooted in Daniel's vision of four successive kingdoms. Daniel saw four beasts coming up out of the sea: first a lion, then a bear, then a leopard, and lastly a terrifying beast with large iron teeth. Centuries later, John saw elements of each of these animals in the form of the beast with ten horns and seven heads.

Daniel's vision of four successive kingdoms represented by different animals (Daniel 7) echoes the elements of Nebuchadnezzar's statue in chapter 2. There, the gold, silver, bronze and iron represented four successive kingdoms, and during the days of the last kingdom God would set up a kingdom that would never be destroyed. A popular view among commentators is that the four successive kingdoms refer to the Babylonian, Medo-Persian, Greek and Roman empires respectively.

We can therefore safely interpret the beast as the Roman Empire. This is further affirmed in chapter 17 of Revelation when the angel explains to John the identity of the beast: 'The seven heads are seven hills on which the woman sits. They are also seven kings. Five have fallen, one is, the other has not yet come' (Revelation 17:9-10).

Rome was universally known as the city of the seven hills, but here the imagery of the seven heads not only identifies the seven hills but also the seven kings, of which the sixth was ruling at the time of John. If we begin by identifying the first Roman Emperor as Julius Caesar, as was the custom of ancient historians like Suetonius and Josephus, then the sixth king was Nero. You can see this from the following table of Roman Emperors:

| | |
|---|---|
| Julius Caesar | BC49 – 44 |
| Augustus | BC27– AD14 |
| Tiberius | AD14 – 37 |
| Caligula | AD37 – 41 |
| Claudius | AD41 – 54 |
| Nero | AD54 – 68 |

Nero was a particularly wicked and profane emperor. His cruelty was not confined to the persecution of Christians, for he had members of his own family brutally murdered, including his wife, who was violently kicked to death. In AD 64 Nero unleashed a ferocious persecution against Christians, whom he blamed for starting a fire which had destroyed large parts of Rome that year.

Among the terrible atrocities committed against the Christian community, believers were sewn up in skins of wild animals for Nero's hunting dogs to savage; they were placed in sacks full of stones and thrown into the River Tiber; they were coated in pitch and set alight to be used as human torches in the palace gardens – the original 'Roman candles'.

The rise of the Caesars was accompanied by the cult of deifying the emperor and worshipping him. We know from contemporary Greek literature that during Nero's reign, a certain day each year was designated as Emperor's Day. The only occurrence of Emperor's

Day in the New Testament is Revelation 1:10. The translators have used the phrase 'Lord's Day' to interpret the Greek, but the term 'Emperor's Day' is an accurate and equally valid translation.

On this day each citizen had to offer a pinch of incense to the divine emperor and declare, 'Caesar is lord'. The citizen was then given a certificate allowing him freedom to trade and, in addition, to worship as many lesser gods as he chose, including Jesus Christ. This practice was overwhelmingly rejected by the Christian community, who pledged their first allegiance to Jesus Christ alone. They thus rejected the mark of the beast.

John states that the mark of the beast is also a number – 666. In Bible numerology, six is the number of man; for example, man was created on the sixth day. The number six also falls short of the number seven which, in biblical terms, indicates divinity and perfection. There are for example, seven lamps blazing before God's throne, representing the seven spirits of God (Revelation 4:5).

John invites anyone who has insight to calculate the number of the beast. To understand this you need to know that in the Hebrew, Greek and Latin languages, letters not only represented sounds, as they do in the English language. Each letter also had a *numerical* value. When the numerical values of the letters were added together it gave a number that could be used to conceal a name or pose as a riddle for the reader to solve.

Graffiti in Pompeii reveals the statement, 'I love the girl whose number is 545'. Obviously the girl herself would recognise the numerical value of her name and other readers would have fun solving the puzzle. This practice was known as *gematria* and it is this exercise that John invites his readers to engage in.

The Hebrew spelling of Nero's name was *Nrwn Qsr*, pronounced *Neron Kaiser*. Since each of the letters has a numerical value, the number of Nero's full name is able to be calculated. The numerical values of each letter are as follows:

| | |
|---|---|
| N | 50 |
| r | 200 |
| w | 6 |
| n | 50 |
| Q | 100 |
| s | 60 |
| r | 200 |
| **Total** | **666** |

According to Richard Bauckham, Professor of New Testament studies at the University of St. Andrews, 'The *gematria* does not merely assert that Nero is the beast: it demonstrates that he is'.[2] We can safely conclude that the mark of the Beast, 666, refers to allegiance to the Emperor Nero, who himself was the sixth emperor to claim divinity. So you need not worry about receiving the mark yourself!

## The man of lawlessness

We noted in our investigation of the millennium that the sole reference to a 1000-year reign of Christ in Scripture occurs in Revelation 20. Similarly, the expression 'man of lawlessness' is found in only one portion of Scripture. Paul refers to this person in his second epistle to the Thessalonians where the first twelve verses of chapter two read as follows:

> *Concerning the coming of our Lord Jesus Christ and our being gathered to Him, we ask you, brothers, not to become easily unsettled or alarmed by some prophecy, report or letter supposed to have come from us, saying that the day of the Lord has already come. Don't let anyone deceive you in any way, for that day will not come until the rebellion occurs and the **man of lawlessness** is revealed, the man doomed to destruction. He will oppose and will exalt himself over everything that is called God or is worshipped, so that he sets himself up in God's temple, proclaiming himself to be God.*
>
> *Don't you remember that when I was with you I used to tell you these things? And now you know what is holding him back, so that he may be revealed at the proper time. For the secret power of lawlessness is already at work; but the one who now holds it back will continue to do so till he is taken out of the way. And then **the lawless one** will be revealed, whom the Lord Jesus will overthrow with the breath of his mouth and destroy by the splendour of his coming. The coming of **the lawless one** will be in accordance with the work of Satan displayed in all kinds of counterfeit miracles, signs and wonders, and in every sort of evil that deceives those who are perishing. They perish because they refused to love the truth and so be saved. For this reason God sends them a powerful delusion so that they will believe the lie and so that all will be condemned who have not believed the truth but have delighted in wickedness.*

It is clear from this passage that Paul had already spoken at length to the Thessalonian believers about coming events and the man of lawlessness while he was living among them. Our own understanding of this passage is difficult since we have no record of what Paul had actually said to them. Instead of repeating it he simply states, 'Don't you remember that when I was with you I used to tell you these things?' (2 Thessalonians 2:5).

As a result, this passage does little to help us know what Paul understood concerning the man of lawlessness. His thinking is abbreviated and he highlights only particular concerns that the Thessalonians clearly understood in the context of his previous comprehensive discussions with them. So what was evident to the church in Thessalonica in this letter from Paul is not so evident to us.

Because readers in subsequent times lack the knowledge of this context, Bible commentators describe this passage as one of the most difficult to understand of any of Paul's writings. Typical is the great Bible commentator Augustine in the 4th century who said candidly: 'I frankly confess I do not know what he means'.[3]

During the 16th century Reformation, when much biblical truth was recovered, some students of the Scriptures proposed that the man of lawlessness referred to the Papacy. Although not so popular today, this view highlights how easy it is to draw bizarre conclusions from a difficult passage of Scripture.

More recently Dr. Leon Morris, a highly-regarded evangelical commentator, has said, 'This passage is probably the most obscure and difficult in the whole of the Pauline writings and the many gaps in our knowledge have given rise to extravagant speculations'.[4]

We believe therefore it is unwise to be dogmatic about any interpretation of the passage and certainly foolish to base any end-times teaching on it. Instead we are going to suggest two possible ways of understanding the man of lawlessness while humbly agreeing with some of the best commentators that no one knows for sure.

### A partial preterist interpretation

We must first consider the possibility that when Paul talks about the 'day of the Lord' here he may not be referring to the end of the world. Indeed, if the end of the world had arrived, would the believers in Thessalonica have required a letter from Paul to inform them of the fact? However, the church at Thessalonica had become unsettled by some purported 'prophecy, report or letter' alleged to have come from Paul. Part of his reason for writing 2 Thessalonians was to assure them that rumours of such a letter or prophecy from him were untrue.

Paul begins his addressing of the issue of the rumours with the phrase, 'Concerning the coming of our Lord Jesus Christ' (2 Thessalonians 2:1). The word for 'coming' is *parousia* which, as we have seen, basically means 'presence'. It is not used exclusively of Christ's second coming; it can refer also to his first coming, and even the physical 'presence' of Paul and Titus, amongst others. Since then, *parousia*, does not necessarily refer to Christ's second coming we should determine the likely meaning of the word by its context.

Similarly, the phrase 'the day of the Lord' often refers to the second coming of Jesus, when he will judge his enemies and reward those who have been faithful. But the phrase often has a broader application to special times of divine judgment in the course of history.

Isaiah, prophesying God's judgment on Babylon in Chapter 13 describes that judgment in verse 6 as 'the day of the Lord'. That day clearly did not bring about the end of the world but it did bring about the termination of the Babylonian Empire.

Although we can be sure that there will be a future *parousia* of Christ, and an accompanying 'day of the Lord' when he will judge all peoples, we cannot assume that every usage of these two phrases refers to Christ's second coming.

2 Thessalonians is one of Paul's earlier epistles, written around AD 51-52. The events described by Jesus in Matthew 24 concerning the destruction of the temple were still future for Paul and his readers. Paul's reference to near-future events in this passage could well have their fulfilment in the siege of Jerusalem in AD 66-70 and its subsequent destruction.

The multiple applications of the words *parousia* and the 'day of the Lord' may cause unease and concern to some Christians, especially those who have been taught that both terms refer exclusively to the second coming of Christ. Such concern is unwarranted. Paul often uses a single word to express more than one meaning. Take for example, his use of the word 'flesh' Greek *sarx*. This word has numerous meanings for Paul and its meaning in a particular passage must be gleaned from its context. He uses 'flesh' to mean mortal body (Galatians 2:20), human descent (Romans 1:3), mankind in general (Romans 3:20), Christ's human nature (Colossians 1:22), and weak human nature (Romans 8:3). Just as there are nuances in Paul's understanding of 'flesh', so we should be aware of the variety of meanings he attributes to other terms like *parousia* and the 'day of the Lord'.

To allay the concerns and uncertainties of the Thessalonians Paul reminded them that the 'day of the Lord' would not come until two things had occurred. These events were the 'apostasy' (NIV 'the rebellion') and the revealing of 'the man of lawlessness'. It is conceivable that the apostasy, or falling away from the faith, that Paul predicts equates with Jesus' prediction in Matthew 24 that before the destruction of the temple many would turn away from the faith and the love of most would grow cold.

Although Paul stated that the man of lawlessness was yet to be revealed, he identified him as a contemporary figure, who at that time was being held back. Among others, N.T. Wright identifies a credible candidate for the man of lawlessness in the person of the Roman Emperor.[5] A decade before Paul's letter, the Emperor Caligula had ordered a large statue of himself to be placed in the temple at Jerusalem. This order was adamantly rejected by the Jewish authorities, and Caligula was murdered early in AD 41, resulting in a temporary respite for the Jewish authorities, who were expecting the imposition of the Emperor's will by force.

Caligula was replaced as Emperor by Claudius, who reigned from AD 41-54. And Claudius was followed by Nero, who reigned from AD 54-68. Nero instigated a severe persecution against the followers of Christ. Like many other Emperors, he suffered from delusions of grandeur and promoted the cult of the Emperor's divinity. The Christians' confession 'Jesus is Lord' ran completely counter to the Emperor's demand that everyone must declare that 'Caesar is Lord'.

Nero, during his time as a rising power on the Roman political scene, was not able to publicly exert his evil influence while the Emperor Claudius was still in power. Interestingly, the name Claudius is derived from the Latin word *claudere* which means 'to shut or restrain'. Once Claudius had died, the restraint on Nero's evil intentions was removed, allowing him to conduct his pernicious campaign against Christians without hindrance. Could Claudius, then, be the one 'holding him [the man of lawlessness] back'?

One thing is clear, when Paul wrote to the Thessalonians, the revealing of the man of lawlessness was expected in the near future.

So if the apostasy and the appearing of the man of lawlessness had their fulfilment in these events leading up to the destruction of the temple of Jerusalem in AD 70, they will not have a future fulfilment for people living today.

This perspective accords with Jesus' own description of life before his second coming when people will still be marrying and giving in marriage right up to the point of his return. Rather than his coming being preceded by cataclysmic events and signs to be observed, everyday life, he said, would carry on as normal.

Just as Paul did not want the Thessalonian church to be unsettled or alarmed by rumours and misunderstandings, so in our day Jesus Christ wants us, his church, to be established in faith and hope about our future and not to be deflected from our primary love and obedience by futile speculation about Scripture passages that causes alarm to God's people rather than inspiring them to fruitful life and service.

## A futurist interpretation

If we take Paul's references to the *parousia* and the 'day of the Lord' as referring to the return of Christ, then the passage is placed firmly in the future! In this case the man of lawlessness could be referring to an actual personality who will emerge some time just before the return of Christ and stand in opposition to his people and his purpose.

Such an interpretation is normally associated with the dispensationalist view that the man of lawlessness will emerge between the rapture of the church and the return of Christ, literally installing himself in a rebuilt temple in Jerusalem and triggering the great tribulation.

But we suggest that this need not be the case. There is a long history of non-dispensational teaching on this passage that is futurist nonetheless. Such teaching simply advocates a satanically-driven personality gaining prominence in the world and heading up severe persecution of believers before the return of Christ. History has thrown up numerous anti-Christian characters like this from time to time, from Nero and Domitian in the 1st Century to Hitler, Stalin or Mao Tse-tung in the 20th century. It would not be unreasonable to view Paul's man of lawlessness in the same light.

In interpreting the passage in this way there is no need to add the trappings of dispensationalism. There is no hint of a raptured church, seven-year interlude, tribulation or subsequent return of

Christ. Having said this, there remain some specific issues of difficulty in the passage that we must address:

## The falling away

Verse 3 refers to a 'falling away' (KJV) or 'rebellion' (NIV) occurring before 'that day'. The word is *apostasia,* from which we get the word 'apostasy'. Futurists have commonly claimed that just before the second coming there will be a massive backsliding of believers from following Christ. They have combined this with other scriptures, like Jesus' words that 'the love of most will grow cold' (Matthew 24:12), to support the idea that however much the church grows, Jesus will actually return for a beleaguered remnant rather than a glorious bride.

But is that what Paul is really suggesting here? The expression carries more of the idea of rebellion than of falling away, and 'rebellion' is how virtually every modern translation renders it. Commentators are divided over who it applies to. It is quite possible that Paul is simply referring to the increasing hostility of those who reject Christ before he comes.

What is contrary to our great hope is the idea that Jesus will return for a church that has largely deserted him. This is wholly inconsistent with our conviction that the glorious gospel will triumph in every nation, winning men and women to Christ in large numbers.

## The temple

What do we make of Paul's statement in verse 4 that the man of lawlessness will 'oppose and exalt himself above every so-called object of worship, so that he takes his seat in the temple of God, displaying himself as being God'…? Is this proof of a rebuilt temple in Jerusalem?

The word Paul uses for 'temple' is not the Greek *hieron* normally used for the physical structure of the temple. Instead Paul uses *naos,* meaning the inner sanctuary. This is the word Paul also uses when describing believers as the temple of God in, for instance, 1 Corinthians 3:16-17: 'Don't you know that you yourselves are God's temple and that God's Spirit dwells in your midst? If anyone destroys God's temple, God will destroy that person; for God's temple is sacred, and you together are that temple'.

1 Corinthians 6:19 and 2 Corinthians 6:16 similarly use *naos* in referring to believers. In Ephesians 2:21 Paul is equally consistent in

describing God's people as a spiritual house: 'in him the whole building is joined together and rises to become a holy temple [naos] in the Lord. And in him you too are being built together to become a dwelling in which God lives by his Spirit.'

It is quite possible, therefore, that Paul has the man of lawlessness 'seated in the temple' in a metaphorical sense. In other words he would be given position in the hearts and lives of men and women, a place intended for God alone.

### The restrainer

The reference to 'the restrainer', or 'the one holding him back', in verses 6-7 has long been a puzzle to Bible students. Many ideas have been proposed as to the identity of this restrainer including the church, the Holy Spirit, law and order and the archangel Michael. No-one can be sure on this matter and speculating on the subject adds nothing to our faith or expectation for the future.

### Conclusion

In closing this chapter we reiterate that no-one knows for certain what Paul was referring to in this difficult passage and we should therefore view any proposals with caution. What we can be sure of is that the passage does not support the dispensational ideas of a seven-year tribulation period separated by a two-stage return of Christ and preceded by the mass falling away of the church. We are confident of better prospects than that!

### End notes

1.  *Vine's Dictionary of New Testament Words*
2.  Bauckham, *The Climax of Prophecy*, p 389
3.  St Augustine, *The City of God*, Book XX, ch.19
4.  Dr Leon Morris, *Tyndale New Testament Commentary: 1 and 2 Thessalonians,* 2nd ed. IVP, 1985, p 125
5.  N T Wright, *Paul for Everyone: Galatians and Thessalonians* SPCK, p 148

# Chapter 11

# The Israel Question

There is a scene in the film *The Hurt Locker* where US bomb disposal expert William James is attempting to defuse a nasty device hidden just below the surface of a Baghdad road. As he pulls on the wire attached to the detonator, from out of the ground appears a network of around seven other devices all interconnected. He stands in the middle of this lethal web of bombs, knowing that his job is not done until he has defused them all.

It is a reminder of the task we face with dispensationalism – you grasp one issue only to find it is connected to a host of others just as volatile. Neither are you safe until every one of them has been tackled, and perhaps the most explosive of all is the subject of Israel.

The place of Israel in the purpose of God is at the heart of our examination of the return of Christ. It is made all the more difficult by the strong emotions generated whenever the subject of the Jewish people is mentioned. Dispensationalism asserts that the Jews have an identity and destiny distinct from that of the church. This belief forms an integral part of their overall scheme that has been woven together using a wide variety of scriptures. In dispensationalist circles unambiguous support for the modern state of Israel is viewed as the duty of every believer. The 'pro-Israel' stance taken by many in Christian media and church circles is so vigorous that you almost fear to consider any other position. Clearly we are walking on eggshells!

Dispensationalists are quick to point out the failings of the church toward the Jewish people over the centuries, citing the Crusades, historic persecution of Jews, the Holocaust and the rise in anti-Semitism. Before we proceed, therefore, we need to state that anti-Semitism cannot be justified in any shape or form. It is an evil that has no place in the church. God loves the Jewish people and has a plan for their salvation.

To question whether the Jewish nation enjoys a divine calling is, however, not anti-Semitic, and the fear of being labelled as such should not hinder healthy debate. It is wrong for dispensationalists to claim that any other biblical position than theirs is somehow anti-Semitic in nature.

## Two issues – the people and the land

Much of the debate over the Jewish people today is centred on the nation of Israel and the respective rights of Israelis and Palestinians. The creation of the modern state of Israel in 1948 and the re-capturing of Jerusalem by Israeli forces in the 1967 Seven Day War are seen by dispensationalists as the fulfilment of Old Covenant promises to Abraham and the positioning of the Jewish people to fulfil a future role in the purposes of God.

Support for the return of the Jewish people to Palestine in order to establish their own nation with Jerusalem as its capital is referred to as Zionism. With its beginnings in the 19th century, it grew into a political movement that continues to flourish today in defence of its original ideals.

Christian Zionism is a particular branch of Zionism that asserts the *divine* right of the Jews to the land that forms the nation of Israel. We should point out that dispensationalists are not the only Christian Zionists. Pre-millennialists generally would fall into this category, enjoying a long and more respectable tradition of supporting the Zionist cause. One of the foremost of these today is UK Bible teacher David Pawson. Although pre-millennialists like Pawson try to distance themselves from their dispensationalist cousins, the arguments used to support the Zionist cause are essentially the same.[1] While acknowledging the difference between the two, we will continue to refer to dispensationalism for the sake of simplicity.

A right to the land is of course conditional upon accepting that the Jews are a special and distinct people in the first place. We are therefore faced with two interconnected questions:

- Are the Jews a special people of God?
- Do the Jews have a divine right to the Promised Land?

We are going to examine these questions using our two interpretive lenses of covenant and kingdom. Dispensationalists assert that Jews are still God's chosen people based on the continued reality of God's *covenant* promises to Abraham. They also claim that the future *kingdom* of God will be Jewish in nature, with Christ ruling personally from Jerusalem for 1000 years.

## Israel and the New Covenant

The issue of covenant is central to our understanding of the place of Israel because biblical covenant is the only basis on which any people may claim to be the people of God.

We noted in chapter 3 that God binds himself to man in a secure relationship through covenant, summarised in Scripture by the often repeated expression, 'They will be my people and I will be their God'. The successive covenants presented in Scripture represent the unfolding of a single purpose of God for the redemption and restoration of humanity. The issue before us is this: if Israel is to be regarded as a people of God today, on which covenant is such a relationship based?

The early dispensational position was that God had granted the Jewish people a permanent status as 'God's ancient people' within the 'dispensation of promise' which ran from Abraham to Moses. The promises of God to Abraham concerning Israel, her national borders and role in the world would be unconditional and permanent.

Early dispensationalists viewed the church as a Gentile domain in which Israel's unique identity could never properly fit. They believed that the church age would culminate in failure with a mass falling away ending in the rapture. Israel would return once more to centre stage as God's primary instrument in the world.

Early dispensationalists recognised the covenants of God; indeed they acknowledged that the Jews became God's people on the basis of the Abrahamic covenant. But the covenants were always seen as secondary to the dispensational structure of Scripture. This created all kinds of theological problems for dispensationalists – problems that were eventually acknowledged and which prompted modification of dispensationalist doctrine.

Progressive dispensationalists place more emphasise on the New Covenant, but insist that God has reserved a special place within it for the Jewish people. But can such a position be defended? We will take a closer look at how the Scriptures view the place of Israel within the New Covenant, to see if this is so. Let's return to the clearest statement in the Old Testament regarding the New

Covenant. This is an important scripture because it is also quoted in full by the writer to the Hebrews in chapter 10:

*The days are coming, declares the Lord, when I will make a new covenant with the people of Israel and with the people of Judah. It will not be like the covenant I made with their ancestors when I took them by the hand to lead them out of Egypt, because they broke my covenant, though I was a husband to them, declares the Lord. This is the covenant I will make with the people of Israel after that time, declares the Lord. I will put my law in their minds and write it on their hearts. I will be their God, and they will be my people. No longer will they teach their neighbour, or say to one another, 'know the Lord,' because they will all know me, from the least of them to the greatest, declares the Lord. For I will forgive their wickedness and will remember their sins no more. (Jeremiah 31:31-34)*

Two observations can be made from this passage. Firstly, the covenant Jeremiah is referring to is none other than the New Covenant in Christ. There simply is no other 'new' covenant to choose from. The 'New Covenant' he speaks of offers a new heart (verse 33), an internal ability to know God not based on the law (verse 34) and the forgiveness of sins (verse 34).

Some early dispensationalists tried to reason that there were two 'new covenants'. Later dispensationalists came to acknowledge that this could not be so but insisted that Israel would maintain a distinct place within the New Covenant none the less.

Secondly, the people to whom God is promising this New Covenant through Jeremiah are his Old Covenant people, the Jewish nation. The startling conclusion we must come to is that the New Covenant in Christ was made for and offered to the Jewish people. The fact that the Gentile world was also in view in the terms of the New Covenant was secondary at this point in time. God wanted his people Israel to know that they had a future and that there was an antidote to their failure to keep the law of Moses; that future lay in the New Covenant and the revolutionary changes it would bring.

Ezekiel also referred to the New Covenant when God spoke of a restored relationship with Israel:

*I will make a covenant of peace with them; it will be an everlasting covenant. I will establish them and increase their numbers, and I will put my sanctuary among them forever. (Ezekiel 37:26)*

Finally, Isaiah reveals that this New Covenant would be centred on and secured by a promised Messiah (in Hebrew *Mashiach*). This anointed one would come as a suffering servant to ransom his people from their sins (see especially Isaiah 42:1-4, 49:1-7, 52:13-53:12).

God speaks of the New Covenant as the next step for the Jews in their relationship with him, their future hope. It was not a second-best option to any of the former covenants, but everything the Jewish people could wish for in order to continue in God's purpose. The early church initially consisted of Jews who had embraced this very revelation.

The introduction of this New Covenant has far-reaching effects on the way everyone, both Jew and Gentile, relate to God. What was once the sole privilege of the Jewish people becomes available to Gentiles too – and on the same terms. The apostle Paul referred to this coming together of Jews and Gentiles as 'the mystery' revealed to him in his day that had not been understood in former times. Let's look more closely at what he has to say in his letter to the Ephesians:

> *Therefore, remember that formerly you who are Gentiles by birth and called 'uncircumcised' by those who call themselves 'the circumcision' (which is done in the body by human hands) – remember that at that time you were separate from Christ, excluded from citizenship in Israel and foreigners to the covenants of the promise, without hope and without God in the world.* (Ephesians 2:11-12)

Here Paul clarifies that, before they received the gospel, the Gentiles were alienated from all that Israel enjoyed through covenant relationship with God. This, he says, is synonymous with being 'separated from Christ'. He goes on:

> *But now in Christ Jesus you who once were far away have been brought near by the blood of Christ. For he himself is our peace, who has made the two groups one and has destroyed the barrier, the dividing wall of hostility, by setting aside in his flesh the law with its commands and regulations. His purpose was to create in himself one new man out of the two, thus making peace, and in one body to reconcile both of them to God through the cross, by which he put to death their hostility. He came and preached peace to you who were far away and peace to those who were near. For through him we both have access to the Father by one Spirit.* (Ephesians 2:13-18)

Believing Gentiles, Paul says, are brought into the actual continuation of God's purpose through Israel. The result is 'one new man', that is, one people – not two! The intended result is unity and peace between Jew and Gentile through union in Christ. Paul continues, addressing the largely Gentile believers in Ephesus:

> *Consequently, you are no longer foreigners and strangers, but fellow citizens with God's people and also members of his household, built on the foundation of the apostles and prophets, with Christ Jesus himself as the chief cornerstone. In him the whole building is joined together and rises to become a holy temple in the Lord. And in him you too are being built together to become a dwelling in which God lives by his Spirit.* (Ephesians 2:19-22)

Paul describes Gentile believers as fully-fledged 'fellow citizens' with believing Jews. This people are none other than the church he has created, his called-out ones, both Jews and Gentiles. So the church is in fact the continuation of Israel. This is different from the teaching known as *replacement theology*, in which the church replaces Israel. The church *is* Israel in its New Covenant form.

It is not so much that converted Jews must join the Gentiles in their covenant with God, but that the Gentiles become part of Israel in the covenant God has provided for both. To allay any remaining doubt over the matter, Paul continues by summing up the position of the Gentiles in the purpose of God:

> *For this reason, I, Paul, the prisoner of Christ Jesus for the sake of you Gentiles –*
> *Surely you have heard about the administration of God's grace that was given to me for you, that is, the mystery made known to me by revelation, as I have already written briefly. In reading this, then, you will be able to understand my insight into the mystery of Christ, which was not made known to people in other generations as it has now been revealed by the Spirit to God's holy apostles and prophets. This mystery is that through the gospel the Gentiles are heirs together with Israel, members together of one body, and sharers together in the promise in Christ Jesus.* (Ephesians 3:1-6)

Paul leaves no option open for anything but one people of God. In the New Covenant there is simply the continuation of his one *ekklesia*. The church is not a Gentile domain, such that the Jewish people should feel the need to perpetuate a distinct identity of their own. It is simply the continuation of the one people of God in the earth, comprising believing Jews and Gentiles but founded now on infinitely better promises. As O. Palmer Robertson puts it:

> He (Jesus) is not, as some suppose, replacing Israel with the church. But he is reconstituting Israel in a way that makes it suitable for the ministry of the New Covenant. From this point on, it is not that the church takes the place of Israel, but that a renewed Israel of God is being formed by the shaping of the church. This kingdom will reach beyond the limits of the Israel of the Old Covenant.[2]

In line with this, Peter takes Old Testament descriptions applied originally to the people of the Old Covenant and unashamedly applies them to those who have embraced the New Covenant and have been sprinkled by the blood of Christ. He regards the Christian community, wherever they may exist throughout the world, as 'a chosen people, a royal priesthood, a holy nation, a people belonging to God'. Sure, there was a time when Gentiles were not considered a people and had not received mercy, but the work of Christ has resulted in their now being known as *the* people of God, recipients of divine mercy (1 Peter 2:10). Note that they are not '*a* people of God' but '*the* people of God'.

The work of Jesus on the cross is so thorough and far-reaching in producing one people of God that the writer to the Hebrews completely identifies believers in Christ as being the fulfilment of Old Testament prophetic imagery. The church of Jesus Christ, whose members' names are written in heaven, is now recognised to be Mount Zion, the place where God dwells. In addition, the terms 'city of the living God' and the 'heavenly Jerusalem' become proper descriptions of the one people of God that has been produced by Christ, his covenant and his kingdom (Hebrews 12:22-24).

Furthermore, Paul sees the community of faith as one 'olive tree'. Gentiles with a faith in Christ have been grafted into the community of God, whereas Jews who have rejected Christ have been, according to Paul, 'broken off'. This is not the end of the story however, for God is able to graft Jews in again as they respond in faith to their Messiah, resulting in one glorious olive tree (Romans 11:17-24).

The emphasis of the New Testament is unequivocal. God has chosen for himself one people, the community of believers in Christ, represented by the imagery of one olive tree, one temple (Ephesians 2:19-22), one body (1 Corinthians 12:12) and one bride (Revelation 21:2), composed of people from every tribe, language, people and nation (Revelation 5:9-10). Here there is 'neither Jew nor Greek' (Galatians 3:26-27), it is 'one' of everything, not two! [3]

N. T. Wright ably explains how the New Covenant has brought about this redefinition of 'Israel':

> Those who now belonged to Jesus' people were not identical with ethnic Israel, since Israel's history had reached its intended fulfilment; they claimed to be the continuation of Israel in a new situation, able to draw freely on Israel-images to express their self-identity, able to read Israel's scriptures (through the lens of Messiah and Spirit) and apply them to their own life. They were thrust out by that claim, and that reading, to fulfil Israel's vocation on behalf of the world. [4]

The destiny of the Jewish people is now found in that covenant. There can never be any going back to the Old Covenant shadows and forms when we have the New Covenant reality. This being so, it is unthinkable that what God has brought together as one new man in Christ should subsequently be peeled apart again on the basis of ethnicity, so that the nation of Israel becomes the primary channel of God's blessing in the world, leaving the church to one side.

The claim by modern dispensationalists that Israel has a special place within the New Covenant is hard to square with the evidence. So, they claim, believing Jews are a remnant of faith within a presently unbelieving nation, and with the mass conversion of Jews 'the nation' itself will resume its former position in readiness to fulfil an end-time dispensational mandate.

The problem with this neat idea, however, is that it continues to mangle our understanding of the New Covenant. If the qualification for such an end-time Jewish purpose is found within the New Covenant, where in Scripture do we find it? We search in vain, for nothing is offered to support it; in fact just the opposite. Everything we have observed highlights the fact that God only has one people.

In addition, if there were indeed an end-time purpose within the terms of the New Covenant for the citizens of the geographical land of Israel, it would have to be open to Gentile converts on the same New Covenant terms as to the Jews, rather than on the basis of ethnicity. But nothing of the sort is even hinted at.

Anything less than the revelation of God's gracious provision that we have outlined undermines the supremacy of the work that Christ accomplished at the cross, in reconciling the world to himself in one body.

## Israel and the Kingdom of God

So much for Israel and the covenant! Now let's look at Israel in relation to the kingdom of God. The kingdom of God is the most central and important theme of the Bible. As John Bright puts it:

> The Bible is one book. Had we to give that book a title, we might with justice call it 'the book of the coming of the kingdom of God.[5]

Scripture presents us with an unfolding picture of the kingdom, from God the King creating the universe to man's rebellion and redemption, right through to the universe being reconciled once more to its Creator.

In Genesis 12 God revealed himself to Abram, made certain promises to him and entered into covenant relationship with him. This point marked a division in the human race because, from here on, all God's redemptive purposes were expressed through Abram and his descendants.

From Abraham's descendants come the people of Israel, whom God redeemed from slavery in Egypt. At Mount Sinai they were described for the first time as a nation with a unique purpose:

> *Now if you obey me fully and keep my covenant, then out of all nations you will be my treasured possession. Although the whole earth is mine, you will be for me a kingdom of priests and a holy nation.* (Exodus 19:5-6)

Here was God expressing his kingdom – his rule – in a specific people, the Jewish nation. This manifestation of the kingdom in Israel reached its climax in the reign of King David and the establishing of Jerusalem as the capital city. David occupied a special place in God's plan for Israel. God said of him, 'I have found David son of Jesse, a man after my own heart; he will do everything I want him to do' (Acts 13:22). And again, 'David served God's purpose in his generation' (Acts 13:36).

So closely was David's throne allied with God's throne that the distinction became blurred. The two were synonymous. Jerusalem was the city of the Great King. It was also where the ark of God rested. Much prophetic expectation of the Messiah, therefore, was expressed in terms of David's kingdom and David's throne:

> You said, 'I have made a covenant with my chosen one, I have sworn to David my servant, I will establish your line forever and make your throne firm through all generations'. (Psalm 89:3-4)
>
> For to us a child is born, to us a son is given, and the government will be on his shoulders. And he will be called Wonderful Counsellor, Mighty God, Everlasting Father, Prince of Peace. Of the greatness of his government and peace there will be no end. He will reign on David's throne and over his kingdom, establishing and upholding it with justice and righteousness from that time on and forever. (Isaiah 9:6-7)
>
> A shoot will come up from the stump of Jesse; (David's father), from his roots a branch will bear fruit. (Isaiah 11:1)

Solomon inherited the throne of David, but he lacked the integrity of his father and the nation of Israel began its painful descent into division, backsliding and ultimately judgment. No further advancement of the kingdom of God can be discerned until John the Baptist appeared on the scene proclaiming, 'Prepare the way of the Lord', for the King himself was about to appear. In the person of Jesus of Nazareth, God's kingdom arrived in bodily form.

The kingdom of God is absolutely central to Jesus' life, teaching and mission. He made his appearance as Israel's king, no less. He came to his own people as their Messiah, the one from David's line who would sit on David's throne. Jesus appeared in order to fulfil the prophetic scriptures we have noted.

Yet he brought radical challenge to Jewish national expectations. Instead of endorsing Israel's divine right to God's kingdom, Jesus upset this idea. In Matthew 21 he related the parable of a vineyard to his Jewish listeners. A landowner rents a vineyard out to tenants. But when harvest time arrives, instead of bringing fruit to the owner, the tenants rebel, killing the servants sent on his behalf. Finally the landowner sends his son, whom they shamefully murder. Jesus continued:

> Therefore when the owner of the vineyard comes what will he do to those tenants? 'He will bring those wretches to a wretched end', they replied, 'and he will rent the vineyard to other tenants, who will give him his share of the crop at harvest time'. (Matthew 21:40-41)

Then, applying this story directly to his Jewish listeners, Jesus quoted Psalm 118:22-23:

> *The stone the builders rejected has become the cornerstone; the Lord has done this and it is marvellous in our eyes.*

He himself was that stone. The Jewish leaders would reject him, but that would not halt God's purpose to bestow upon him the highest honour as King. Finally Jesus made one of the clearest and most profound statements about the kingdom of God. To the Jews he said:

> *Therefore I tell you that the kingdom of God will be taken away from you and given to a people who will produce its fruit.* (Matthew 21:43)

An inheritance is transferred from one people to another, from the Jewish nation to the church of Jesus Christ comprising believing Jews and Gentiles. A New Covenant would require a New Covenant people to express God's kingdom. Dispensationalists find this difficult to accept. They argue that Jesus was only speaking to the Jewish rulers, not to the nation. But the kingdom of God was never given to the Jewish leaders alone in the first place but to the nation. In addressing the leaders Jesus was addressing the whole nation that they represented and explicitly said that the kingdom would be given to a 'people', not just a leadership.

Or they argue that the sentence Jesus pronounced was applied for a time, until the kingdom would be restored again to Israel. But the whole weight of Scripture is against such an idea. Peter writing to believers scattered throughout the Roman Empire takes the word of God to Israel at Mount Sinai and ascribes it now to *all believers*:

> *But you are a chosen people, a royal priesthood, a holy nation, God's special possession, that you may declare the praises of him who called you out of darkness into his wonderful light.* (1 Peter 2:9-10)

The kingdom the New Testament writers speak about is not ethnic, political or geographic. It has its roots in a right relationship with God. Paul said, 'For the kingdom of God is not a matter of eating and drinking, but of righteousness, peace and joy in the Holy Spirit' (Romans 14:17). And it goes on to express itself in supernatural and moral dimensions that encompass every area of life.

Again Paul says, 'For the kingdom of God is not a matter of talk but of power' (1 Corinthians 4:20). Our ability to operate in the power of the Spirit is evidence of the continuing presence of the kingdom of God. Healing the sick and casting out demons are signs of the kingdom coming in power, as it did through Jesus. This is the church's privilege and prerogative.

All of this is a far cry from the dispensationalist view that the nation of Israel is still God's kingdom people, a view that has produced some definitions of the kingdom that are novel, to say the least.

Early dispensationalists claimed, as we have seen, that there is not one kingdom of God but two! Since the church is God's *spiritual* people, they claimed, there is a secret and inward aspect of the kingdom of God expressed in the church. But Israel remains God's earthly people, and for her there will be nothing less than an earthly future aspect to the kingdom of God. This is the millennial kingdom that they reckon will be set up when Christ occupies his throne in a rebuilt temple in Jerusalem and reigns there for one thousand years.

As with other aspects of dispensational doctrine, this dualistic view of the kingdom became increasingly untenable and recent dispensationalists have concluded that the millennial kingdom could not really be a distinct kingdom. Instead they claim it must be a future stage of the one kingdom of God.

The following diagrams will hopefully make the various views clearer:

## *Comparative views of Israel today*
### Classical dispensationalism

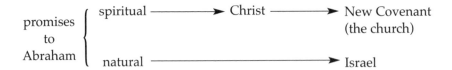

Classic dispensationalists proposed that God's promises to Abraham fell into two categories: the 'spiritual' promises were for the church and the 'natural' promises for the nation of Israel. Therefore today the New Covenant is viewed as 'for the church' but natural Israel is still governed by promises made under the Abrahamic covenant. This belief still carries popular support today.

## Progressive dispensationalism

promises to Abraham { spiritual / natural } → Christ → New Covenant { spiritual (The church) / natural (Israel) }

Progressive dispensationalists, realising the flaws in the classic position, proposed instead that the Jewish people have a special place reserved for them within the New Covenant whereby the promises made to the nation of Israel in the Abrahamic covenant could find fulfilment today. The fundamental problem remains, however, in that the New Covenant speaks only of Jews and Gentiles being united as one on equal terms as God's people in Christ.

## A kingdom/covenant approach

promises to Abraham { spiritual / natural } → Christ → New Covenant { Jews and Gentiles are 'one new man' in Christ }

A kingdom/covenant position recognises that every Old Testament promise is inherited by Christ, 'the seed of Abraham' (Galatians 3:16). Every promise then finds fulfilment in the New Covenant where 'there is neither Jew nor Gentile' (Galatians 3:28). In Christ, all are Abraham's offspring (Galatians 3:29). There is no evidence for two separate peoples.

All agree that the kingdom of God will come in its fullness only at the return of Christ. At present we live in an overlap of the 'already' and the 'not yet'. We have tasted the powers of the age to come but we await the consummation of the kingdom at Christ's return. We must resist the idea that the kingdom as revealed by Jesus and inherited by the church will, in the future, revert to an Old Testament form of Jewish political kingdom.

Instead the picture the New Testament paints is of the kingdom of God filling the earth before Jesus comes back. A Jewish millennial kingdom could never adequately represent the glory of the kingdom of God that we have already been brought into through Christ. It would be a backward step.

Dispensationalists are increasingly struggling with the theological basis of their views. Progressive dispensationalism is an attempt to address these issues, but with limited results. In their book *Progressive Dispensationalism*, Bock and Blaising argue passionately that the future millennial blessing on the Jews will be entered by faith[6]. But the Scriptures they use to support this argument have nothing to do with a future millennial kingdom of Israel but are all about the blessing of the gospel of Christ. The hope of Israel of which Paul speaks so powerfully in Romans 9-11 is their salvation by faith in Christ – his consistent theme throughout the book of Romans.

## The question of the land

The arguments surrounding the political situation in the Middle East are complex and highly emotive and this tragic conflict remains no closer to a resolution than ever, demonstrating that there is no cut and dried solution. Our treatment of the issue of the land will be brief but for those who want a more in-depth analysis we strongly recommend Colin Chapman's book *Whose Promised Land?*

Tackling this subject has not been easy and it is doubtful that we will avoid raising the hackles of some who fear we are abandoning the Jewish people to their enemies. This is not our desire. Indeed, we affirm the right of the nation of Israel to exist in peace and with secure borders. Our case for stating this, however, is not religious or theological but legal and historical. Although the story of the formation of the modern state of Israel is tortuous, to say the least, we believe a strong case exists for its legitimacy and protection under international law.[7]

### Promises about the land

Having demonstrated that God has only 'one people', it should follow that no *divine* right to the land of Palestine can be claimed for the Jewish people today. But scriptural references to 'the land' provide dispensationalists with particular focus for their defence of the nation of Israel. They assert that promises made by God to the Jewish people concerning the land under the Abrahamic Covenant still hold good today as an eternal title deed. How do we respond to this claim?

We saw earlier that all the Old Testament covenants find their fulfilment in Christ. They then emerge reinterpreted by the New Covenant he inaugurated. Nothing remains untouched by Christ.

This includes the promises of God to Abraham. On three occasions the New Testament refers to the fulfilment of those promises but always in respect to Christ and the gospel, not to the issue of land ownership. Firstly under the inspiration of the Holy Spirit Zechariah proclaims that Christ will fulfil the promises of God to Abraham. He says Jesus' birth will bring:

> *salvation from our enemies and from all who hate us – to show mercy to our fathers and to remember his holy covenant, the oath he swore to our father Abraham to rescue us from the hand of our enemies, and to enable us to serve him without fear in holiness and righteousness before him all our days.* (Luke 1:73-74)

Secondly, Peter, after healing the crippled beggar, announces to his Jewish listeners that Christ fulfilled the Abrahamic covenant and they are heirs of that covenant because of the salvation brought through Christ:

> *And you are heirs of the prophets and of the covenant God made with your fathers. He said to Abraham, "Through your offspring all peoples on earth will be blessed." When God raised up his servant, he sent him first to you to bless you by turning each of you from your wicked ways.* (Acts 3:25)

Finally in his letter to the Galatians, Paul is at pains to emphasise that:

> *The promises were spoken to Abraham and to his seed. The Scripture does not say 'and to seeds', meaning many people, but 'and to your seed', meaning one person, who is Christ.* (Galatians 3:16)

He concludes his argument by declaring that 'If you belong to Christ, then you are Abraham's seed, and heirs according to promise' (Galatians 3:29). Paul didn't divide the Abrahamic promises into two categories, some for ethnic Israel and some for the church. He simply affirmed that everything is summed up in Christ. Abrahamic promises concerning the land take on a new dimension in the New Covenant as with every other promise. In Romans 4:13 we discover that the land Abraham was promised has expanded to embrace the whole world. In Hebrews 11:16, we read that the Patriarchs 'looked for a better country, that is, a heavenly one'. The promise of the land cannot be separated from other components of the Abrahamic covenant that are fulfilled in Christ.

## Predictions concerning the land

In addition to the *promises*, dispensationalists appeal to Old Testament *predictions* of a return by the people to their historic land which they claim have been fulfilled in the formation or the modern State of Israel. Let's look a little closer at some of the key scriptures used to support this idea.

*Jeremiah 32:37-40*

> *I will surely gather them from all the lands where I banish them in my furious anger and great wrath; I will bring them back to this place and let them live in safety. They will be my people, and I will be their God. I will give them singleness of heart and action, so that they will always fear me and that all will then go well for them and for their children after them. I will make an everlasting covenant with them: I will never stop doing good to them, and I will inspire them to fear me, so that they will never turn away from me.*

It is often pointed out that prophecies like this speak of a return of the people from exile preceding a spiritual awakening. Reasoning is applied to claim that as the awakening has not taken place yet, the passage must refer to the modern day re-gathering of the Jewish people. But again and again the original context of such passages was the immediate exile of the Israelites to Babylon and their subsequent return in order that God could inaugurate his New Covenant, which he did in Christ.

Ezekiel 37:15-28 is another example of a return from exile followed by spiritual renewal. But again this is tied to the introduction of the New Covenant, something that took place in Christ 2000 years ago. And here's another:

*Isaiah 11:11*

> *In that day the Lord will reach out his hand a second time to reclaim the surviving remnant of his people, from Assyria, from Lower Egypt, from Upper Egypt, from Cush, from Elam, from Babylonia, from Hamath and from the islands of the Mediterranean.*

Dispensationalists assert that Old Testament prophecies like this one speak of *two* returns from exile for the people of Israel and that the second return culminated in the formation of the modern State of Israel. They claim that the expression 'a second time' must refer to this latter-day re-gathering as distinct from the ones which occurred under Nehemiah and Ezra. But the explanation is found in verse 16:

> There will be a highway for the remnant of his people that is left from Assyria, as there was for Israel when they came up from Egypt.

In other words the first occasion was the deliverance of the people from Pharaoh under Moses and their occupation of the land of promise under Joshua. So the second is their return from exile in Assyria/Babylon. There is no room to read modern events into the passage.

### Zechariah 8:7-8

> This is what the Lord Almighty says: I will save my people from the countries of the east and the west. I will bring them back to live in Jerusalem; they will be my people, and I will be faithful and righteous to them as their God.

The context of these verses is a word of encouragement for the remnant who had returned from exile under Ezra the priest and who were rebuilding the temple in Jerusalem. The verses that precede and follow it all affirm that God was speaking to his people at that time. People would continue to return 'from east and west', and in the course of time Christ would come to the re-gathered nation of Israel in order that a believing remnant may accept their Saviour. How this happened is described in Acts and the rest of the New Testament. We do not need to superimpose events another 2500 years into the future to support our own ideas of the modern State of Israel.

### Ezekiel 36:24-28

> For I will take you out of the nations; I will gather you from all the countries and bring you back into your own land. I will sprinkle clean water on you, and you will be clean; I will cleanse you from all your impurities and from all your idols. I will give you a new heart and put a new spirit in you; I will remove from you your heart of stone and give you a heart of flesh. And I will put my Spirit in you and move you to follow my decrees and be careful to keep my laws. Then you will live in the land I gave your ancestors; you will be my people, and I will be your God.

This passage and others from the book of Ezekiel (such as 36:8-15 and 37:11-14, 21-28) speak graphically of a return to the land from exile accompanied by spiritual renewal, material prosperity and a restored nation. What do we make of them? Dispensationalists would have us believe that we are staring at conclusive predictions of the modern-day re-establishment of the state of Israel. But what is the context?

The first section of the book of Ezekiel is concerned with the failure of Israel to live up to the Old Covenant and God's judgment on her as a consequence. It culminates with the glory of the Lord departing from the temple in chapter 10. The latter part of the book is concerned with the introduction of the New Covenant and the success of the New Covenant people living under its provisions. The climax is the return of God's glory to a new temple in chapter 43.

In a nutshell, the second half of the book containing the crucial prophecies is a depiction of New Covenant realities expressed in Old Covenant language. The description of the temple, the allotment of land, renewed institutions and water flowing from under the altar, are all prophetic motifs for God's people enjoying spiritual regeneration – something found only in the New Covenant. They were never meant to be taken literally and simply don't make sense if we try to!

Attempting to overlay 20th century political history onto these texts violates the meaning God intended to convey. The temptation to force Old Testament scriptures on our contemporary situation must be resisted and instead we should continually ask, 'What did this passage mean to the original hearers'? Then we can profit from the passage without violating it.

### Serious questions

It is difficult to square the process by which modern Israel came into existence and current conditions in the Middle East, with the biblical vision of the coming of the kingdom of God. The New Testament revelation of God's kingdom is not political, militaristic or ethnic. It is manifest through righteousness, peace and joy in the Holy Spirit (Romans 14:17). Ethnic privilege has been replaced with grace for all through faith in Christ.

To claim that the modern state of Israel is God's 'elect nation' would force us back to the Old Testament where the Jews invaded the land by divine decree, mass killing was justified in the name of

Jehovah and you could be dispossessed of land and property because of your ethnicity. It seems amazing that Bible-believing Christians today can justify such a position while claiming to belong to a kingdom characterised by compassion, humility and justice.

## A final word

Christian Zionism today is woven into the fabric of much evangelical Christianity, particularly in the USA, where millions of Christians believe that the Israeli government should be defended without question. This view is so widespread that it has even shaped American foreign policy over recent decades. Indeed, at least three modern presidents (Jimmy Carter, Ronald Reagan and George Bush Jr.) held to a dispensational view of the end times, a view that directly affected their attitude toward the Middle East.

We believe this attitude is blinding the eyes of believers to the wider Middle East crisis and causing a stumbling block to Arab Muslims receiving the gospel. Worse still, some Arab Muslims vent their anger toward Western Zionists on their Arab Christian neighbours in the form of discrimination and violence.

Christians who continue to take a literalistic approach to Scripture in regard to the modern state of Israel have nothing to offer to break the deadlock in the Jewish-Palestinian conflict. Indeed, some Christians are found to be actively opposing the peace process on the grounds that God has decreed war, not peace, for the Middle East. As Timothy Weber points out, 'dispensationalism depends entirely on the belief in the divine right of Jews to the land, re-establishing the state of Israel'.[8] Until the church moves from this simplistic position to the moral and spiritual foundations of God's kingdom, believers will continue to defend the indefensible.

There is no doubting the deep-seated animosity of some extreme Arab and Muslim groups toward Israel, but what should the church anticipate – military conflict or revival? The dispensationalist approach to the Middle East is to deny the Palestinian people any rights of their own. Too often their priority is not to evangelise the Middle East but to defend the Israeli government. Christians, however, should be driven by a love for all peoples and a vision of the kingdom of God filling the earth, which will involve the mass conversion of Israel's Arab and Muslim neighbours as well as the Jews themselves.

The church is called to the role of peacemaker. Our aim should be to stand for the rights of all peoples in an even-handed way. Israel, which remains under daily threat from extreme elements hostile to its very existence, should be defended unreservedly. The legitimate rights of the dispossessed Palestinian peoples occupying the two territories should also be defended. Furthermore, we must acknowledge that both sides have suffered terrible injustices over the decades and that there can be no lasting resolution until each recognises the suffering and injustice endured by the other.

In seeking to expose the idea of a distinct end-time purpose for the Jewish nation, it is important at the same time, to affirm God's love for the Jews. Dispensationalism has fostered the idea that loving the Jewish people means accepting them as a divinely elect nation and giving unqualified support to the Israeli government. We disagree.

The reality is that the Jewish people largely rejected their Messiah. The Jewish authorities opposed and persecuted the early church. Paul even refers to them as 'enemies of the gospel' (Romans 11:28). Yet immediately after, he states that they are 'beloved of God for the sake of their forefathers'. Our attitude should be the same. We should pray for them as lost sinners while seeking the welfare and security of the Jewish people as a whole – as we would for any other nation.

Finally, God clearly does have a plan for the Jewish people. Paul says that 'God did not reject his people, whom he foreknew' (Romans 11:2). There is today a remnant of faith – a small proportion of believers within the unbelieving nation. But this remnant will not remain as such for ever. Large-scale salvation among the Gentiles will trigger the opening of the spiritual eyes of the Jewish people and their return in great numbers to God (Romans 11:13-16). Equally it will occur among Jewish communities all over the world, not just in the nation of Israel.

But here precisely is the point. This coming to faith will take place on the same terms as the Gentile believers and for the same purpose. Paul has not departed from the great theme of his letter to the Romans – salvation from sin through faith in Jesus Christ. The election Paul speaks of is not concerned with national identity but with the grafting back of believing Jewish people into the promises of Abraham by faith in Christ.

Paul says absolutely nothing in Romans 9-11 about land ownership or a Jewish millennial kingdom. The plan of God for the

Jews is their salvation and inclusion in Christ. In view of this we should love them and reach out to them with the gospel.

## End notes

1.  Pawson's book, *Defending Christian Zionism* (Terra Nova, 2008) is a passionate and sometimes emotional defence of the pre-millennial version of Christian Zionism. It is interesting to note however that he agrees almost entirely with arch-dispensationalist John Hagee of Cornerstone Church, San Antonio, Texas. Commenting on Hagee's fiercely Zionist book *In Defense of Israel*, Pawson can only disagree with one highly controversial chapter (see *Defending Christian Zionism*, p 84).

2.  O. Palmer Robertson: *The Israel of God*, p 118.

3.  In *Defending Christian Zionism*, David Pawson repeatedly appeals to Paul's epistles in seeking to distinguish between the Jews and the church. However the scriptures he uses emphasise the exact opposite. For example:

    *   Page 77: He appeals to Ephesians 2:19 to claim that 'Gentile Christians are fellow citizens *with* God's people, not *instead* of'. But Paul is arguing the exact opposite. He is saying Gentile believers are indeed part of the *one man* (verse 15) with Jewish believers. Furthermore, the basis of inclusion by both groups is faith in Christ. So ethnicity has no bearing whatsoever on the final position.

    *   Page 79: He appeals to Romans 2:28-29 to claim that a 'real Jew' is not a description of a Gentile believer but a Jewish person who has believed in Christ. But the issue is the same, faith in Christ not ethnicity. A believing Jew is part of the one same people as a believing Gentile – the church of Jesus Christ.

    *   Page 80: He appeals to Romans 9:6 to claim that Paul's use of the word 'Israel' here is not referring to the Gentile church but the believing remnant within natural Israel. Again, all that does is reinforce the point that Jewish believers are part of one body in Christ with Gentile believers. To claim otherwise would actually create three groups of people; ethnic Israel, believing Gentiles and believing Jews!

4.  N.T. Wright, *The New Testament and the People of God*, pages 457-458

5.  John Bright, *The Kingdom of God*, page 197

6. *Progressive dispensationalism,* Darrel Bock and Craig Blaising, pages 192-194
7. From the time of its establishment in 1897, the Zionist Organisation canvassed the international community to recognise the historic title of the Jewish people to a national homeland in the territory known as Palestine. The aftermath of the First World War and the collapse of the Ottoman Empire gave impetus to this process through what is known as the Balfour Declaration. In 1917 the then British Foreign Secretary, Arthur Balfour, wrote a letter in which he expressed the British Government's support for the establishment of a Jewish homeland in Palestine. This was formally adopted as government policy in 1922. The Paris Peace conference of 1919 and the Treaty of Versailles gave opportunity for the settlement of territorial aspirations of both Arabs and Zionists in the aftermath of the First World War and the collapse of the Ottoman Empire. At the conference both affirmed each other's national interests in a homeland. The Covenant of the League of Nations, formed at that time, recognised in Article 22 the principle that territories not yet ready for sovereign statehood could be ruled by a mandated power in the interim. Such was the situation for the territory of Palestine under British protection. At the Saint Remo conference of 1920 the leaders of five key nations – the US, the UK, France, Italy and Japan – made a decision on the basis of the Balfour declaration to give political rights to Israel, provided the religious and civil rights of the Arab peoples were upheld. Various other treaties made in this same era mandated the formation of the modern day Arab nations of Iraq, Syria and Lebanon. The nation of Jordan was also formed as a further concession to provide a home for Palestinian Arabs. As time went on Britain's mandate to rule Palestine became unworkable and in 1947 a special commission of the UN made recommendations for the creation of separate Jewish and Arab states. The plan was rejected by the Arab people as unfair and when the British mandate ended on 14th May 1948 the Jews went ahead and proclaimed their own national state. This triggered all-out war between Jews and Arabs and by the time of the ceasefire in January 1949 Israel had gained occupation of seventy-seven percent of the land (from its ownership of approximately 6% prior to the war). Between 700,000 and 800,000

Arabs fled or were driven out of their homes by the Jewish forces in the aftermath of the collapse of the 1947 UN Partition plan. Since then we have witnessed successive wars and conflicts, notably Suez in 1956, the Six Day War in 1967, the Yom Kippur War in 1973, the annexation of Golan Heights in 1981, the invasion of Lebanon in 1978 and 1982, and the Intifada from December 1987 to September 1993. At present the territorial conflicts surrounding the formation of modern-day Israel have focused on two tiny areas of Palestinian territory, the West Bank and Gaza Strip. That situation offers a daily reminder of an ongoing human tragedy, the resolution of which can only come through negotiated settlement, although this appears as distant as ever.

8.   Timothy Weber, quoted in *Whose Promised Land*, page 276.

# Chapter 12

# Faith, hope and love

The book of Second Kings records the life story of King Hezekiah who reigned in Jerusalem from 715 to 686 BC – a particularly crucial time for the southern Hebrew kingdom of Judah.

Hezekiah had been a good king who walked in the ways of the Lord. With considerable courage he had dealt with the threats of the king of Assyria against him and his people. But suddenly he faced a different kind of enemy – terminal illness – and the prophet Isaiah's words to him only confirmed the prognosis when he said, 'Put your house in order, because you are going to die; you will not recover' (2 Kings 20:1).

Hezekiah was dismayed and sought God for mercy. Appealing on the basis of his faithfulness and devotion, he pleaded for an extension to his life. The answer appeared swiftly: Isaiah had scarcely left the palace when the word of God came again to him:

*Go back and tell Hezekiah, the leader of my people, "This is what the Lord, the God of your father David, says: I have heard your prayer and seen your tears; I will heal you. On the third day from now you will go up to the temple of the Lord. I will add fifteen years to your life. And I will deliver you and this city from the hand of the king of Assyria. I will defend this city for my sake and for the sake of my servant David".* (2 Kings 20:5-6)

Sure enough, the king was healed and God confirmed his promise to extend his life through a supernatural sign: the shadow on the palace steps retreated by ten paces and Hezekiah looked forward to another fifteen years.

Now let's compare this scene with what follows next. Hezekiah was paid a visit by envoys from the emergent and territorially ambitious Babylonian kingdom, supposedly to congratulate him on the news of his healing. Somewhat surprisingly, Hezekiah gave these visitors a guided tour of the kingdom's treasuries, holding back nothing from their eyes. No sooner had they left than the King found himself standing once more before the prophet Isaiah, who asked him:

> 'What did those men say, and where did they come from?' 'From a distant land,' Hezekiah replied. 'They came from Babylon'. The prophet asked, 'What did they see in your palace?' 'They saw everything in my palace,' Hezekiah said. 'There is nothing among my treasures that I did not show them.' (2 Kings 20:14-15)

Hezekiah had disclosed the wealth of the nation to a potential enemy. It was an extraordinary thing for a king to do and betrayed an attitude of pride and selfishness that God was about to expose through a warning given by his servant Isaiah:

> The time will surely come when everything in your palace, and all that your fathers have stored up until this day, will be carried off to Babylon. Nothing will be left, says the Lord. And some of your descendants, your own flesh and blood, that will be born to you, will be taken away, and they will become eunuchs in the palace of the king of Babylon. (2 Kings 20:17-18)

What followed is one of the most shocking revelations of a man's true state of heart. Without a hint of concern for his children or the fate of the nation, Hezekiah replied:

> 'The word of the Lord you have spoken is good,' Hezekiah replied. For he thought, 'Will there not be peace and security in my lifetime?' (2 Kings 20:19)

Now consider this: when Hezekiah faced premature death he prayed and wept bitterly before God for his life. However when the dreadful destiny of the entire nation was revealed he said, 'The word of the Lord is good'. No pleading for the next generation, no fight, no intercession – just passive acceptance. When the issue was his personal welfare, Hezekiah responded with faith for a change of the prophecy. When the issue was the nation's welfare, he took it as fate and accepted the prophecy!

Hezekiah is a sober reminder of today's generation of believers. The furthest horizon for many in the church today is about fifteen years. By that time they expect the rapture will have taken place and the church will have been whisked away to safety. Until then, Christians are prepared to exercise faith in God for their personal blessing, protection, health and prosperity. Beyond this limited time frame, they give little thought to preparing for future generations of spiritual children or to our commission to invade the world with the kingdom of God. Once the rapture has occurred the church will be gone and those left behind will be judged!

In the meantime the focus of much church evangelism is on reaching as many people as possible 'before it is too late'. Christians pray that military and political events in the Middle East will steer us toward the rapture. Tragically, some even pray *against* peace in the Middle East, in the belief that God wants Armageddon, not peace! Like Hezekiah, they respond to the pessimism of today's end-time prophecy teachers by saying, 'The word of the Lord is good'. And their reasoning is the same as his: our generation will be safe from tribulation and distress because the rapture will deliver us from whatever occurs beyond that.

An urgent prophetic wake-up call is needed for the church to rouse itself from this form of spiritual short-sightedness and become concerned with leaving a legacy for our children's children. While living each day in a state of readiness, we should focus more on the next fifteen generations than on the next fifteen years. Sadly, dispensational assumptions and rapture theology have conditioned Christians to abdicate from any further role in the world.

In many church settings, a 'What's the point?' attitude stifles global thinking and long-term planning. 'Jesus is coming anytime now, so it is unrealistic to expect the kingdom of God to increase before then.' So goes the logic! In his day Hezekiah effectively cursed the nation's future through his fatalistic response to the word of judgment. We do the same today when our vision extends no further than the church being raptured away from the world it is called to reach.

Preoccupation with personal well-being has robbed the body of Christ of its mandate to take the kingdom of God to every nation. It is time to realise that Jesus will not return for a half-completed job. The great ideologies and religions that presently blind nations to the light of the gospel must crumble and fall before the return of Christ. But this will not happen overnight. It may be a multi-generational work.

Many nations are currently being changed by the gospel of the kingdom of God but it is taking several generations to achieve this. Latin America continues to experience a powerful spiritual awakening. Many nations of Africa are enjoying an unprecedented spiritual harvest. Similar stories could be told about the Asian continent. South Korea for example, had but a handful of believers 100 years ago, whereas today nearly half the population professes Christ. Until around 1980 you could measure the number of Christians in Mongolia on one hand. Today it runs into the tens of thousands.

It will be no different for the secular strongholds of Europe and the Muslim strongholds of the Middle East and South Asia. They too will open to the gospel and multitudes will be delivered from spiritual darkness before Jesus returns. Our task is to equip our spiritual sons and daughters to advance the kingdom of God throughout the whole earth until the task is finished whether it takes five years or five hundred!

Despite the dire problems the world faces, Scripture is far from laden with doom about the future. Many Christians seem to revel in prophecies of imminent judgment and the destruction of civilization as signs of the times. We contend that there is no place for celebrating bad news and the works of a defeated devil as signs of the coming of Christ. Instead the Bible holds out the most positive and optimistic picture of the sovereign God working all things toward his ultimate purpose.

## The sovereignty of God

The climate of fear and pessimism that pervades dispensationalism is in direct contradiction to the stated intentions of the sovereign God of the Scriptures. Before his return to the Father, Jesus unequivocally declared, 'All authority in heaven and on earth has been given to me' (Matthew 28:18). If Jesus is the ruler of heaven and earth, then it is impossible for world events to occur that ultimately run completely counter to the reality of his universal reign.

Of course dispensationalists acknowledge the sovereignty of God. But they limit God's intervention in history to rescuing a failing church and setting up a millennial kingdom. God is sovereign *in spite* of the church's failure rather than *through* the church's success. Thus they absolve the church of its mandate to bring in the kingdom while claiming to uphold the sovereignty of God.

Liberated from the assumptions of dispensationalism, we can easily see from Scripture that God has destined his people to carry his divine life and blessing to the nations of the world before the return of Christ.

When God chose Abraham he promised, 'I will bless you ... and you will be a blessing ... and all peoples on earth will be blessed through you' (Genesis 12:2-3). In writing to the Galatians, Paul makes it clear that those who belong to Christ are similarly chosen, so that 'the blessing given to Abraham might come to the Gentiles through Christ Jesus' (Galatians 3:14). The Christian community in other words, is destined both to know God's blessing and to be a blessing to others, in order that all the peoples of the earth will be blessed through us.

According to Scripture the church, rather than being fruitless and impotent, is God's chosen means through which, 'the manifold wisdom of God should be made known to the rulers and authorities in the heavenly realms' (Ephesians 3:10).

Understanding God's promise that has come to us through Abraham and Christ positions the church not only to receive God's blessings, but to carry those blessings to the world, with the expectation that society itself will be transformed by the power of Christ. This perspective radically alters our approach from pessimism to faith for the world's future as the church of Jesus Christ becomes aware of her role and is empowered by the Holy Spirit to accomplish it.

Normal Christian living is living in the blessings of our heavenly Father. Paul identifies some of these blessings in his letter to the Corinthians: 'Now these three remain: faith, hope and love. But the greatest of these is love' (1 Corinthians 13:13). As these blessings become an abiding reality in the lives of believers, they act as an antidote to the pessimism that has caused the church to become withdrawn and ineffective.

- Faith is the antidote to doubt
- Hope guards against the entry of despair
- Love drives out fear

Pessimism about the future will keep producing doubt, despair and fear. As it did with Hezekiah, it will narrow God's blessings down to the short-term, personal level. We dare not limit God that way since he has called us to live in his blessings of faith, hope and love. This is the environment in which God himself lives, and he beckons his people to share in these same heavenly blessings and to communicate these riches to society around us.

## Love

In identifying faith, hope and love as God's provisions for our lives, Paul affirms that the greatest of them is love. The apostle John helps us understand that God himself is love, and that everything in his kingdom is motivated and sustained by that love (1 John 4:7-8). God's kingdom is unlike any other kingdom because it is described as 'the kingdom of the Son he loves' (Colossians 1:13). God's love so thoroughly fills his kingdom, that love becomes the quality that distinguishes his realm from any other.

When Jesus came to earth, his whole life and ministry flowed as a love-gift from the Father. In the upper room, at the end of his earthly ministry, he told his disciples that he had obeyed his Father's commands and had lived in his Father's love. And the love that he had received from his Father he expressed fully to his disciples, with whom he had shared his life. As they had seen him live in his Father's love, so he encouraged them to live in the love that he had for them (John 15:9-10; 17:23-26),

More than that Jesus commanded each of them to love one another just as he himself had loved them (John 13:34-35; 15:12-17). And this command to love one another did not stop with the twelve disciples; *every* disciple of Jesus has the privilege of daily experiencing his love and communicating it to those around. In fact, this life of love is the means by which all people will know that we belong to Christ and are truly his disciples (John 13:35; 17:23).

Living in Christ's love and exploring its unfathomable proportions will extinguish fear from our lives. Nothing in the present or the future is beyond the scope of his redeeming love. As Paul sums it up: 'Love never fails' (1 Corinthians 13:8). Instead of looking to the future with apprehension, we can live with confidence, knowing nothing that we will ever encounter is beyond the capacity of God's love to heal, restore and overcome.

The gospel of conquering love tells us that God has not given up on the world and that evil will not triumph. It delivers us from preoccupation with our own protection and safe passage to heaven. Instead, it constrains us to get our hands dirty in demonstrating his love to the hurting and broken, thereby transforming society itself.

Furthermore a gospel of love cannot view any race or people as end-time enemies to be opposed by military conflict. Love believes in the mass conversion of the heathen, including Muslim peoples. Love does not require the coming of Christ to be preceded by their destruction in warfare. This love will not give up but will continue to meet the needs of humanity rather than backing off and waiting for it to be judged.

## Hope

Hope springs from God's nature and forms the environment in which God lives. He is 'the God of hope' (Romans 15:13). Just as a natural father desires his children to enter into all their inheritance, so our heavenly Father desires that we, his children 'may overflow with hope by the power of the Holy Spirit' (Romans 15:13). Hope is the 'happy anticipation of good' and it relates to our vision of the future. According to Paul, the future will be characterised by Christ being all in all, and so he describes Christ Jesus as our hope as we make our way there (1 Timothy 1:1). His coming again is 'the blessed hope' (Titus 2:13).

John was no less excited than Paul at the prospect of that coming. When Jesus returns, he enthuses, we shall be changed to be like him, for we shall see him as he is (1 John 3:2). What an incentive for us to become increasingly purified as we anticipate meeting our Lord who is completely pure!

Clearly in the minds of the apostles there existed not a trace of foreboding regarding the future. Rather, this hope filled them with confidence and an expectation of eventual good. Yes, they experienced difficulties and setbacks but they were infused with an optimistic outlook which they sought to communicate to us through their writings.

For too many believers today, the hope of Christ's coming extends no further than that he will rescue the church from tribulation and bring in his millennial kingdom. It certainly does not extend to the church being the blessing of God to the nations before Jesus comes. Bill Johnson has put it like this, 'It is hard for us to bring solutions to the world's dilemmas when our hope (end-time theology) lies in eagerly anticipating the destruction of the planet'.[1]

The classical Christian hope of our spiritual forefathers in past centuries was for the gospel to fill the earth and the kingdom to increase *until* Jesus returned. Note what the great preacher George Whitfield wrote in 1763 after he had seen thousands brought into the kingdom of God on both sides of the Atlantic:

> The Scriptures are so far from encouraging us to plead for a diminution of Divine influence in these last days of the gospel

that on the contrary, we are encouraged to expect, hope, long, and pray for larger and more extensive showers of Divine influence than any former age hath ever yet experienced. For are we not therein taught to pray, 'That we may be filled with all the fullness of God', and to wait for a glorious epoch, 'when the earth shall be filled with the knowledge of the Lord, as the waters cover the sea.' [2]

Revivalists like Whitfield, John Wesley and Jonathan Edwards were fully convinced that the church would be the instrument to bring in God's kingdom before Christ returned. Against all the odds they gave their lives to pioneer missionary work and revival across the world. For them, the Christian hope was that Christ would come for a converted world and a ready bride.

The emergence of dispensationalism in the mid 19th Century eroded that hope until the church became obsessed with preserving its purity in a corrupt world rather than being salt and light to influence that world. We praise God that we live in days when truth is being restored to the church and, with that truth, a truly biblical view of hope. Christian hope is supernatural. It does not exist at the level of human expectation, but is an expectation of the kingdom received by revelation and entered by faith. As Paul puts it:

> ... that the eyes of your heart may be enlightened in order that you may know the hope to which he has called you, the riches of his glorious inheritance in his holy people, and his incomparably great power for us who believe. (Ephesians 1:18-19)

Today we are closer to the return of Christ then ever before. Nations are being won by the gospel and the influence of Christianity continues to increase. There are more Christians worldwide today than at any time in previous history! Pessimism and fear have no place in the church, for God is moving so wonderfully in the world. It is time to believe him for the completion of all that Christ died to accomplish, and to give our lives to that end.

## Faith

The third sphere of abiding blessing that God has provided for his people is faith. Habakkuk announced that, 'the righteous person will live by his faithfulness' (Habakkuk 2:4). Paul and the writer to the Hebrews both quote this statement as applicable to those who have believed in Christ (Romans 1:17; Galatians 3:11; Hebrews 10:38). And the writer to the Hebrews adds that faith is an essential requirement for a person who desires to please God (Hebrew 11:6).

Faith in God and his word is a hallmark of the kingdom. Angels are mighty ones who do God's bidding and obey his word (Psalm 103:20), and their faith in who God is and what he says is total. Since God intends his kingdom to come on earth as it has already been established in heaven, he is looking for this environment of faith to ever increase in the lives of his children. Their faith in the unchanging nature of God and the power of his spoken word makes them like salt, both changing the flavour of society and preserving it.

The faith that results in our being saved is a gift from God. It does not come from our own abilities and efforts, so that no-one may boast (Ephesians 2:8-9). Faith comes to us as we 'hear the word of Christ' (Romans 10:17) and humbly accept the measure of faith that God gives to each of his children (Romans 12:3).

But it is the responsibility of every Christian to ensure that the measure of faith they have received continues to grow and influence every aspect of their thinking and living. With the shield of faith we can extinguish the fiery darts of the enemy – lies, deceit, distortions of the truth. This way we can overcome his hostile activity and create around us an environment of faith, hope and love.

Our faith is to be in what God himself has said to us and not in what men may say through their teaching and traditions. Jesus rebuked the Pharisees for that very thing: they neglected to hear and obey what God had said in order to obey the traditions of men (Matthew 15:3). Such an attitude will never produce wholeness in our lives or blessing in society.

The Pharisees were strong in external rules and traditions and weak in internal reality. Their lips expressed devotion to God but their hearts were far from him. And when Jesus said that their disciples were twice as much sons of hell as their teachers, he was clearly indicating that the teachings of men are of no value in establishing a godly environment. Only the words of Jesus express spirit and life, and only faith in what he says can result in heaven's environment coming to earth.

## The light of the world

Allow the precious graces of faith, hope and love to increase in your life! As you do, they will overflow to a world that longs to experience them, but has been searching in all the wrong places. Paul was delighted that the Thessalonians' faith was growing more and more, and their love for each other was increasing (2 Thessalonians 1:3). There are untapped dimensions of faith, hope and love that your heavenly Father is encouraging you to appropriate and enjoy, for it is these qualities that speak so eloquently about his nature and the environment of his kingdom.

While on earth, Christ declared that he was the light of the world (John 8:12). Now that he lives in his church, it is we who are called the light of the world (Matthew 5:14). Our faith, hope and love are to shine out from his church, bringing light to those who live in darkness, and comfort to those who are hurting.

Isaiah's promise comes to you today with all its original freshness:

> *Arise, shine for your light has come, and the glory of the Lord rises upon you. See, darkness covers the earth and thick darkness is over the peoples, but the Lord rises upon you and his glory appears over you. Nations will come to your light, and kings to the brightness of your dawn.* (Isaiah 60:1-3)

Let gloom, despair and dead traditions be banished from our lives so that God's wonderful provision in Christ can flow into the church, fill our lives and flow out from us to bless all the nations

## End notes

1. Bill Johnson, *Face to Face with God*, p 193
2. *Works*, vol 1, p 246. Quoted in *The Puritan Hope* by Iain Murray, p 149

Appendix

# Understanding Bible interpretation

The subject of Bible interpretation is called hermeneutics. It is derived from the Greek word *hermeneuo*, which means to explain, interpret or translate. The word *hermeneuo* is found in the New Testament itself in John 1:42, 9:7 and Hebrews 7:2.

Hermeneutics is concerned with establishing the meaning of what we read in a text. It is a vast subject. Here we cannot cover it in depth but we suggest you refer to the selective bibliography in the end notes for further reading.[1] Instead, we intend to give just a brief overview of the subject, with particular reference to issues concerning Christ's return.

When considering subjects like Israel, the antichrist or the rapture, the temptation is to rush immediately to what we consider to be the key Bible passages and draw a conclusion on what they mean. (In reality, our choice of passages and how we read them is often determined by someone else's view of the subject.) We should resist such urges because we can only interpret the Bible with integrity and consistency when the ground rules for doing so are securely in place. Possibly the most important part of our book is therefore this appendix. Not only will it explain the basis for our study of the return of Christ, but the principles it highlights will equip you to better understand any passage or subject in God's Word.

Of course, because we all want to get to the true meaning of a given Bible text, we will approach that text with absolute sincerity. But we do so from a predetermined set of suppositions. These suppositions are like lenses through which we read the Scriptures. We may well not even be conscious of them, but they are present nonetheless and exert a powerful influence on our minds.

Understanding this helps explain why even the religious cults can get away with using God's Word as their text book! Having decided what they believe, it is not difficult to overlay those beliefs onto a text of Scripture and read into it everything they want to see.

Hermeneutics is therefore crucial, because when we adopt sound rules of Bible interpretation, any matter can be settled over against personal preferences and prejudices.

## Literal versus non-literal interpretation

As we have seen, one of key features of dispensationalism is its literal interpretation of the Bible. In fact this is the foundational principle of its whole system of belief. Herman A. Hoyt insisted that 'The literal method of approach to the teaching of the premillennial, dispensational doctrine of the kingdom is absolutely fundamental'[2]. At first sight this seems a 'no-brainer'. Who would question the merits of taking the Bible at face value? Surely the old maxim is right, 'The Bible says what it means and means what it says'?

Of course there is truth in this. For on the positive side the literalistic position has been a powerful voice in defending the Scriptures from attack by the forces of liberalism and 'higher criticism'. But sadly, literalists have sometimes implied that only those who agree with their view can claim to be faithful to the inerrancy of Scripture. Indeed John Walvoord linked those who question literalism with all manner of heretical teachings when he said, 'The diverse theological systems of Roman Catholic, modern liberal and modern conservative writers are found to be using essentially the same method'[3], that is a method that refuses to be tied to literalism.

He is not alone. Many voices today assert that only the 'literal dispensationalist' view of Scripture is valid. We contend, however, that it is not liberalism to believe in the inspiration of Scripture yet disagree with dispensationalists! Those who accept that there is non-literal content in the Bible are no less committed to the inspiration of Scripture than those who take it all literally. Rather, they recognise that the words of Scripture can only be taken literally within accepted principles of interpretation.

The plain fact is that no-one takes the entire Bible literally. We all accept that figures of speech, styles of writing and cultural context make such a notion impossible. We know that when Isaiah says, 'the trees of the field will clap their hands' (55:12) he wasn't suggesting that they will grow arms! Similarly, we accept that when Jesus sent out the twelve in Mark chapter 6, telling them to 'wear sandals', he was not prescribing a pattern of footwear for evangelists in every culture and climate (or even proposing nude evangelism!).

As we explore our subject we will discover that dispensationalists themselves fail to adhere consistently to the principle of literalism. Often, their 'literal' interpretations change according to the political landscape of the time. Sometimes there are even several 'literal' interpretations in circulation at the same time!

For example, one preacher maintained that when Isaiah wrote, 'In the day of great slaughter, when the towers fall, streams of water will flow on every high mountain and every lofty hill' (Isaiah 30:25), he was speaking of the 9/11 attack on New York's twin towers: 'After all, isn't that what the verse literally says?'

Similarly, during the 1993 US invasion of Iraq, more than one Bible teacher claimed that Daniel 8:5-6 was describing the USA's use of low-flying Scud missiles against Iraqi forces when it says, 'As I was considering, behold, a male goat came from the west across the face of the whole earth, *without touching the ground*. And the goat had a conspicuous horn between his eyes. He came to the ram with the two horns, which I had seen standing on the bank of the canal, and he ran at him in his powerful wrath.'

Where is the line to be drawn between the literal and allegorical? On its own, the question is unhelpful. We must broaden the argument to embrace all the principles of Bible interpretation and not force every passage through the 'literal versus non-literal' sieve. We cannot set literalism above the whole range of hermeneutic tools available to us, so that when a cherished belief is questioned, literalism trumps every other principle.

## Guiding principles of Bible interpretation

Our first task then, is to understand the ground rules by which the Bible should be interpreted, rather than to defend our familiar belief system. This can be uncomfortable. The authors of this book can think of times when, after sober consideration, we have had to change our position on an issue because, in the light of what we were seeing, it could no longer be defended. We may not have liked the result that confronted us and have been tempted to retreat behind the security of our tradition. But in such circumstances courage must prevail. This book is in part the story of such a journey for both of its authors, whose own understanding has grown with the passage of time.

What follows is an overview of hermeneutic principles, sufficient to demonstrate our approach to the biblical material we have presented in this book. These principles fall into several categories:

- Historical and cultural issues
- Grammatical issues
- Theological issues
- Literary style and genre
- Principles of application

## Historical and cultural issues

This group of principles ask the question, 'What did this text mean to the original writer and his audience?' Until this is answered, we cannot move on to the question, 'What does it mean to me?' The Bible text was written thousands of years ago in a very different cultural setting from our own. We must cross the historical and cultural divides and get into the shoes of the original audience.

Henry Virkler provides a good example of the challenge we face:

> Proverbs 22:28 commands; "Do not move an ancient boundary stone set up by your ancestors."
>
> Which of the following sentences best convey the true intent and meaning of this verse in its context?
>
> a. Do not make changes from the way we have always done things.
> b. Do not steal.
> c. Do not remove the guideposts that direct travellers from town to town.
> e. None of the above.
> f. All of the above.
>
> The answer is (b).
>
> In its historical context, the landmark refers to the boundary marker that separated one man's land from his neighbour's. It was relatively easy to increase your acreage by moving such markers and therefore a form of stealing.[4]

Here is another example of the need to understand what the passage (in this case, Revelation) meant to the original reader.

> A perennially best-selling work, Christian or otherwise, in the United States has been Hal Lindsey's The Late Great Planet Earth, yet over and over again he violates fundamental

hermeneutical principles. He asserts that in Revelation 9:7-11 John was describing helicopters and their tail gunners! Now to be sure, Lindsey draws some striking parallels between John's locusts and modern-day flying machines, but in so doing he ignores the meaning that would have occurred to John's original readers in favour of one that could never have been imagined until a few decades ago. This violates the most basic principle of hermeneutics: seek the meaning of the text. What is more, his interpretation unwittingly 'demythologises' the text. Instead of depicting supernatural, demonic creatures coming out of the Abyss (vv.2-3) ruled by Satan their king (v.11), Lindsey reduces John's vision to one about mere human warfare.'[5]

Typical questions that we need to ask under the historical and cultural heading are:

### The background

What is the historical situation behind the text, the circumstances facing the author and his readers? What knowledge of ancient customs will clarify what I am reading? What was the condition of the audience?

### The book

Who was the author of the book, his background and experience, and to whom was he writing and why?

### The passage

Where does the passage I am reading fit into the major sections of the book and contribute to the whole?

### The author

What is the perspective of the author? (For example, Jeremiah wrote about the exile of Judah as one experiencing it. Ezekiel wrote about it after the event as he sat with the exiles). Is the passage describing events or teaching prescriptive truth? Who is the passage addressing? (For example, Matthew wrote his gospel with a Jewish audience in mind. John wrote his that people might believe in Jesus personally).

These historical and cultural principles form the bedrock to understanding the Bible. Only when we have grasped what the author intended in his writing, are we able to move on to study the passage for its significance to us.

## Grammatical issues

We come to understand a passage by studying the words used (the lexical aspect) and the way those words are put together (syntax). A key factor here is that, 'Although words take on a variety of meanings in different contexts, they generally have but one intended meaning in any given context'[6]. An understanding of the meaning of words and their context in the biblical passage is essential to understanding what God intended us to hear.

For example, 1 Thessalonians 4:14 says, 'We believe that Jesus died and rose again and so we believe that God will bring with Jesus those who have fallen asleep in him'. Is this passage supporting the idea that believers who die exist in a semi-conscious state (soul sleep) until Christ returns? Not when we understand that the word 'sleep' is being used in a figurative sense and that the context does not support such an idea.

In the preceding chapters you will have observed how we have employed these principles to establish the meaning of disputable texts. We will now look at these two, the lexical and syntactical aspects of a bible passage in more detail.

### Lexical

Once we have understood the background of the author and the book along with the author's thought processes we are ready to understand the meaning of individual words – the lexical structure. This is achieved by comparing words with similar meanings (synonyms) and examining the way the words were used at the time of writing.

Today there are many excellent lexical tools such as concordances and lexicons to help us understand the meaning of biblical words when we don't know the original Hebrew or Greek languages. Bible software is also readily available to assist in the process.

The next step is to ascertain how the word in question is employed in the context of the passage itself. This is important because words can often carry a number of meanings or shades of meaning. Only in the context of the sentence can we know for sure which meaning was intended.

For example the word 'flesh' in the New Testament – the Greek word *sarx* – is used in numerous ways. It can mean:

- The fleshly part of the body, Revelation 19:18
- The whole body, Galatians 4:13
- The whole person, 2 Corinthians 7:5
- Physical existence, Ephesians 2:15, Galatians 2:20
- The sensuous nature of man, Colossians 2:18
- Human nature dominated by sinful desires, Romans 7:18

There are several methods for determining how a word was intended to be used in a particular context. We can:

### a) Examine what meaning the author himself gives to a word

For example, we know that the word 'tribulation', Greek *thlipsis*, used in 2 Thessalonians 1:4 means 'persecution' and not 'God's wrath', because Paul makes it clear in that verse.

### b) Determine if the subject and the predicate of a sentence may explain each other

For example the Greek word *mÿranthÿ* in Matthew 5:13 can mean either 'to become foolish' or 'to become insipid'. We know the subject of the sentence is salt ('…if the salt has lost its savour'), so the second option is the correct one.

### c) Examine any parallelism that may be present

Much Hebrew poetry is characterised by a style known as parallelism. Basically, this means saying the same thing in two different ways. Understanding if parallelism is being used, and what type, will help us understand the meaning of the word we are examining.

Louis Berkhof illustrates this point from Isaiah 46:11: 'The Lord says of himself "From the east I summon a bird of prey;" and this finds its explanation in the parallelism: "the man that executeth my counsel from a far country".'[7] So the bird represents a person.

### d) Determine if the word is being used as part of a figure of speech

Figures of speech have, by definition, a meaning other than the literal meaning. For instance in English we may say, 'His eyes were bigger than his stomach' or 'I'm broke'. Figures of speech are common in Scripture and require careful handling. Giving a literal interpretation to a Bible passage when a figure of speech is present can land one in deep trouble.

The book of Ezekiel is full of such examples where literal interpretations have been forced upon highly figurative passages to justify dispensational teaching about the end times, for example the promise of a rebuilt temple and city in chapters 40-48. But Ezekiel's references to God's glory filling the temple and water flowing from the throne demonstrate that God had a far greater purpose for us than the restoration of a physical temple and priesthood. This whole section of Ezekiel must be taken as a whole and viewed as a description of New Covenant realities given in Old Covenant language.

### Syntax

Syntax is the way thoughts are expressed through grammatical forms. Each language has its own particular pattern and it is vital that we respect the language form of the original text. Hebrew (the language of the Old Testament) is an analytical language like English. The meaning of a sentence depends largely on the word order. Greek (the language of the New Testament), on the other hand is a synthetic language; meaning is derived only partly from word order and mostly from word endings or 'case' endings.

Fortunately there are a variety of tools available to aid the student in this process:

- Interlinear Bibles: The Hebrew or Greek text and English translation are set out side by side.
- Analytical Lexicons: These identify the specific variation of a word (e.g. speak, spoke, spoken) and say which part of speech it represents.
- Grammars: Hebrew and Greek grammars explain the various forms that words can take.

## Theological issues

This aspect of Bible interpretation asks the question, 'How does this passage fit into the total pattern of God's revelation to man?' None of us reads a passage in a total vacuum; we approach it from our overall understanding of God and his purposes. As we examine a passage in the light of our theological framework, we may encounter questions that challenge those beliefs. We need humility to reassess our beliefs in the light of the passage. When a passage throws a cherished belief into question, we need to resist the temptation to try and make the passage fit our understanding.

A classic example relating to the return of Christ is the way Daniel 9:26 is interpreted. Belief in a two-stage return of Christ requires this verse to be separated from its preceding verses by a time gap of at least 2,000 years. Yet the passage itself offers not a shred of evidence that it should be interpreted in this way! Only a willingness to lay aside the dispensational time-grid will enable the Bible student to understand the plain reading of the passage.

The greatest question theological analysis raises is also one very relevant to our subject: the matter of *continuity versus discontinuity* between the Old and New Testaments. God has revealed himself in two testaments of Scripture. How do these testaments relate? Is God treating the people of the New Testament in the same way as, or differently from, those of the Old Testament?

Those who stress the continuity of Scripture tend to see the people in the two Testaments as God's one people through history, and regard the promises of God to Israel as finding their fulfilment in the church. They emphasise the covenant structure of the Bible. They also see the kingdom of God as progressively filling the earth until Christ comes. The Jewish people were originally God's kingdom people, but since the introduction of the new covenant, that privilege has been granted to both Jews and Gentiles on the basis of faith in Christ. These new covenant people are here to display the kingdom of God and see it fill the earth.

Those who stress the discontinuity of Scripture emphasise the distinction between the Old and New Testaments, between the Jewish nation and the church and they view the Bible dispensationally. They believe the old covenant contains promises yet to be fulfilled exclusively in Israel as an ethnic nation. Consequently the kingdom of God awaits a future dispensation that will be revealed in and through the Jewish nation. What follows this position is an essentially pessimistic view of the world; things go from bad to worse and the church has no ultimate role in bringing in the kingdom here and now.

This basic choice over the way we understand God's plan of salvation will determine our hermeneutic approach to the whole

Bible. There is no middle ground. The challenge, therefore, is to constantly ask the key question: are we fitting the Scripture into our system or allowing our system to bend to the biblical revelation?

## Literary issues

Perhaps the single most important hermeneutic principle of all is this: *Each statement of Scripture must be understood according to its natural meaning in the literary context in which it occurs*. What do we mean by 'literary context'? The Bible consists of a number of literary forms or genres and every Bible text should be interpreted accordingly. Those literary forms are:

| | |
|---|---|
| Old Testament: | Narrative |
| | Law |
| | Poetry |
| | Prophecy |
| | Wisdom |
| New Testament: | Gospels |
| | Acts |
| | Epistles |
| | Revelation |

Let us briefly examine each of these.

### Narrative

Much of the Old Testament is written in narrative (straightforward account) form, beginning with the description of creation, through to the calling of Abraham, and on to the formation of the nation of Israel and its subsequent history. In the Old Testament narratives we see God acting in history and, in so doing, revealing his character and unfolding his redemptive purpose in the earth.

In interpreting narrative, it is vital that we respect the following:

### *Distinguish between what is descriptive and prescriptive*

It is easy to read into a narrative a certain theological perspective that isn't intended. For instance, the battle between Israel and Amalek in Exodus 17 is a rich illustration of the reality of the natural and spiritual worlds. The lifting of Moses' hands speaks of prayer but we should not deduce from this that prayer is only effective by the raising of hands. The account *describes* what happened on this occasion but doesn't *prescribe* it as a pattern for all at all times.

## Interpret the Old Testament in light of the New Testament

This principle applies in particular to narrative, where it might be easy to read more into the text than is intended. For example we know that Abel's offering of 'the firstborn of his flock' was accepted by God whereas his brother Cain's offering of 'the fruit of the ground' was not (Genesis 4:1-7). What are we to make of the difference in these offerings? Hebrews 11:4 explains that faith was the issue at stake here, not God's preference for lamb stew over bread rolls! 'By faith Abel offered to God a more acceptable sacrifice than Cain'.

## Avoid dogmatism over areas of dispute or uncertainty

For example, there are various interpretations of the creation account even amongst those who believe in the inerrancy of Scripture. We are all united, however, on the truth that *God created the heavens and the earth'*.

### Law

The first five books of the Old Testament are known as the Pentateuch and contain the law embedded in them in the form of narratives. Today we tend to think of *law* as restrictive rules, but the Old Testament books of the law are highly positive, presenting us with a view of God's community blessed by living according to God's way. In them we see the values of covenant living, the blessing that attended it and the grim consequences of departing from it.

At the heart of God's law is a God who wants the best for his children. The Ten Commandments are the epitome of this. They present principles by which human society may live happy and harmonious lives. Cecil B. DeMille once commented that, 'You don't break the ten commandments so much as break yourself against them'.

Dispensationalism views much of the Old Testament as belonging to a special *dispensation of the law*, later replaced, from the day of Pentecost onward, by the *dispensation of the church*. The dispensationalist view of the law was that it served its purpose in its time but does so no longer. The opposite view would be the extreme covenantal position known as reconstructionism, which anticipates a total restoration of the Old Testament law in this age.

How should we handle the law genre in the matter of interpretation?

### a) The law is ultimately fulfilled in Christ

Paul says, 'Christ is the culmination of the law so that there may be righteousness for everyone who believes' (Romans 10:4). We know that Jesus did not come to abolish the law but to fulfil it (Matthew 5:17). The righteousness that the law demanded has been met in Christ. Therefore, we do not look to the law as the means of attaining right standing with God.

### b) At the heart of the law is love

Both Jesus and Paul made it clear that the law and the prophets are summed up in the commandment, 'Love your neighbour as yourself' (Romans 13:8-10). Behind the law is a God of love and the person who loves has fulfilled the law. It is this that the Pharisees missed so widely and that Jesus identified when he said of them, 'You give a tenth of your spices – mint, dill and cumin. But you have neglected the more important matters of the law – justice, mercy and faithfulness' (Matthew 23:23).

### c) We should accommodate to specific laws which are upheld in the New Testament

For instance, Paul appeals to the requirement of two or three witnesses in bringing an accusation against an elder (compare 1 Timothy 5:19 with Deuteronomy 17:6).

### d) We should try to discover the ethical and moral principles behind specific laws

For example, Exodus 19:9-10 forbids harvesting to the edges of your field or picking up fallen fruit at harvest. Practical compassion for the poor is what lies behind these regulations, which would otherwise be irrelevant to people in developed nations.

### e) We should aim to uphold the greater spiritual truths behind the laws

For instance, we no longer sacrifice animals for sin because we celebrate the ultimate sacrifice of Christ for sin.

### Poetry

The poetic books are principally the Psalms, the Song of Solomon and Lamentations, although poetry as a literary style occurs throughout the Old Testament. As such it takes various sub forms:

| | |
|---|---|
| Prayers: | many of the Psalms in particular take the form of prayers. |
| Songs: | for instance, the song of deliverance from Egypt in Exodus 15, or the song of Deborah and Barak in Judges 5. |
| Liturgies: | A liturgy is a prescribed text used in worship, often involving two or more speakers responding to each other, for example Psalm 118. |
| Wisdom Psalms: | These are a particular category of Psalms giving instruction for living, such as Psalm 1 which contrasts the ways of the righteous with those of the wicked, symbolised by two trees. |

Poetry requires careful handling as it contains literary devices and figures of speech that were not intended to form doctrinal statements. David's cursing of his enemies and his cry to God to harm them, for example, causes consternation to some but should be viewed as the heart-cries of a tormented soul, not as a theological statement on how we relate to the unrighteous.

## Prophecy

Prophetic ministry features prominently in the purposes of God, not only in the large volume of prophetic material in Scripture, but also in the impact the prophets made in salvation history and in particular on the nation of Israel.

The prophet was the spokesperson of God, declaring his word and will in the world. Several categories of prophets can be identified in the Old Testament:

| | |
|---|---|
| The former prophets: | functioning as described in Joshua, Judges, 1 & 2 Samuel, and 1 & 2 Kings. |
| The latter major prophets: | Isaiah, Jeremiah, Ezekiel and Daniel. |
| The latter minor prophets: | Hosea, Joel, Amos, Obadiah, Jonah, Micah, Nahum, Habakkuk, Zephaniah, Haggai, Zechariah and Malachi. |

The terms 'major' and 'minor', of course refer only to the length of their writings, not to their relative importance. For the sake of space, we will select just some of the points of care requiring attention when it comes to interpreting prophecy and the prophetic books of the Bible.

### Predictive prophecy

Not all Old Testament prophecy is predictive. The prophets were not only fore-tellers but forth-tellers of God's word. They came to reveal the heart and mind of God. Often the very circumstances of their lives, as well as their words, spoke of God and his will for his people. Yet the predictive element does feature in their ministry and must be handled with care.

The temptation for the casual reader is to feel that predictive prophecy must be fulfilled in their own time and experience. This leads to the forcing of interpretation onto the text. Church history is littered with such examples, some quite tragic! The bold assertions of Christian TV's prophecy teachers are a prime example of this treatment of prophecy today.

Predictive prophecy is, in fact, often conditional in nature. God told Jonah to declare that 'in 40 days Nineveh will be destroyed' (Jonah 3:4). The fact is that God, being merciful, relented on this word in response to the repentance of the Ninevites, even though this did not figure in the original prophetic message.

Good prophetic promises, particularly those to Israel, were also conditional on the people's righteousness, justice for the poor and obedience. Even though God made promises to Israel concerning the land, their expulsion from it was the consequence of their backsliding. That condition has not changed since. Although God's love for the Jewish people is unquestionable, Israel today is a secular and materialistic state, not a theocracy.

Most predictive prophecy has already been long fulfilled and the reader's task is to look back rather than forward for the point of fulfilment. Prophecies about the return of Israel to her land are a case in point. The return of the exiles from Babylon, not the founding of the modern state of Israel, represents the fulfilment of such passages.

### Multiple and deeper meanings

It is commonly accepted that prophecy can contain several levels of fulfilment and may sometimes have an even deeper meaning (or *sensus plenior*). Like superimposed acetates on an overhead projector, shown on the screen as a single picture, multiple layers of fulfilment can often be discerned in a single prophecy. For example, 'Rachel weeping for her children' in Jeremiah 31:15 originally referred to grief over the slaughter of Israel due to God's judgment in the days of King Nebuchadnezzar. But Matthew takes it also as prophecy of Herod's slaughter of the infants of Bethlehem (Matthew 2:18).

Sometimes Old Testament prophecy has fulfilment at the same time in the nation of Israel, in Christ and in the church, for example the 'servant' prophecies of Isaiah.

### Literal versus non-literal

This distinction is highly relevant when it comes to interpreting prophecy. Everyone accepts that a mixture of literal and non-literal language is often present; the challenge is where one draws the line. Dispensationalists treat vast tracts of Old Testament prophecy as literally referring to the future millennial kingdom. Highly allegorical passages are often treated in this way, leading to all kinds of interpretive problems. Dispensationalism claims for example, that Isaiah 65:17-25 describes a future idyllic life on earth in the millennium. Yet verse 17 states, 'See I will create new heavens and a new earth. The former things will not be remembered, nor will they come to mind' clearly identifying it as the eternal state of the age to come, not an intermediate millennial kingdom.

### Wisdom

The main idea behind biblical wisdom literature is that by observing creation and human behaviour one can acquire wisdom for successful living. The wisdom books of the Old Testament include:

Proverbs – The book of Proverbs contains pithy, memorable statements of truth in the form of descriptions, comparisons and contrasts.

Job – The book of Job takes the form of a number of 'dispute speeches' on the subject of Job's suffering. The outpourings of the various speakers reflect their limited human perspectives and should not be taken as absolute revelations of truth.

Ecclesiastes – The scepticism of the book of Ecclesiastes acts as a foil to the more optimistic certainties of the book of Proverbs. Its sometimes worldly pessimism has been compared to the black velvet pad on which the jewels of God's ways stand out.

## Gospels

The significance of the Gospels is that they offer a first-hand record of the life of Jesus, 'the Word made flesh'. The record of our Saviour's life and passion is the centre and hub of the Scriptures. Everything that came before anticipates him, and everything that follows flows from him.

Without doubt, the coming of God's kingdom is the subject the Gospels are most concerned with – and one that is central to our study. Jesus himself proclaimed that in his own person the kingdom had broken into the world (Matthew 4:17, 12:28). Yet it is obvious, too, that the kingdom did not come in its fullness.

This observation is at the root of the debate over the nature and timing of the coming of the kingdom. We have already seen that early dispensationalists distinguished between a 'kingdom of heaven' and a 'kingdom of God'. That view has now largely been discredited and replaced with the idea that there is *one* kingdom administered in different ways, at present through the church but in the future through the nation of Israel.

A balanced kingdom theology, however, not only sees one kingdom of God but also holds that it is non-ethnic in nature. This approach is known as *inaugurated eschatology*. Jesus inaugurated his kingdom on earth at his first coming. We now await his return for the fulfilment of that reign. So we live in the 'already but not yet'[8] aspect of the kingdom of God. There is no need to distinguish a separate Jewish component to this kingdom.

## Acts of the Apostles

The book of Acts describes the continuation by the apostles of the work Jesus began in his life and passion. It follows the story of the early church from its roots in Jerusalem to its expansion through 'Judea, Samaria and to the uttermost parts of the earth'. In doing so, the book of Acts documents the expansion of the kingdom of God through the apostles and the early church.

The supernatural 'signs of the kingdom' evidenced in the life of Jesus are present in abundance throughout the book of Acts. Here we observe the kingdom, freshly inherited by the new covenant community, enlarging to fill the earth by the power of the Spirit.

A key issue for our study is the inclusion of Gentile believers into the predominantly Jewish Church. This took place by supernatural design when a group of Gentiles, who had gathered at the home of the Roman Centurion Cornelius, received the Spirit in the same way as the disciples had done on the day of Pentecost.

The reverberations of this episode were felt for years to come as the Jerusalem-based church tried to come to terms with Gentile converts now being included in the New Covenant by faith in Christ regardless, of submitting to circumcision or keeping Jewish laws. By this means God was creating 'one new man' in his Son.

## Epistles

The epistles were letters written mainly by apostles to churches or individuals. They are rich in theological teaching and practical instruction for young believers. The letters of Paul dominate this genre and are the source of much of Christianity's teaching.

But in studying them we must be ever diligent to separate timeless principles from teaching given just for specific situations. The epistles were written to particular churches and individuals and not everything we read in them is applicable to us. For example few would dispute that Paul's exhortations to the Corinthian church over head coverings and hair length are highly culture-specific.

Similarly, when Paul writes to the Thessalonian church on the return of Christ, he is doing so in answer to questions and concerns raised by that church, to which we have access only through Paul's replies. This makes the issue of interpretation challenging, and should guard us from being dogmatic about future events.

## Revelation

The book of Revelation falls into the category of 'apocalyptic literature'. We examined it in more detail in a chapter of its own and here will just make some general comments. The Greek word for revelation, *apokalypsis*, means 'uncovering'. The focus of apocalyptic literature is the disclosure of what has been hidden. Apocalyptic books like Revelation may be viewed as a sub-genre of prophecy and therefore have much in common with it.

The book of Revelation is characteristic of all apocalyptic literature in that:

- It is highly symbolic
- It warns of inevitable judgment and destruction
- God uses an intermediary messenger, in this case John
- It calls for a faithful remnant to persevere

The book of Revelation is undoubtedly the most controversial and most challenging book of the Bible to understand! There are several classic schools of interpretation:

Preterist: The book was written predominantly for its 1st century readers.

Historicist: It is a commentary on world history from the first to the second advent of Christ.

Idealist: It contains general principles relevant to every age throughout history.

Futurist: It is concerned with still-future events surrounding the return of Christ and the end of the world.

Of these the futurist view is the most widespread held today, popularised in the Christian media. The book of Revelation is the manual of choice for many 'prophecy teachers', who confidently interpret it through their dispensational lens. It is of great concern that this wonderful book, whose subject is Christ, has been reduced to that of speculation over the end times.

So far in this chapter we have looked at nine literary forms, from OT narrative to the book of Revelation. Apart from these the Bible also contains a variety of special literary devices or figures of speech which are important to note. These include:

### Similes and metaphors

A simile expresses comparison and frequently uses the words 'like' and 'as'. For example, 'The kingdom of heaven is *like* treasure hidden in a field' (Matthew 13:44). Metaphors are also comparisons but do not use the words 'like' or 'as'. Instead the comparison is intertwined. The Bible is full of metaphors and Jesus himself frequently used them, for instance, 'I am the good shepherd' (John 10:11); 'You are the light of the world' (Matthew 5:14).

Louis Berkhof points out that Psalm 18:2 contains no less than six metaphors when it states that, 'The Lord is my rock, my fortress and my deliverer; my God is my rock, in whom I take refuge, my shield and the horn of my salvation, my stronghold'.[9]

### Parables

A parable is an extended simile. Comparisons are drawn and the subject compared in greater depth with the thing being compared. A typical parable uses a familiar scene from everyday life to illustrate a moral or spiritual truth.

The danger with parables lies in trying to interpret all the details, when that was rarely the intention. The story of the Good Samaritan is a classic example. This parable has a long tradition of serving as a teaching aid on salvation and the return of Christ, with each component of the story viewed as a pointer to a sequence of events, something like this:

| | |
|---|---|
| Jerusalem | = godliness |
| Jericho | = ungodliness |
| 'Going down' | = slippery road of sin |
| Robbers | = temptations |
| Priest | = religion, unable to save |
| Levite | = good works, unable to save |
| Samaritan | = Jesus |
| Oil and wine | = peace and joy |
| Donkey | = fellowship |
| Two coins | = Bible study and prayer (or bread and wine, or the two thousand years until Christ returns) |
| Innkeeper | = pastor |
| Inn | = local church |
| Reimbursement | = reward at Christ's return |

We can safely say that none of this was intended when Jesus answered the question, 'Who is my neighbour?' This simple story conveys the call to act with love and compassion to all, even to those we consider the least deserving, in this case a Samaritan helping a Jew.

There are a few exceptions to this 'no meanings in the detail' approach, for example, the parable of the wheat and weeds in Matthew 13:24-30, 36-43. The details here, however, are explained by Jesus himself, and serve to strengthen the central point of the parable rather than add secondary teaching.

Parables are an intriguing means of communication. They reveal truth, often in a confrontational way as when Nathan challenged David over his adultery and murder through the story of a king stealing a poor man's lamb. But they frequently depend on the heart condition of the hearer as to whether they will be understood. This is especially so with the parables of Jesus. Jesus said:

*The secret of the kingdom of God has been given to you (speaking to his disciples). But to those on the outside everything is said in parables so that, "they may be ever seeing but never perceiving, and ever hearing but never understanding; otherwise they might turn and be forgiven!"* (Mark 4:11-12)

Henry Virkler points out, 'By its nature a parable demands a response. When the response is one that rejects God's truth, the parable serves as a means of exposing the condition of the heart'.[10]

Jesus frequently used parables in his teaching and the majority of them concerned the kingdom of God. This is relevant to our subject. Dispensationalists have frequently used Jesus' parables to teach a future millennial kingdom, but nowhere is this notion explicitly contained in the parables themselves.

## Allegories

An allegory is like a metaphor that has been extended into a story. The comparison is unexplained; the subject is mingled with that being compared, and all in the form of a narrative conveying a message. Frequently the characters and components of the story carry detailed information about the lesson.

Whereas in a parable the story itself is the focus of attention, directing the listener to one principal lesson, in an allegory the main elements of the story have a spiritual meaning too. A good example is the allegory of the faithless bride in Ezekiel chapter 16. Here Israel is compared to a woman whom Jehovah loves, woos and marries but who is unfaithful. It is both a love song and an historic record of Israel's failings.

## Types

Typology is a fascinating subject. It recognises a relationship between an initial event that foreshadows a later event in salvation history.

One of the best definitions identifies a type as 'a solid event, person or institution which serves as an example or pattern for other events, persons or institutions'.[11] The deliverance of Israel from Egypt, for example, is a type of our salvation in Christ. The sacrificial animals of the Old Testament are types of Christ and his sacrifice for sin in the New Testament.

Typology recognises that New Testament realities can be discerned in shadow and pattern form in the Old Testament. God's work of salvation is prefigured in the Old Testament through types which are then fulfilled in the New Testament in corresponding antitypes. The rock that followed the Israelites through the wilderness is the type; Christ is the antitype. The Sabbath is the type; the believer's rest in Christ is the antitype.

The nation of Israel may be viewed as a type of a greater New Covenant reality at two levels. Firstly, Israel is a type of Christ who came to fulfil the role that Israel failed to play as God's son and servant. Secondly, Israel is a type of the church, God's New Covenant people. Types fall into several categories:

Events –         The crossing of the Red Sea
Institutions –   The Passover, the Day of Atonement
Offices –        The priesthood, the kingship of David, Moses as
                 prophet
Actions –        The bronze serpent on the pole

## Principles of application

Finally, we must bring to our interpretation of Scripture various principles that because they don't fall neatly into any of the other groups, we will categorise as general rules of application. Some of them overlap in part with the preceding sections, and since the exact number of such principles is open to debate, we have listed some of the undisputed ones. These are the following:

### Interpret Scripture with Scripture

This principle recognises that the Bible is its own best interpreter. God has provided the means for us to understand Scripture by cross-reference. This is in fact the foundation stone of reformed (i.e. non-Roman Catholic) hermeneutics where it is called 'the analogy of faith'.

Jesus practised this himself when being tempted by Satan in the wilderness. When the devil encouraged Jesus to throw himself from the temple by quoting Psalm 91:11-12, Jesus replied by interpreting this passage in the light of Deuteronomy 6:16 to show that such an action would be tempting God.

## Interpret the obscure in the light of the clear

This principle naturally follows from the last one. Luther first acknowledged that not all parts of Scripture are equally clear. The path to heresy is paved with obscure scriptures! The foundation for belief and practice can only be laid with what is clear and explicitly stated. The interpretation of scriptures that are difficult to understand should be based on what is clear.

For an example let's consider 1 Corinthians 15:29, where Paul refers to the practice of 'baptising on behalf of the dead'. Clearly there were groups in existence who practised this, and the passage has been taken by some to justify such a practice today, e.g. the Church of Jesus Christ of Latter Day Saints (Mormons).

On closer inspection however, we see that Paul is not at all advocating baptism by proxy for the dead. He is using the practice of such fringe groups to strengthen his argument for the resurrection of the dead. In effect he is saying, 'If even those who baptise on behalf of the dead believe in the resurrection of the dead how much more should we!'

## Interpret the Old Testament in the light of the New Testament

It was Augustine who first coined the phrase, 'The New is in the Old concealed, the Old is in the New revealed'. Both testaments are God's inerrant word. If we believe that revelation is progressive, then we must place a premium on the New Testament as the fullest revelation of God.

This principle has constant relevance to our study of the return of Christ for the Old Testament, particularly the Prophets, has become the battleground for settling issues such as the role of Israel and the millennial kingdom, as we have seen. Dispensationalists want to elevate the Old Testament to a position where it carries as much weight in interpreting the New Testament as the New does for the Old[12]. This we reject.

## A subject cannot be fully understood until every scripture on that subject has been considered

This is sometimes difficult to put into practice because we instinctively build a solid case for our views from selected scriptures while conveniently ignoring those that don't quite fit in!

For example, on the subject of the role of women in ministry, great stress has been put on certain proof texts that at first sight seem to consign women to silence. One such passage is found in 1 Corinthians chapter 14, where Paul says, 'As in all the congregations of the Lord's people, women should remain silent in the churches. They are not allowed to speak, but must be in submission, as the law says (verses 33-34).

However elsewhere in the same book, Paul writes, 'Every woman who prays or prophesies with her head uncovered dishonours her head' (11:5). Whatever else it means, one thing is certain here, Paul anticipates the active participation of the women. Then in chapter 14 verse 5 Paul says, 'I want you all to prophesy'. It is clear when we take all the relevant scriptures into account, that women were very much part of the vocal congregation.

We have deliberately spent some time working through these important principles in an attempt to show the reader that Bible interpretation is not merely a matter of chance or guesswork. Although we must always approach God's Word with humility, we can be confident and certain about a great deal. God gave us his Word to bring us to maturity and fullness, not to reduce us to squabbling and confusion.

## End notes

1. *Introduction to Biblical Interpretation*, Klein, Blomberg, Hubbard, published by Thomas Nelson; *Principles of Interpretation*, Louise Berkhof, published by Baker Book House; *Hermeneutics*, Henry A Virkler, published by Baker Academics
2. *The Meaning of the Millennium*, IVP p 67
3. *The Millennial Kingdom*, p 312
4. Henry Virkler, *Hermeneutics*, p 81
5. Klein, Blomberg, Hubbard, *Introduction to Biblical Interpretation*, p 442
6. Virkler, op. cit., p 98
6. Berkhof, *Principles of Interpretation*, p 79
7. *The Gospel of the Kingdom*, G. Eldon Ladd.
9. Berkhof, op. cit. p 83
10. Virkler, op. cit. p 154
11. David Baker, *Typology and the Christian Use of the Old Testament*
12. Herman A. Hoyt said, 'The Old Testament is not complete apart from the New Testament, and the New Testament cannot be comprehended apart from the Old.'

# Glossary

**Abomination that causes desolation** – A phrase first used by Daniel (11:31; 12:11) and referred to by Jesus in the Olivet discourse (Matthew 24:15; Mark 13:14). Luke's account of the discourse makes the phrase's meaning clear: 'When you see Jerusalem being surrounded by armies...' (21:20). In AD 70, Roman armies surrounded the city, soon to raze it and the Temple to the ground. The Roman soldiers carried ensigns displaying eagles and images of the Emperor, which they worshipped. The 'abomination' was thus the offering of worship to something other than the one true God.

**AD 70** – The significant and fateful year in which the Romans sacked Jerusalem and destroyed the Temple. This, and the events leading up to it, were prophesied in some detail by Jesus in the first part of the Olivet discourse (Matthew 24:1-35). Details of these terrifying events were documented by the Jewish historian Josephus. AD 70 is not mentioned in the New Testament writings because they were completed shortly before then, and Christians have been prone to wrongly attach Jesus' prophecies in the first part of the Olivet discourse to the events leading up to Christ's second coming. AD 70 is important in that it cut the umbilical cord tying the early church to its Jewish origins, enabling it to range unfettered throughout the world.

**Age to come** – Scripture distinguishes two 'ages' or periods in human history: 'this age' and 'the age to come'. Christ's second coming marks the dividing line between them. But there is a complication in that, according to the New Testament, Christ's *first* coming has a bearing on the distinction. With his ascension and the pouring out of the Holy Spirit on the church, the 'age to come' invaded history backwards into 'this age' so that Christians today 'taste the powers of the coming age' (Hebrews 6:5). But it is only a taste, not yet the full banquet. For the most part, the 'age to come' refers to the eternal state after Christ comes again.

**Amillennialism** – One of the schools of thought concerning the millennium, the thousand-year period mentioned in Revelation 20. In Greek the prefix 'a-' is a negative, like the English 'un-', so the term literally means 'no millennium'. Amillennialists believe there will be no millennium, at least not in the sense of a literal thousand-year earthly reign of Jesus. They view the millennium as a symbol for the whole period between Christ's first and second comings, with Jesus reigning at the Father's right hand in glory and believers seated there reigning with him, while the devil is unable to prevent the nations of the world from hearing and responding to the gospel.

**Antichrist** – A term that occurs only in the writings of John. The Greek prefix *anti* means both 'opposed to' and 'instead of', and antichrist is anybody or anything that opposes or undermines Christ and his supremacy and sets itself up in his place. In his letters, John indicates that 'many antichrists have appeared'—false teachers in the early church who denied Christ's incarnation and deity. Traditionally, some Christians have identified the name 'antichrist' with what Paul calls in 2 Thessalonians 2:3 'the man of sin'. But this association is arbitrary, and certainly John himself gives no indication of any future evil individual to be called *'the* Antichrist'.

*Apantesis* – A specialised Greek noun meaning 'meeting'. It occurs in Matthew 25:6, Acts 28:15 and, most significantly, in 1 Thessalonians 4:17. An *apantesis* took place when a king or dignitary visited a town in his domain. To honour him, the leading citizens of the town would go out of the city gates and travel some way down the road, where they would formally greet the visitor and welcome him. Then, formalities over, they would join his entourage and accompany him back into town. Paul's use of this term in connection with Christ's return shows that, when we are caught up to 'meet' the Lord in the air, it will be to accompany him back to where we left from: the earth—not to go with him into heaven.

**Apocalyptic literature** – A biblical genre with no equivalent in modern writing. The books of Daniel and Revelation are considered to be at least partly of this genre. Apocalyptic works were common among Jewish and Christian communities between 250 BC and 150 AD. They are marked by a great deal of colourful imagery and symbolism, portraying the struggles of God's people and the ultimate triumph of good over evil. Usually the main human character receives revelation through an other-worldly being like an angel, and the revelations are intended to encourage God's pressured people during times of suffering or persecution. It is vital, in interpreting apocalyptic books, to be aware of the conventions of this type of writing and not read into their language meanings that were never intended.

**Apocalypse** – See *Apokalypsis* below.

*Apokalypsis* – A Greek term meaning 'uncovering', 'unveiling' or 'revelation'—it is the first word in the original Greek text of the book of Revelation, which is 'the revelation of Jesus Christ', that is, the revealing of him as the supreme King that he is. The English transliteration is 'apocalypse', and some English versions of the Bible name the last book of the New Testament the *Apocalypse*.

**Armageddon** – A word that appears only once in the Bible, in Revelation 16:16. It comes from a Hebrew expression meaning 'Mount Megiddo', probably referring to the town of Megiddo in northern Palestine. Because this town was the scene of many key battles in Israel's history the name Megiddo came to symbolise a battlefield. Oddly, there is no 'mount' at Megiddo; indeed, the town is on a plain (2 Chronicles 25:22). The reference in Revelation is hard to interpret with any precision but seems to indicate a future great battle in which 'the kings of the East' are involved. We should be wary, however, of giving too material an interpretation to this, as in the scenarios in popular prophecy books that warn of a coming dreadful 'battle of Armageddon'.

**Beast** – A character in the books of Daniel and Revelation. In Daniel, especially in chapter 7, the beast symbolises a world ruler who oppresses God's people. Revelation picks up this theme and develops it further, presenting it as an obvious reference to the Roman Empire and its persecution of Christians. See also *Mark of the beast*.

**Chiliasm** – Another word for millennialism: the belief that, at some stage in the future, there will be a literal thousand-year period in which Jesus will reign on earth from a base in Jerusalem. The term *chiliasm* comes from the Greek word for 'thousand', while *millennium* comes from the Latin word.

**Continuity and discontinuity** – A way of viewing major theological differences between the Old Testament and the New, and determining how much of the Old Covenant law and teaching remains binding upon believers under the New Covenant. For example, eating pork was forbidden in the Old Testament, but Jesus later 'declared all foods clean' (Mark 7:19) – an example of discontinuity. Conversely, the eighth commandment declared, 'You shall not steal' (Exodus 20:15) and the New Testament teaches the same (e.g. Ephesians 4:28) – an example of continuity. Christians arrive at different schemes of biblical interpretation depending on how they view continuity and discontinuity in reference to, say, God's promises of territory to Israel.

**Covenant** – A binding agreement between two parties, with penalties for breaking the agreement and benefits for adhering to it. The Bible structures itself around the major covenants that God entered into with the likes of Noah, Abraham and Moses, and most importantly the New Covenant established in Christ, which supersedes and fulfils all the earlier ones. To replace this overt covenantal structure with a dispensational one as the basis for understanding God's purpose is to neglect the Bible's own declared framework in favour of an artificial one of human invention.

**Dispensationalism** – A framework for understanding the Bible and God's eternal purpose. It divides human history into a series of periods or 'dispensations', during each of which God allegedly deals with human beings according to a particular criterion. This scheme is relatively modern, having been developed in the mid-nineteenth century and popularised by the *Scofield Reference Bible*. It is an artificial structure that takes little account of the covenantal structure in the Bible. Dispensationalism makes a hard distinction between ethnic Israel and the church, favouring the former over the latter as the key to God's developing purpose.

*Epiphaneia* – One of several Greek words used for the return of Christ in glory. This one – which gives us the English 'epiphany' – means literally a 'shining out' and emphasises the splendour of his arrival. Used of his first coming in 2 Timothy 1:10, it more commonly refers to his glorious return, as in 2 Thessalonians 2:8 and Titus 2:13.

**Eschatology** – The study of the 'last things', that is, the events to do with the last days and the winding up of human affairs with the return of Jesus. The word comes from the Greek *eschatos*, 'last'. Strictly, the 'last days' began with Christ's *first* coming (e.g. Hebrews 1:2), making the whole of this current period the eschatological age, but in common parlance the term tends to be applied to events still future.

**Fundamentalism** – A movement that grew up in the late nineteenth century to defend the Bible and Christian truth against the upsurge of modernism: evolutionary theory, biblical criticism and liberal theology. It re-emphasised what came to be called the 'five points of fundamentalism': the verbal inerrancy of the Bible, the deity of Christ, his virgin birth, the substitutionary view of his atoning work and his bodily return in glory. This movement has been strongest in the USA.

**Futurism** – One of several schools of thought on the interpretation of the book of Revelation. Futurists hold that the book is chiefly, if not entirely, describing events which are for us still future and which will unfold at the very end of time, leading up to the return of Christ.

**Great tribulation** – A phrase used by Jesus (Matthew 24:21, KJV); (the NIV has 'great distress') in his Olivet discourse. The context makes it clear that it refers to the horrors leading up to and culminating in the events of AD 70, when the Roman armies, after a long siege of Jerusalem, sacked the city and destroyed the Temple. The same phrase occurs in Revelation 7:14, and dispensationalists take it to mean primarily a pouring out of God's wrath during the second half of an alleged seven-year period between the rapture and Christ's return in glory.

**Hermeneutics** – The art/science of Bible interpretation, from the Greek *hermeneuo*, 'interpret'. What the Bible actually *says* – its words and phrases – is clear, but Christians often have different views about what it *means*, and all of us bring, whether consciously or not, some underlying interpretive scheme to bear on the Scriptures when we read and study them. Widely-accepted hermeneutical principles include the need not to take metaphors and similes literally, the importance of context, and the recognition of the New Testament writers as the inspired interpreters of the Old.

**Historicism** – One of several schools of thought on the interpretation of the book of Revelation. Historicists hold that the book portrays human history sequentially from Christ's first coming to his return. This approach has lost popularity, partly because Revelation itself gives no hint that it should be interpreted this way, but chiefly because of the difficulty of clearly identifying modern events with the symbols and imagery in the book.

**Idealism** – One of several schools of thought on the interpretation of the book of Revelation. Idealists hold that the book has no progressive storyline but is a collection of cameos that highlight principles of enduring validity which Christians of every generation can apply to themselves.

**Kingdom of God** – One of the major themes, if not *the* major theme, of the New Testament in general and of the teaching of Jesus in particular. The kingdom of God refers not to a territorial region but to the *rule* of God; wherever his will is done, there the kingdom is. The Old Testament prophesied its arrival, which came in the person of Jesus himself (Luke 11:20); he is the King of the kingdom. And it will be seen in its fullness when Jesus returns and every knee bows to him.

**Literalism** – The view that we should read and interpret the Bible literally. This naïve approach can lead to ridiculous conclusions when applied to poetic language. No Christians takes *every* passage of Scripture literally, but a generally literal approach is the keystone of dispensational teaching and accounts for the complex nature of some of its claims about Israel, the millennium and the kingdom of God.

**Man of lawlessness** – A character mentioned by Paul only once, in 2 Thessalonians 2:3, and alluding to previous discussions with the Thessalonian believers (2 Thessalonians 2:5) which we are not privy to. Many believe he is referring to the Roman Emperor and to future events surrounding the fall of Jerusalem in AD 70. We should certainly be very cautious about building a major doctrine around this obscure figure, as some do, and making him a key player in still-future events.

**Mark of the beast** – A feature in Revelation chapter 13, where the beast (most likely representing the political power of the Roman Empire) puts a mark on people's right hand and forehead, without which they may not buy or sell. Later in the chapter the mark is identified as '666'. Because of the apocalyptic nature of Revelation we should avoid interpreting this too literally. '666' is, many believe, a numeric reference to Nero, the Roman Emperor (reigned 54-68 AD) and persecutor of Christians, who would not acknowledge Nero as Lord. See also *Beast*.

**Millennium** – The phrase means '1000 years' and appears solely in Revelation chapter 20. Though it appears only once, and in the most obscure and symbolic book in the New Testament, three main schools of thought about its meaning have developed: see *amillennialism, postmillennialism* and *premillennialism*.

**Olivet discourse** – A long address by Jesus recorded in Matthew 24-25, Mark 13 and Luke 21. The longest treatment is in Matthew's Gospel. The discourse is so-called because Jesus gave it while he was with his disciples on the Mount of Olives (Matthew 24:3).

**Parenthesis** – A period of time that is 'in brackets', that is, a temporary diversion from the main purpose of God. Dispensationalists believe that God's purpose has always been concerned with the nation of Israel; hence the church is a parenthesis in it and his purpose will in future revert to giving Israel prominence once again. The Bible teaches, however, that there is, and has always been, just one people of God: those who share the faith in God's promises that Abraham showed. Far from being a parenthesis in God's dealings with humanity, the church as fully revealed in the New Testament and embracing believing Jews and Gentiles, has always been in the mainstream of his eternal purpose.

*Parousia* – A Greek word meaning 'presence', 'arrival' or 'appearing', and the most common term used by the New Testament writers to refer to Christ's return in glory. In the secular Greek of the day it referred to the arrival of a king or dignitary to honour a town with a personal visit.

**Postmillennialism** – One of the schools of thought concerning the millennium, the thousand-year period mentioned in Revelation 20. Postmillennialists believe that the return of Jesus will take place *after* (Latin *post*) the millennium, which they interpret to be a golden age (not necessarily a literal thousand years in duration) this side of his return when the gospel will have unprecedented success and the world will effectively become Christianised. This view makes postmillennialists optimistic about the prospects for the gospel and the church.

**Premillennialism** – One of the schools of thought concerning the millennium, the thousand-year period mentioned in Revelation 20.

Premillennialists believe that the return of Jesus will take place *before* (Latin *pre*) the millennium, which they interpret to be a literal thousand-year period when Jesus will rule with a rod of iron from his base in Jerusalem. Only after this, and subsequent conflict, will the eternal state be introduced. Despite the popularity of this view at various times in Christian history, including today, it must be suspect in that it inserts an additional long period between 'this age' and 'the age to come'.

**Preterism** – A view of the 'last things', holding that not just some but all of the New Testament's prophecies were fulfilled in the events surrounding AD 70. It thus leaves no room for any still-future fulfilments such as Christ's visible return in glory and the resurrection of the dead for final judgment. This is *full* preterism. There is, by contrast, much to commend *partial* preterism, which, while granting that *some* prophecies were fulfilled in the events of AD 70, holds that others still await fulfilment in the future. The term 'preterism' comes from a Latin word meaning 'past' or 'gone by'.

**Rapture** – The 'catching up' of believers to meet the Lord in the air, as described by Paul in 1 Thessalonians 4:17. For many Christians today the term has unfortunately come to mean *'secret* rapture'—a sudden, silent and mysterious disappearance of believers from the earth. The context, by contrast, talks of 'a loud command', the 'voice of the archangel' and the 'trumpet call of God', which place the rapture in a setting that is the very opposite of secret, and this is in line with other New Testament passages on Christ's return.

**Reconstructionism** – A view of Christian history propounded by Rousas J. Rushdoony and others. It sees the church as Christianising the world chiefly through the introduction of a legal system based on the Old Testament law as given to ancient Israel. Only after this process is complete – which they reckon could take many thousands of years – will Jesus return.

**Replacement theology** – The view that, in the purpose of God, the New Testament church replaces Israel as the people of God. In contrast, the Bible reveals the church as the redefined Israel. The church today is the one true Israel, made up of the spiritual descendants of believing Abraham, both Jews and Gentiles, and it is with these that God's purpose is concerned today and in the future, not with ethnic Jews or with the modern State of Israel.

**Restrainer** – The person who will 'hold back' or restrain the 'man of lawlessness', according to 2 Thessalonians 2:1-7. Some believe this refers to God himself, others that it means some human ruler such as the first-century Roman Emperor Claudius who, while he remained in power, prevented the ambitious and evil-intentioned Nero from persecuting the church.

**Scofield Reference Bible** – An edition of the Bible (King James Version) first published in 1909 and revised in 1917 with detailed explanatory notes by Cyrus I. Scofield alongside the text. Scofield was a dispensationalist and his commentary gives a dogmatically dispensational interpretation through its comments and cross-references. This Bible became very popular and was a major factor in the spread of dispensational ideas. A further revision in 1967 removed some of the more outlandish aspects of Scofield's theology. See also *Dispensationalism*.

**Seventy weeks** – A phrase from Daniel 9:24-17, rendered 'seventy "sevens"' in the NIV. The angel Gabriel gave Daniel an insight into the future using a time-frame based on 'weeks' of years, that is, seven-year periods. Taken at face value, the 490 years involved bring us to the time of Christ's incarnation and ministry, and it is in them that we should see the prophesied events being fulfilled. Dispensationalists, by contrast, insert a gap between the sixty-ninth and seventieth weeks, a gap that has already lasted over two thousand years.

**Signs of the times** – A commonly-used phrase referring to alleged signs that the return of Jesus is fast approaching. It is taken from the disciples' question to Jesus in Matthew 24:3. Jesus explained to them that a whole range of signs would precede the grim events of AD 70 (verses 4-35), but then pointed out that, by contrast, his ultimate return in glory would be preceded by no signs at all (verse 36 ff); it would be sudden and unexpected, and life in society would carry on as normal right up to the moment of his appearance.

**State of Israel** – The modern State of Israel was established in 1948 and expanded as a result of the Six Day War of 1967, at enormous cost to the Palestinian inhabitants of the territory. Whether or not its establishment was a fulfilment of biblical prophecy is strongly disputed, but dispensational theology makes it a major plank in its eschatological system. Indeed, some dispensationalists oppose any peace negotiations between Israelis and Palestinians on the grounds that, in their view, God has decreed war in the Middle East and therefore to work for a peaceful settlement is to oppose his declared will.

**Temple** – Originally the temple built by King Solomon in Jerusalem, which became the focus of Israel's worship. This structure, known as the First Temple, was destroyed by King Nebuchadnezzar of Babylon around 587 BC. After Israel's exile a replacement, the Second Temple, was built by Zerubbabel and the returnees from exile. Much later, at the time of Jesus, King Herod extended this temple and lifted it to a high level of grandeur, only for it to be totally destroyed a few years later by the Romans (AD 70), as predicted by Jesus (Matthew 24:1-2). The supernatural tearing of the sanctuary curtain when Jesus died could be regarded as a sign that God was finished with this localised temple. From now on he would position his presence in a temple consisting of his redeemed people, wherever they might be (2 Corinthians 6:16; Ephesians 2:21). Dispensationalists, however, expect God to revert in the near future to operating from a rebuilt temple in Jerusalem, complete with animal sacrifices and Israelite-style worship.

**'This generation'** – A phrase from Matthew 24:34. There Jesus, after predicting the destruction of the temple and associated events, declared: *'This generation* will certainly not pass away until all these things have happened.' The plain meaning is that these events would take place in the lifetime of those to whom Jesus was speaking and of their fellow-Jews. And that indeed came to pass in the events surrounding AD 70. Dispensationalists, however, maintain that Jesus' predictions are still awaiting fulfilment, and interpret 'this generation' to mean 'this race of people', namely the Jews. Matthew's use of the term elsewhere in his Gospel seems to rule out this interpretation.

**Typology** – The way in which an Old Testament person or event pictures a person or event in the New Testament. The Old Testament picture is the 'type', the New Testament fulfilment the 'antitype'. For example, Israel's crossing of the Red Sea, after the Passover and exodus from slavery in Egypt, is a type of our baptism as Christians following the shedding of the blood of Christ, our Passover lamb, and our deliverance from slavery to Satan (see 1 Corinthians 5:7;

10:2). We must exercise caution over seeing types where the New Testament itself does not make them explicit.

**Wrath** – The wrath of God is specifically his judgment on sinners because of their sin. It must be distinguished from 'trouble', 'distress' or 'tribulation', which are the normal lot of God's people, surrounded as they are by a hostile, often anti-Christian society.

# Bibliography

Adams, Jay E., *Preterism: Orthodox or Unorthodox* (Timeless Texts)

Adams, Jay E., *The Time of the End, Daniel's Prophecy Reclaimed*

Augustine, *The City of God*

Baldwin, Joyce G., *Commentary on Daniel*

Baker, David, *Typology and the Christian Use of the Old Testament*

Barton Payne, J., *The Imminent Appearing of Christ*

Bauckham, Richard, *The Theology of the Book of Revelation*

Bauckham, Richard, *The Climax of Prophecy*

Berkhof, Louise: *Principles of Interpretation* (Baker Book House)

Blaising, Craig, and Bock, Darrell, *Progressive Dispensationalism* (Baker Book House)

Blomberg, Klein Hubbard, *Introduction to Biblical Interpretation* (Thomas Nelson)

Bright, John, *The Kingdom of God* (Abingdon Press)

Bruce, F. F., *1 and 2 Thessalonians, New Bible Commentary*

Chapman, Colin, *Whose Promised Land?* Lion Publishing

Clouse, Robert G, *The Meaning of the Millennium* (IVP)

Conner, Kevin J, *Interpreting the Symbols and Types* (City Christian Publishing)

Dallimore, Arnold, *The Life of Edward Irving* (Banner of Truth)

Eberle, Harold and Trench, Martin, *Victorious Eschatology* (Worldcast Publishing)

Elliott, E.B., *Horae Apocalypticae, A commentary on the Apocalypse*

Eusebius, *The History of the Church*, Penguin Classics

Fee, Gordon, *Paul, the Spirit and the People of God* (Hendrickson)

Feinberg, John S., *Continuity and Discontinuity* (Crossway Books)

France RT, *The Gospel of Matthew, New International Commentary on the New Testament*, Eerdmans

Grier, W. J., *The Momentous Event* (Banner of Truth)

Gundry, Robert H., *The Church and the Tribulation* (Zonderman)

Gundry, Stanley N. *Three Views on the Rapture*, Zondervan

Harrison, Norman B, *The End, Re-thinking the Revelation*

Johnson, Bill, *Face to face with God* (Destiny Image)

Josephus, *The Jewish Wars: The Jewish Antiquities*

Kik, J Marcellus, *Matthew 24: An Eschatology of Victory*

Kittel, G., *Theological Dictionary of New Testament Words* (Eerdmans)

Ladd, G. Eldon, *The Gospel of the Kingdom* (Eerdmans)

Morris, Dr Leon, *Commentary on 1 and 2 Thessalonians*

Murray, Iain, *The Puritan Hope* (Banner of Truth)

Oliphant, Margaret, *The Life of Edward Irving* (first published London, 1862)

Robertson, Palmer O., *The Christ of the Covenants*

Robertson, Palmer O., *The Israel of God*

Pawson, David, *Defending Christian Zionism* (Terra Nova)

Pawson, David, *When Jesus Returns* (Hodder & Stoughton)

Philips, J. B., *Translation of the New Testament* (Geoffrey Bles, Presbyterian and Reformed)

Ryken, Leland, Wilhoit, James C, and Wilhoit, Tremper Longman III (editors), *Dictionary of Biblical Imagery* (IVP)

Ryrie, Charles C., *Basic Theology*

Sandeen, Ernest R., *The Roots of Fundamentalism* (University of Chicago Press)

Sproul, R.C., *The Last Days According to Jesus* (Baker Book House)

Weber, Timothy, *Living in the Shadow of the Second Coming*

Wright, N. T., *Paul for Everyone.*

Wright, N. T., *The New Testament and the People of God*

Vine, E. W., *Expository Dictionary of the New Testament* (Riverside)

Virkler, Henry, *Hermeneutics* (Baker Academic)